BLOOD STRIPES

THE GRUNT'S
VIEW
OF THE
WAR IN IRAQ

DAVID J. DANELO

Foreword by Steven Pressfield

STACKPOLE
BOOKS

0 11557 03393 9

Cover design by Tracy Patterson

Printed in the United States of America

10 9 8 7 6 5 4 3 2 1

ISBN 978-0-8117-3393-9 (paperback edition)
ISBN 0-8117-3393-9 (paperback edition)

The Library of Congress has cataloged the hardcover edition as follows:

Danelo, David J.
   Blood stripes : the grunt's view of the war in iraq / David J. Danelo ;
foreword by Steven Pressfield.
      p. cm.
   Includes index.
   ISBN-13: 978-0-8117-0164-8
   ISBN-10: 0-8117-0164-6
   1. Iraq War, 2003—Personal narratives, American. 2. Danelo, David J.
3. United States. Marine Corps—Biography. I. Pressfield, Steven. II. Title.

   DS79.76.D354 2006
   956.7044'342092—dc22

                                                    2005036247

For those who fought the Muj in Iraq,
and for all who follow the Spartan Way

Honor to those who in the life they lead
Define and guard a Thermopylae
Never betraying what is right,
Consistent and just in all they do
But also showing pity and compassion;
Generous when they're rich
And when they're poor,
Still generous in small ways;
Always speaking the truth
Yet without hating those who lie.

—Konstantinus Kafavis,
Greek poet (1863–1933)

Table of Contents

Foreword

T his book is about enlisted Marines, specifically infantrymen
ranked corporal or above. Its author, David J. Danelo, is a
Naval Academy graduate who served as a Marine captain in Fallujah and Al Anbar Province from February to September 2004. He
tells us in these pages of the sergeants and corporals he knew and
served with, what they were up against, how they responded—and
what it means, or should mean, to us as citizens who will give or
withhold our consent to our country's military enterprises in the
coming decades of a post–9/11 world.

Wars of the twenty-first century will not be won from the top
down. Success, if it comes, will be produced by the street-level
troops, the men and women who are engaged day-to-day in the
life of the community and with its citizens on a face-to-face basis.
Victory will come, if it does, from soldiers and Marines acting in
their capacity as individuals and human beings as much as in
their roles as warriors or occupiers.

This is Captain Danelo's subject. His heroes are regular
American guys from Iowa and New Hampshire, Kentucky and
South Dakota. Not captains and generals, but NCOs. Non-Com-

missioned Officers. The "blood stripes" of the title refer to the two-inch-wide scarlet strips that run from cuff to waist on the outseam of Marine Corps dress-blue trousers. Only corporals, sergeants, and up may wear these.

NCOs are the heart and soul of the Marine Corps and always have been. How could it be otherwise in any outfit fighting on the ground? The man who makes the life-and-death decision has to be the man right there in the dirt, on the spot. A popular and, I think, very interesting concept these days is that of Fourth Generation Warfare, meaning counter-guerrilla, counter-insurgency, "low-intensity conflict"—the kind where a tactical victory like wasting a neighborhood and killing a few dozen bad guys can turn out to be a moral defeat, producing alienation of the populace, boosting recruiting for the enemy, destroying the village in order to save it. One of the concepts of Fourth Generation Warfare is "the strategic corporal"—that is, the twenty-year-old E-4 in Najaf who sees a Shiite funeral coming down the street and decides in the moment (this is a real incident, by the way) to pull his patrol off to the side and have them lower the muzzles of their rifles and remove their helmets as a gesture of respect. And who, by this act, makes friends instead of enemies and turns a potentially incendiary situation into an opportunity for progress and engagement. In other words, an NCO making a decision that captains normally make. And of course making such decisions a hundred times a day.

But when has it ever been different? When have corporals and sergeants been less important? In Al Anbar Province today, the smart move may be to defuse a potential crisis, to dial down the level of aggressiveness; on Guadalcanal, it may have been to cut loose with every ounce of firepower you've got. Either way, it's the squad leaders and platoon sergeants who most of the time make the call. In peacetime they hold the Marine Corps together;

they train its recruits; they provide the role models for the next generation. In wartime . . . well, we know what they do in wartime.

All this is to take nothing away from Marine officers, at the company level or on up the food chain. I've gotten to know quite a few over the last couple of years, and I can testify that they are, without exception, outstanding individuals who would be just as successful in business or civilian life if they had elected to follow such a course but who, for reasons of service, honor, and maybe a little adventure, have taken up the profession of arms instead. And that's what they are: professionals. Not just hard-core physical specimens who can hold their own with the gnarliest of the grunts beneath them, but thoughtful, well-read, multidimensional leaders who are dedicated to their trade eighteen hours a day and who hold themselves to a standard of fidelity equal to that of "the Greatest Generation" or of any generation to wear the Eagle, Globe and Anchor.

David Danelo is one of those officers. An Annapolis grad who chose the Marine Corps, Captain Danelo served in Iraq alongside the NCOs he so expertly and empathetically depicts in these pages. As a rule, NCOs don't write books. (A few do, like Anthony Swofford, but not many.) Our corporals and sergeants need someone to speak for them, to represent their side in the public forum and to the councils of power. Captain Danelo is that man. He's the ideal guy to step up for squad leaders and platoon sergeants because he's one of them himself. An NCO at heart. You can take it from me, an old E-3 grunt myself, that Dave Danelo is "one of us." And that's the highest praise an enlisted Marine can bestow.

Steven Pressfield
Los Angeles, 2006

Author's Note

Since Iraq is an Arabic word, the English equivalent has no proper pronunciation; the closest would be "eee-rock." The word derives from the Arabic *uruq*, which means *root*. Iraq, a modification requiring the addition of a single letter in the Arabic alphabet, literally translates as "Root of All." To aid the reader in deciphering the nuances in both Iraqi and U.S Marine Corps culture, a glossary of terms has been appended.

Paying special attention to the corporal and sergeant point of view, *Blood Stripes* highlights selected characters and events that took place in western Iraq from February–September 2004. Marines referred to this foray into the Root of All as OIF II-A. This story expresses the grunt's view of the Marine Corps, the infantry, and OIF II-A, specifically the regions of Fallujah, Ramadi, and the Syrian border.

Many units, skirmishes, individuals, and facts that some Iraq veterans might consider important are glossed over or not discussed. This book does not profile any events surrounding the Battle of Najaf in August 2004 or the Second Battle of Fallujah in

November. Absent as well are any combat engagements in 2005 or thereafter.

Of the dozens of Marines interviewed, only four ranked above captain while in Iraq (two generals and two field-grades). Other than these individuals, all material was obtained from enlisted men, company-grade officers, open-source research, and personal observations.

David J. Danelo

December 2005

Dramatis Personae
Al Anbar Province, Iraq

February–September 2004
(in order of appearance)

Sergeant Dusty Soudan—platoon sergeant, 3rd Platoon, Lima 3/7

Corporal Peter "Link" Milinkovic—squad leader, 3rd Platoon, Lima 3/7

Second Lieutenant Benatz*—platoon commander, 3rd Platoon, Lima 3/7

Corporal Brian Zmudzinski—squad leader, 3rd Platoon, Kilo 3/4

John Zmudzinski—father, Brian Zmudzinski

Corporal Daniel Amaya—squad leader, Kilo 3/4

Krista Lance—girlfriend, Sergeant Dusty Soudan

Captain Bill Anderson*—Marine officer

Lieutenant Frederick Stokes—platoon commander, 3rd Platoon, Kilo 3/4

Lieutenant Isaac Moore—anti-armor platoon commander, 3/7

Captain Richard J. Gannon II—company commander, Lima 3/7

Gunnery Sergeant Sandor Vegh—company gunnery sergeant, Lima 3/7

---

* Pseudonym.

Corporal Craig Atkins—fire team leader, 1st Platoon, Fox 2/4

Gordon, Bev, Garrett, and Mitch Atkins—family of Corporal Craig Atkins

Deborah Edwards—girlfriend, Corporal Craig Atkins

Major General James N. Mattis—commanding general, 1st Marine Division

Corporal Dustin Schrage—squad leader, 1st Platoon, Fox 2/4

Lance Corporal Justin Oliver—SAW gunner, 1st Platoon, Fox 2/4

Commander Bill Devine—senior chaplain, 1st Marine Division

Corporal Jarod "Shady" Stevens—humvee driver, I MEF Headquarters Group

Corporal Jason Howell—squad leader, 1st Platoon, Bravo 1/5

Captain Jason Smith—company commander, Bravo 1/5

Lance Corporal "Dirty Steve" Nunnery—fire team leader, 1st Platoon, Bravo 1/5

Lieutenant Stephen Lewis—platoon commander, 1st Platoon, Bravo 1/5

Captain Morgan Savage—company commander, Kilo 3/4

Muhammad*—jihad-worshipping paramilitary fascist

David and Kacey Carpenter—parents, Corporal Daniel Amaya

Corporal Bob Dawson—squad leader, 1st Platoon, Bravo 1/5

Lieutenant Dominique Neal—executive officer, Lima 3/7

Toby Keith—popular country-western musician

Ted Nugent—avid hunter, gun enthusiast and 1970s rock and roll musician

Fatima*—female Iraqi translator, Camp Fallujah

H-Money—male Iraqi translator, Bravo 1/5

---

* Pseudonym.

Grunts

grunt: [noun]
(1) a deep, short throaty sound
(2) a U.S. Army or Marine foot soldier
(3) one who routinely does unglamorous work

At midnight on April 5, 2004, Sgt Dusty Soudan and Cpl Peter "Link" Milinkovic sat outside a mosque in Husaybah, Iraq. A brick wall that unfolded into a courtyard surrounded the Islamic house of worship. Dressed in regular desert camouflage without body armor and carrying only their rifles, the pair of Marines from Lima Company 3/7 carried a handful of pro-American posters written in Arabic and a roll of black electrical tape.

"Boost me up," Link said. Soudan took a knee and cupped his hands.

Link vaulted onto the wall and lay down, sprawling belly first onto the concrete. He extended his hand. Soudan tossed the posters up to Link and then shimmied over the obstacle.

Link, a stocky but fit Marine who spoke with a Chicago accent, was always coming up with some kind of scheme. He would talk to anyone he could—Soudan, his fellow squad leaders, or even Lieutenant Benatz—and tell them his latest plan to win the guerrilla war in Iraq, or at least the one they were fighting in Husaybah on the Syrian border. Soudan was quieter, but ready to try anything he thought might work.

Weeks before, MajGen James N. Mattis's 1st Marine Division—also known as Blue Diamond—had relieved the soldiers from the Army's 82nd Airborne in Iraq's western Al Anbar Province.* The soldiers had told the Marines that the Mujahideen, or Muj, were using the mosques as bases of operation. Marines had seen the men marching in and out of the house of worship carrying packages and staring sullenly at the Americans. Soudan and Link wanted to remind them a new sheriff was in town.

In January 2004, Major General Mattis and his key aides had gone on a leaders recon of the Al Anbar Province. A leaders recon is an information-gathering journey taken to examine the enemy, terrain, and other important variables in the military planning process. After the recon, Mattis decided to place his division headquarters in the town of Ramadi. Located between Baghdad and the Syrian border town of Husaybah, Ramadi is the political capital of Al Anbar and a key trading post along the Euphrates. In 2003, after Saddam Hussein's reign had ended, Army major general Charles Swannack, the commander of the 82nd Airborne Division, had also placed his headquarters there. In counterinsurgency warfare, occupying a region's political center is a fundamental tenet. "Putting the headquarters in Ramadi is a no-brainer," Swannack had told Mattis.

---

* The 1st Marine Division's official logo is a blue diamond superimposed with a red "1" bearing the stamp of Guadalcanal and the Southern Cross constellation. The icon originated in World War II, soon after the division was formed, to commemorate the heroic actions of the men who fought on Guadalcanal.

Hundreds of miles west of Ramadi, Soudan and Link were on a leaders recon of their own initiative. Although they hoped to catch someone building or handling explosives, their unsanctioned foray into the mosque had another purpose. They wanted to show the Muj that they could not continue their activities in the neighborhood without suffering some consequences. *That was how the Army did things,* they thought. *We're Marines. We'll square this place away and they'll love us. After all, they loved us down in southern Iraq last year. We'll be different.*

Although service rivalries have faded over the years at senior military levels—"joint" is the ever-present Pentagon buzzword—young Marines like Soudan and Link arrived in the Al Anbar Province in early 2004 without the same inclusive attitude. They believed the only reason they had to come back was because the Army hadn't done its job. Events would soon change their mind. The corporals didn't think the soldiers had their Spartan discipline.

To focus their energies away from this unhealthy type of rivalry, Major General Mattis had given his Marines three simple mottos to operate by. *First, do no harm:* like a city policeman, make every effort to de-escalate a volatile situation before using violence. *No better friend:* find ways to build common cause with the people of Husaybah and all of Iraq. *No worse enemy:* if some bastard wants to fight, hunt him down and kill him (or her) before they do the same to you. They were easy creeds for young students of the Spartan Way to understand, even if, at times, they took liberties with them.

In ancient Sparta, boys were sequestered from society at the age of seven for training in the *agoge,* the Spartan warrior training camp. Stripped of their possessions, mothers, and egos, the children were barely given enough food to survive. Within their first few weeks in the *agoge*, the Spartans learned that if they wanted to live, they would have to steal food, which was against Spartan law. Those who surreptitiously pilfered food and got away with it not only survived, but they performed better than their peers. In this way, generations of Spartans—and, later, Marines—passed on the lessons and ironies of war as they had learned them. Like many young grunts, Soudan and Link thought that redeeming Iraq might require them to bend a few rules, such as not entering mosques.

The posters Soudan and Link carried into the mosque had pictures of smiling Americans handing out food, medical supplies, and other necessities to grateful Iraqis. They showed Iraqis and Americans working together on projects. "Join the Liberation of Iraq," said the pictures and the Arabic script. By placing up the placards, the pair of Marines were hoping to impose the first of Blue Diamond's mottos on the locals. Their efforts, however, were independent of the chain of command.

Soudan and Link ran past the courtyard and peered into the mosque. They carried their rifles at the ready, but found no reason to raise them. They stopped, looked, listened, and even smelled. All was quiet and still. They taped up the posters near the mosque entrance, glanced quickly, and slid back over the compound walls.

They returned to Camp Husaybah as quickly and quietly as they had exited. Only the gate guard, a lance corporal whose silence was easily secured, knew what had happened. Then they went back to their concrete bunkers, removed their gear, stretched out on their green cots, and went to sleep.

The next morning, 3/7's battalion commander, LtCol Matthew Lopez, was patrolling the town. As the acting viceroy for Husaybah and Al Qaim, Lopez was the senior American for a huge chunk of Iraqi territory. Each day he met with sheikhs, imams, and notional law enforcement officials to advance solutions to problems of water, sewage, security, education, electricity, and fuel. Like recalcitrant privates, the Iraqis in Husaybah—and in many other parts of Al Anbar Province—were long on complaints but short on industriousness.

Lieutenant Colonel Lopez stopped the patrol when he saw the posters. An angry sheikh who Soudan and Link had sensed was up to no good was pointing and gesturing.

"The sheikh wants to know why you have insulted him," an interpreter said. "He says this building is reserved for God. Americans should not be in here."

Lopez went to Camp Husaybah, where one of Lima's platoon commanders happened to be on duty.

"Who was out in town last night?" Lopez demanded. In keeping with the overall Marine strategy, the battalion commander had planned to approach Husaybah with a careful eye towards cultural sensitivities.

The lieutenant was confused. Lima's Marines had been on the other side of the town. No one had said anything about a night observation post. Sometimes the Marines from the reconnaissance platoon would head out into Husaybah on covert missions. It must have been them.

"Sir, I heard Recon was out on patrol."

Lopez nodded, accepting the duty officer's explanation.

"Thanks, lieutenant," Lopez said. "I'll go have a talk with Recon. Those guys are always hard to keep under control."

CHAPTER 1

Go Tell the Spartans

*I think the Army is much more connected to society than
the Marines are. The Marines are extremists.*

—Assistant Army Secretary Sara Lister,
October 26, 1997

They packed their gear during their last week at Camp
Pendleton, an enormous military complex nestled between
Los Angeles and San Diego. Marines thrive on gear. They
acquire it, trade it, buy it, sell it, and cover it with green duct
tape. Marines talk and brag incessantly about their gear. Some
even refer to their girlfriends or wives as "a good piece of gear."
Prior to and after field training exercises, Marines spend days
preparing and cleaning both weapons and gear.

They purchased or acquired—that is, stole—all the special
items they would need. They rigged them onto the webbing of
their flak jackets, along with things like K-bars, CamelBaks, GPS
systems, magazine pouches, and first-aid kits. After inserting the
bulletproof Kevlar plates in the front and back, the entire appa-
ratus, which they called their rig, weighed about twenty-five
pounds. Most gear the grunts used remained attached to the flak

jacket using metal clips, Velcro, or thick green string known as 550-cord.

The most important pieces of gear for any grunt are his good luck charms. The only people more superstitious than men in combat are professional gamblers and baseball players on a hitting streak. Marines carry pictures of lovers and family, wear lucky jewelry, tattoo themselves with lucky symbols, and adorn themselves with manifestations of potentially good karma. One Marine's favorite trinket was the boar's tooth.

The boar's tooth—a scimitar-shaped fragment about four inches long—was taken off a boar in North Carolina in the late 1930s. The heirloom had survived multiple firefights and accidents in World War II, Korea, and Vietnam. Apparently, every man who ever carried the boar's tooth into harm's way returned alive—not necessarily unscathed, but alive—and, most importantly, with male-specific equipment intact.

Thousands of grunts around Camp Pendleton assembled their gear at the same time, in the same way. They packed and repacked, checked and double-checked. They set their gear off in the corner of their barracks rooms and went out to taste alcohol or women one last time before boarding the World Airways jet at March Air Force Base, California, that would take them back to the Root of All.

They had large formations, organized pep rallies that invariably began with the ranking officer asking inanely, "How we doin' Marines?"

How are we doing, sir? Tired—it's February 2004, and we've been either fighting or training for a year. Now we have to go back to do the Army's job for them. *How are we doing, sir?* Angry—we didn't join the Marine Corps to be peacekeepers. We joined because we wanted to kill. *How are we doing, sir?* Envious—most Americans our age are getting either drunk or laid in bars or dorm rooms every night, and we're heading to Iraq for our second tour. Don't these people give a shit that we're at war?

Then again, that's the whole reason they signed up to be grunts in the first place. They didn't want anything to do with the soft, nasty civilian life. They wanted to be men. They wanted challenge. They wanted to fight. They wanted to bear the burdens others were too weak to shoulder. They wanted to live a grunt's life.

Thousands of these grunts packed their gear in the infantry battalions of 1st Marine Division. Actually, they packed their "trash" or their "shit," but for the tender civilian ears of their mom, wife, or girlfriend, "gear" would suffice. They had returned home in triumph in September 2003, but one month later, they were preparing to fight the insurgency in Operation Iraqi Freedom II. The official title for their February 2004 deployment was OIF II, with each letter and number spoken separately. The invasion of Iraq in 2003, as well as the months of immediate aftermath, was called OIF I.

When OIF I ended, Cpl Brian Zmudzinski—a lanky, rawboned, thoughtful Marine who would later deploy for OIF II—was stationed at Marine Security Forces in Bangor, Washington, a submarine base located about an hour west of Seattle. After enlisting as an infantryman with security forces, Zmudzinski had spent almost a year in schools and two years guarding "national strategic assets" at a secret, undisclosed location.*

After he finished his time at Bangor, Corporal Zmudzinski would spend the last year of his enlistment with an infantry battalion. This was different than most young grunts. Infantrymen who were not on security forces spent three-quarters of their

---

* The United States Navy neither confirms nor denies the existence of nuclear weapons at this facility.

enlistment with their battalion. When the Marines attacked into Iraq in March and April 2003, Zmudzinski—stuck at Bangor and away from the war—was bitter. He thought he had missed his big chance. His hopes faded further when Saddam's regime fell so quickly. The corporal thought he would never get into the fight. Zmudzinski would get more than he had ever anticipated.

Three things define Milwaukee: beer, motorcycles, and patriotism.

Brian Zmudzinski grew up in Muskego, about twenty miles south of the original Miller Brewing Company and Harley-Davidson factories. Milwaukee's Major League Baseball team, the Brewers, is the only American professional sports team named to honor the production of alcohol—and they generally give their fans plenty of reasons to drink. In 1903, William Harley and Arthur Davidson produced their first motorized bicycle, which has led devoted fans of the Harley-Davidson Motor Company to easy ride Milwaukee-manufactured hogs across the nation ever since.

Because servicemen enthusiastically welcome both booze and choppers, it comes as no surprise that a town built on such all-American virtues also takes pride in the military. Milwaukee boasts one of the largest locally funded war monuments in the entire country. Located downtown on Lake Michigan, the ninety-four-acre Veteran's Park, War Memorial Center, and Vietnam Veteran's Memorial could be worth millions to real estate brokers or venture capitalists. But in 1957, Milwaukee authorities dedicated the War Memorial Center "To Honor the Dead by Serving the Living" in recognition of those who had served in both World Wars and Korea. Over time, the area expanded. City life in Milwaukee revolves around this sacred terrain.

Brian's father John—a tall, strong, athletic man with a thick, carefully trimmed black mustache—used to take him to the War Memorial when he was young. Brian was the youngest of John and Fran Zmudzinski's three children and their only son. Brian and his father had always been close. Sometimes when they went to Veteran's Park, John would tell a story from his days as a Marine in Vietnam, but usually father and son would just sit together, quietly pondering life the way fathers and sons often do. In 1991, when the city opened up the Milwaukee Vietnam Veteran's Memorial, Fran paid for a brick engraved with John's name. They placed it in the inner circle of the monument, between a series of large and small granite columns.

Brian Zmudzinski attended Milwaukee Area Technical Center, a two-year college where he completed a police science degree in 2000. Because he had always planned to follow his father into military service, Zmudzinski thought about finishing his degree and becoming an officer. As he considered his options, he decided if he did earn a commission, he wanted to get it by coming up through the ranks.

Enlisting later that year, Zmudzinski volunteered for the infantry and requested a special assignment: security forces. Security forces duty meant that he would receive a government clearance, attend an advanced self-defense and weapons school, and guard some high-value asset belonging to the United States Navy. After completing his security forces tour, Zmudzinski would finish the remaining year of his enlistment in the Two Numbers of an infantry battalion.

Earlier that same year, Daniel Amaya from Odessa, Texas, also signed up for security forces. Daniel Amaya was a blend of Jon Stewart, Toby Keith, and John Wayne. Tanned and muscular,

Dan, the family prankster, stood three inches over six feet. He had sandy hair and loved to make others smile. Called "magnetic," "spiritual," and "a natural leader" by his peers, Dan the Man spun off wisecracks and one-liners with balanced, relaxed gestures and classic how-ya'll-doin' Texas facial expressions.

Amaya was a bit of an iconoclast. Instead of playing football at gridiron-crazed Odessa High School—not to be confused with Permian, their crosstown rival depicted in *Friday Night Lights*—he became a cheerleader and played the euphonium in the band. In addition to joking and cheerleading, Amaya loved shooting guns. He had always dreamed of becoming a Marine, then moving on to a life as a professional comedian. After graduating from Odessa in 2000, Dan Amaya joined the Marine Corps.

As with most young men who pursued the Marines, Brian Zmudzinski and Daniel Amaya yearned for some authentic human experience beyond their sanitized, postmodern, X Box–filled, suburban routine. They wanted a rite of passage that confirmed both their transition from adolescence and the indisputability of their manhood. The Marine recruiter stated up front that joining the Corps meant they would live in austere conditions, endure lengthy deployments, and perhaps even see combat. Other services promised educational benefits, world travel incentives, or retirement perquisites. The Marines offered only one thing.

The Spartan Way.

According to an ancient Greek fable, an old man wandering around the quadrennial games on Mount Olympus was looking for a seat. Intoxicated with sport and with an eye toward the evening revelry, the mostly Athenian crowd amused itself by jeering him. The man walked over to a small crowd of Spartans. Clad in their distinctive red tunics, every Spartan stood, offering the old man their entire bench.

Stunned, the Athenians applauded the Spartans for their unhesitating demonstration of respect. The old man turned to the Spartans. Their expression was neither compassionate nor angered. "All the Greeks know what is right," he said, "but only you Spartans have the discipline to do it." He took the seat. The Spartans guarded him as their own for the rest of the Olympics.

The warrior religion, inculcated into every Marine for life, represents this same unflinching code of honor. The samurai called it Bushido, the way of the warrior. Although Marines venerate the history of many warrior cultures, the Spartans—especially as described in Steven Pressfield's novel *Gates of Fire*—have had a profound effect in defining the Marine ideal of leadership, valor, and citizenry.

Since its publication in the fall of 1998, *Gates of Fire*, a work of historical fiction based on the Spartans' heroism and sacrifice at the battle of Thermopylae in 480 B.C., has become the unofficial Bible of Marine infantry. Gen James L. Jones, who was then Commandant of the Marine Corps, called it "a book that every Marine should read." The Spartans in *Gates of Fire* define the antidote to fear, the Highest Good, as the greatest of warrior virtues. They believe this Highest Good can be discovered only on the battlefield. Nothing else—no job, challenge, amount of money or revelry—could replace the purity of this Highest Good when shared monastically with the warrior's mates.

Who would volunteer to become a Spartan? Why would they choose to forsake comfort and seek this mysterious Highest Good? Some find the Spartan Way because they want to protect, lead, and serve. Some want to prove to themselves and the rest of the world that they have earned their citizenship and voice in their republic. Some want to use military service as an honorable rite of passage; they define their maturity simply by wearing the uniform. And some young men, like Dusty Soudan, want a validation of their masculinity like no other: passing the test of mortal combat.

Dusty Soudan has sandy hair, intense blue eyes, and a pugnacious face. At Girard High School, Soudan played inside linebacker and fullback, partied hard, and got into trouble. His grades were mediocre. Soudan hated studying and thirsted for physical activity. Besides football and parties, his girlfriend Krista Lance was the other bright spot in his life. Krista is short and petite, with blue eyes, curly shoulder-length brown hair, and an impish smile. As high school classmates at Girard, they had been dating since their sophomore year.

As Dusty drifted, he frustrated his parents, brothers, and Krista. The youngest of four boys with a father who had served in the Army, Soudan had always planned on joining the military in a nebulous sort of way. Located south of Erie near the Pennsylvania-Ohio border, the rugged town of Girard was a place where yards spanned several acres, fathers worked blue-collar jobs, and houses displayed the stars and stripes.

One day during the last semester of his senior year, a Marine recruiter stopped him in the hallway. The recruiter, a sergeant, was wearing a khaki short-sleeve shirt, black shiny faux-leather shoes, and heavy blue pants with a red stripe down the side. Marines called it the blood stripe, in memory of the valor displayed at the 1847 Battle of Chapultepec during the Mexican-

American War. Only Marines ranked corporal and higher—on average, it took three years for a solid grunt to rise from private to corporal—wore the blood stripes on their uniform trousers.

The sergeant stopped him in the hallway. "You're Dusty Soudan, right? The football player?"

"That's me." Soudan puffed his chest a bit, like the cocky teenage jock he was. The Girard newspaper had written a few articles about his gridiron accomplishments.

The Marine pulled him aside, lowering his voice. "Would you like to miss seventh period?"

I could miss Social Studies and not get in trouble? "Hell yeah!"

"Meet me down in the gym."

Soudan went with a handful of other guys to listen to the recruiter's pitch. Because of his father's service, Dusty had harbored thoughts of joining the Army since childhood. But now the Marines were starting to intrigue him.

Dusty Soudan liked the recruiter. He wasn't pushy, like a used car salesman. He was interesting, relaxed, confident, and cool. He looked sharp and spoke well.

Most of all, he kept giving Dusty opportunities to miss class. After the presentation, he pulled Soudan aside.

"Would you like to miss school tomorrow?"

"The whole day?"

"Sure," the recruiter said. "We'll take you down to Cleveland to visit the MEP Station just to talk over a few things. We'll pay for your hotel for the night. Meals too. You could use some time away from your parents, right?"

That brought another laugh from Soudan. "So . . . am I signing up?"

"Not officially." The recruiter downplayed the event. "The military just has to do some paperwork to make sure your enlistment can go through. You don't have any background with drugs, do you?"

"Do they consider alcohol a drug?" Soudan was still a little hung over from a bender two days before.

The recruiter laughed. "No, you're fine. I'll see you tomorrow at the MEP Station."

Dusty Soudan spent the next day filling out paperwork, attending an interview, and taking a physical at the Military Entrance Processing (MEP) Station in Cleveland. After it was finished, the recruiter drove him back to Girard and shook his hand.

"So what happens next?"

"Well, that's it. If you want to be a Marine, you need to be here on this date," the recruiter pointed, handing Dusty some forms. "If you don't, don't show up."

Soudan thought about it.

"I'll show up."

Dusty Soudan, Brian Zmudzinski, and Dan Amaya—who eventually became the kind of squad leaders that generals depended on to get business done on the battlefield—began their initiation into the Spartan Way with the cleansing ritual of Marine recruit training, which is more commonly known as boot camp. Part tribal initiation and part Protestant tent revival, boot camp is a rebirth. At Parris Island, South Carolina, or San Diego, California, "nasty" civilians repent from their sinful lives of laziness, weakness, and sloth, and are born again with evangelical fervor as Marines—disciplined, strong, and efficient. People serve in the Army, Navy, and Air Force. Marines *become* Marines.

Once through boot camp, each Marine receives a four-digit number that corresponds to the military occupational specialty (MOS) they have earned. Zmudzinski and Amaya were 0311s. The first pair of numbers in the MOS represents the broader field, such as administration (01), intelligence (02), infantry (03), or communications (06). The last two digits designate a Marine's specific job: 0311 signifies infantry rifleman; 0331, machine gunner; 0341, mortarman; and so on. When asked for their job, grunts often say to friends and family, "I'm just a basic oh-three," forgetting that their listener does not know exactly what an oh-three is.

As recruits, they also learned the Spartan worship songs. Every recruit memorizes all three verses of the primary paean, The Marines' Hymn, during boot camp. Billy Joel's "Goodnight Saigon," an anthem of battlefield devotion during Vietnam, is a familiar refrain at Spartan gatherings. Most Spartans know Lee Greenwood's "God Bless the USA" by heart. Toby Keith's renegade country ballads "American Soldier" and "Courtesy of the Red, White, and Blue" often get airplay in Spartan crowds. Out in the field, grunts invariably rig speakers to a humvee or tank and blast heavy metal—Metallica, AC/DC, or "Bodies," an ode to violence by the band Drowning Pool.

Fresh from indoctrination, the first test for a newborn 0311 begins at the School of Infantry. The Corps runs two schools, one near Camp Lejeune in North Carolina, the other at Camp Pendleton in California. At the School of Infantry, the young warriors—each one with hair scalped and burred two inches above their ears, fading into a small patch of scruff on the top of their head known as a high-and-tight—learn their trade. They learn to patrol, attack, and defend. They memorize acronym after acronym: The Six Troop-Leading Steps, Artillery/Mortar Call For Fire, Machine Gun Employment, The Five Paragraph Order.

They punch, gouge, kick, and choke each other during Marine martial arts training, informally known as "semper fu." They sit in discussion groups and think through tactical decision games: "You are guarding an embassy in the Middle East and a group of Arabs are massing in angry protest. Gunfire erupts in the air. Do you shoot at them or not, private?"

Weekend liberty at the School of Infantry is like a boot camp in sex and economics. Those in California ramble around the hip surf town of Oceanside. They scare pelicans, flirt with local girls on the pier, rummage through elite overpriced–but–cool-looking military gear shops, and get their first of many grunt tattoos.

Those on the East Coast explore exotic Jacksonville, North Carolina, where signs advertising strip clubs and churches exist in equal ratio. Having the largest concentration of military bases in the region, North Carolina markets itself as "America's most military friendly state." The Marine expatriate complex comprises a majority of the civilian population of Onslow County, where the region seamlessly blends southern hospitality with the centuries-old Bible Belt traditions of hell-raising on Saturday followed by forgiveness on Sunday.

Regardless of church, region, or liberty experience, by the time they headed for security forces school in Chesapeake, Virginia, and then to their first duty station in Bangor, Washington, Amaya and Zmudzinski had figured out they had joined a religion as well as a military service. Like Taoist monks, the grunts of the Corps nurture their devotion through faithfully practicing Spartan precepts, which revolve around reconciling the twin yin/yang cultural imperatives of Order and Disorder.

Non-commissioned officers—corporals and sergeants—are the stalwart laity of the Spartan Way. They assume responsibility for imbuing the Way's sacred tenets of Order and Disorder into every young boot that crosses their path. Finding the balance within this dichotomy is tricky; both cultures exert a strong pull on Marines. The twins call like sirens from opposite banks of a river, singing for the Marine to listen to their virtues and ignore their vices.

The culture of Order is the Marine in dress blues, spotless and pristine, medals perfectly measured, hair perfectly trimmed. Any rule, code, or tradition that has echoed down from Tun Tavern in 1775 throughout the Marine Corps' storied existence is obeyed rigorously, to the jot and tittle.* Sharp creases with starched uniforms; drill with gleaming, spit-polished boots; razor-sharp haircuts; junk-on-the-bunk inspections with buffed canteen cups; entrenching tools spray-painted black for an extra shine; coming to parade rest when addressing a superior: these types of things comprise the culture that is Orderly, functional, prepared, and disciplined. This represents strength and power and everything stereotypically military.

However, as anyone who has endured the beach landings of World War II, the tundra of Korea, the fierce jungles of Vietnam, or the gritty desert fight in Iraq would affirm, war is anything but Orderly. Combat is filled with uncertainties, half-truths, bad information, changing directives from seemingly incompetent higher headquarters, and unexplained explosions. War is chaos, the ultimate form of Disorder.

The culture of Disorder embraces this. Loves it, really. These are Marines who live to be covered with dirt and sweat, wearing filthy clothes in hideous weather. They are happiest when they haven't slept in days and their rations are low and they are hun-

---

* On November 10, 1775, the Continental Congress ordered Samuel Nicholas to raise two battalions of Marines. That afternoon, Nicholas began performing his duty in Philadelphia's Tun Tavern. Marines are very proud that the Corps was born in a bar.

gry and thirsty and under attack with bullets and RPGs and somebody expects them to *perform* or *decide* or *figure it out.* That's the reason they joined in the first place. These folks, these amours of Disorder, really don't care about whether their ribbons are worn one-eighth or one-sixteenth of an inch from the pocket of their dress blues or about the proper step, cadence, and movement to form for physical training. They join for the Disorderly trials and adrenaline rushes that only war can provide.

Even more so, the champions of Disorder join not just to experience war, but also to lead others in it. They start out as young boots, craving to be sent on that *one dangerous mission,* the one that is hard and difficult and nearly impossible, but their own strength and cunning and intellect enables them to get it done. Maybe they must find a land navigation box or transport a secret message or steal something for their platoon sergeant. No matter. After getting the job done, the boot has demonstrated he can *accomplish the mission* in the midst of this uncertainty and chaos. Soon enough, that private first class or lance corporal will blossom into a corporal, a non-commissioned officer, a leader completely responsible for the lives and actions of other Marines, and in the midst of the craziness of bullets and explosions, Marines will look at him with *that look:* What do we do now, corporal? Sergeant? Staff sergeant? Lieutenant? Captain? General?

The first time Amaya, Zmudzinski, and Soudan had younger Marines give them *that look* was during their years at Bangor, Washington. Nestled amidst cedars, pines, and Douglas firs, Naval Submarine Base Bangor was home to several Trident missile submarines that carried national strategic assets. Marines from security forces could neither confirm nor deny that they guarded those assets.

They could also neither confirm nor deny that their routine was filled with long posts, frustrating superiors, and mundane

Orderly tasks. In their two years with security forces, the men slogged through enough days of guard duty to fill a six-month deployment. Worse, some of their leaders were not faithful to the Spartan Way. When Zmudzinski and Amaya were at Bangor, their sergeant major—a bulbous, loud martinet who had spent over twenty-five years in infantry units without seeing combat—insisted on a white-glove room or uniform inspection at least once a week. The men had to display every item of their polished gear in a methodical manner. Called a junk-on-the-bunk inspection, this only made them feel like they were that much more removed from the "real" Marine Corps, where grunts actually used their entrenching tools to dig real fighting holes instead of spray-painting them to a blackened shine to impress their lazy boss.

After September 11, 2001, when the rest of the Marine Corps went on the warpath, the Bangor routine remained unchanged. If anything, the Marines at Bangor became even more demoralized. They had signed up for security forces after the recruiters had said they would be going on exciting excursions all over the world. ("You'll be stationed with the Navy! You'll see foreign ports! You'll get the best missions in the Marine Corps!") Instead, they had been trapped in a life of boredom, shackled to strategic assets, while their buddies from boot camp prepared for war with infantry units.

Of course, not everyone was happy with the idea of preparing for war. In particular, most of the parents of young men who thirsted for action had seen their sons volunteer for military service before the events of 9/11. Like others in America, many of these parents thought they had seen the so-called End of History, where democracy had been proven to be the only logical form of government and war would become little more than an occasional nuisance. When the families of young boys like Brian Zmudzinski, Daniel Amaya, Jason Howell, Dusty Soudan, and

Craig Atkins sent their sons into the Marines in 2000 and early 2001, they thought the most action they would see might be a peacekeeping mission.

While Zmudzinski and Amaya were at Bangor, they were promoted to corporal. Although promotion to lance corporal is a rubber stamp affair, attaining the rank of corporal is difficult. More than a dozen variables—physical fitness, leadership ability, marksmanship, uniform appearance, conduct, and even academic performance in correspondence courses—are factored into a number called a composite score. Various algorithms nestled somewhere in Quantico, Virginia, are computed every three months to produce the magical cutting score. All Marines with composite scores higher than that are promoted.

The day a Marine becomes a corporal, he also earns his Blood Stripes. After the promotion ceremony, all sergeants and below in the unit will drag the new corporal into his barracks room, dog-pile him, and take turns throwing punches to both sides of his legs. The event is an informal Marine Corps sacrament to remind the new corporal of his responsibilities as an NCO: that he is now a leader in a warrior tradition that pre-dates the nation itself. More fraternally, it's also one of the few times lance corporals can get away with pummeling someone they will eventually take orders from.*

One day in December 2002, the Bangor sergeant major held a formation for all the enlisted Marines.

---

* Technically, the Blood Stripes ceremony was banned in 1996 when a new sheaf of Marine Corps hazing regulations was imposed in the wake of a brutal "blood pinning" televised on a popular American news program. However, only a handful of officers and staff NCOs made any effort to outlaw the corporal's rite of passage. To maintain plausible deniability, platoon and company commanders and their staffs have an unofficial "don't ask, don't tell" policy. Staff NCOs and officers rarely participate in the Blood Stripes ritual.

"HEY YOU NASTY GRUNTS! OOOOHHHRAHHH! CAN YOU GIMME AN OOOOHHHRAHHH!"

"Ooh-rah sergeant major," the men offered.

"THAT AIN'T LOUD ENOUGH! YOU DON'T SOUND VERY MOTIVATED TO ME! HOW ABOUT A REAL OOOOOOOHHHHRAHH!"

"Ooh-RAH ser-GEANT ma-JOR!" Their voices dripped with the nasal inflections of false enthusiasm.

"Okay, Marines," said the sergeant major, who had decided that the motivation level was high enough for his tastes. "Here's the word. The infantry battalions need more bodies. Rumor is that there's gonna be another war with the ragheads. Anyone who has less than three months to go until the end of his two-year security forces contract can volunteer to leave early and go kill camel jockeys. Now I know all ya'll hard-chargers wanna go out there and get some. Any takers?"

Several corporals, including Dan Amaya and Dusty Soudan, raised their hands. They had no intention of spending their four years in the Marine Corps stuck at Bangor if a war was happening. All Marines on security forces spent the last year of their enlistment with infantry battalions. In the past, many had arrived to their grunt units unprepared for the rigors of training, which had given security forces a bad reputation. Amaya and Soudan did not want to miss out on anything. Furthermore, they were certain that wherever they were going, the Bangor sergeant major wouldn't be.

Corporal Zmudzinski, who would not be free to leave Bangor until the following September, felt left out. A few days later, Amaya and the other volunteers held a farewell party to say their goodbyes to Zmudzinski and the others they would leave behind. The party was at Dusty Soudan's apartment. Another Marine at the party who was angry at remaining behind was a corporal named Jason Howell.

They drank a lot of beer and had themselves a good time. *After all*, they thought, *we might never see each other again.*

Since the men knew little of the Marine Corps beyond the clandestine world of Bangor, officers taught a class to Marines leaving for their units about the Fleet Marine Force, the part of the Marine Corps that comprised the infantry. They were encouraged to ask questions about the basic elements of an infantry battalion; their officers did not want corporals to appear foolish or poorly trained to the squads they would lead in battle.

"What does 3/4 mean?" Cpl Brian Zmudzinski asked. The Marines often called him Z-Mud, or simply Z. Grunts with complicated ethnic surnames often find their identity reduced to a couple of easy-to-pronounce syllables. Quintanablea becomes "Q." Olofunmike becomes "Foomz." Garcia-Torresramirez becomes "Hey You."

"3/4 is pronounced 'Three Four,'" replied the briefing officer, Capt Bill Anderson, a typical Marine officer who often answered with guttural, monosyllabic responses such as "check," "roger," or "noted."

Anderson continued: "Three Four stands for 3rd Battalion, 4th Marines. 'Marines' means 'Marine regiment.' An average battalion is a little over 1,100 Marines. A regiment has three battalions, plus several supporting elements. The division comes after regiment. There are only three divisions in the entire active duty Marine Corps. Do you know what division your battalion is in?"

"The 1st Marine Division, sir."

"Check. What's their nickname?"

Zmudzinski glanced at the PowerPoint slide. "Blue Diamond?"

"Nice guess. They're also called 'The Old Breed.' Do you know who the commanding general of Blue Diamond is?"

"MajGen James N. Mattis." The room grew quiet at Zmudzinski's invocation of the grizzled, plainspoken warrior. Stories flew throughout the Marine Corps about Mattis. Some of them were even true. One Marine swore that Mattis had spent five years fighting in the French foreign legion under a *nom de guerre* before becoming a Marine officer.

The spread of rumors and stories through the Marine Corps is called the Lance Corporal Network. Lance corporals are the mouthpieces of the Corps. They trade information constantly, the way stockbrokers swap tips and students discuss final exams. In August 2002, the Blue Diamond Lance Corporal Network buzzed about their new commanding general. He's awesome! He's crazy! He walks the lines at night and talks to his Marines! He sleeps on the ground, right next to them! He's not afraid of anything or anybody! He fires bad officers on the spot! He used to be in the French Foreign Legion!

Anything that comes through the Lance Corporal Network is probably half true. But that's the point: if an idea reaches the Network, there is usually some margin of truth to it. Mattis really did walk the lines at midnight and chat up the young troops. He really did sleep the same way his Marines did—if they were on the ground, so was he. He really did mandate that all burdens were equally distributed. He was never a French legionnaire.

"Z-Mud, which battalion are you going to again?" Anderson asked once more. Like high school teachers, Marine leaders often repeat important points for the sake of emphasis when they give classes.

"Three Four, sir."

"Do you know their motto?" Zmudzinski did not.

Anderson explained that each Marine infantry battalion has a motto, nickname, or legend associated with their traditions of heroism in battle. Battalion mottos evolved during World War II, Korea, and Vietnam. 2/4, an infantry battalion that would later distinguish itself in Ramadi, is called "The Magnificent Bastards." 3/7 is known as "The Cutting Edge." 1/5's motto is "Make Peace or Die." Not all slogans are original: 3/4 shares their moniker, "Thundering Third," with at least one other Marine battalion, 3/1, and with several assorted Army units.

An infantry battalion defines a grunt's experience and identity; the battalions are the grist of the Marine Corps. Officers and enlisted infantrymen might spend three years with the same platoon or bounce back and forth between the three rifle companies and the larger weapons company. Unlucky souls wind up in headquarters and service units, referred to as "H and S"—or condescendingly by grunts as "hug and suck" or "hot dogs and Snickers." The nicknames remind their non-infantry brethren, whom they derisively call pogues, of their place in the Marine Corps caste system.

A grunt considers his infantry battalion as the primary clan to which loyalty is pledged. Regiment is too far removed, but the battalion is close enough to become an extension of oneself. The clan goes to war together. Marines who combated the Iraqi insurgency in 2004 trained, deployed, and returned to the comforts of home as battalions. This was not always the case. During the Vietnam War, men rotated back and forth from 'Nam to the World as individuals rather than units.

Whenever Marine infantrymen ask each other, "What unit are you with?" they mean, "Which battalion are you in?" The response is Two Numbers. Marines wage war in small units as squads, platoons, and companies. Nonetheless, when queried for his unit's title, a grunt invariably replies with the Two Numbers—One Five, Two Four, Three Seven, Three Four—that serve to designate his particular tribe.

The rhythm and intensity of deployments, referred to as the operations tempo, increased dramatically for grunts after December 2002. That date marked the initial major call-up of Marine reserve units required to augment the active duty for OIF I.* Every active duty infantry battalion that deployed for OIF II in 2004 had spent more than half a year overseas, either in Iraq or Okinawa, for most of 2003.

"What's a rifle platoon like?"

An infantry officer and former platoon commander himself, Captain Anderson offered a cursory description of the interpersonal dynamics of Marine rifle platoons. He explained that they are commanded by second lieutenants and that the senior enlisted man, typically a staff sergeant, is the platoon sergeant. The relationship between this pair affects the entire platoon. If both men are strong leaders, the platoon generally performs well. Weakness in either is a kiss of death, unless the squad leaders step in and fill the void.

The politics of a rifle platoon seem straightforward but are actually complex. By title and job description, the platoon commander and platoon sergeant wield the most power among the forty Marines that comprise a standard platoon. Each platoon has three squads of about a dozen, normally led by corporals or sergeants. Each squad has three fire teams.

A fire team has four men: the rifleman (a boot), the assistant SAW-gunner (a junior lance corporal), the SAW-gunner (a senior

---

* Reserve infantry battalions have distinctive nomenclature. In the 4th Marine Division—the Marines' only reserve division—the reserve battalions come from regiments in the double digits. For example, 2/23, 3/24, and 1/25 are Marine reserve units. Active duty infantry battalions come from single digit regiments.

lance corporal), and the team leader. The fire team is built around the SAW, which stands for squad automatic weapon. The SAW is a lightweight machine gun with bipods that fold out and extend. Marines carry it across their back with a wide, black strap. The weapon has an interchangeable barrel, which is carried by the assistant SAW-gunner. The SAW also has an unfortunate reputation for jamming constantly.

When a private first class reports to an infantry battalion, he is called a boot. All Marines of this lowly rank are considered boots, unless a newer, younger group of fresh fish arrives before the boots are promoted to lance corporal.* The only exception to this is a private first class that used to be a lance corporal but is punished with reduction in rank—"busted down"—for some type of misbehavior.

A Marine who is busted down might still remain a cool guy in the platoon—perhaps he was merely caught drinking underage by a "dickhead" officer who wanted to make an example of him. If this is the case, he maintains respect; the jarhead was only dumb enough to get caught. If he was busted down for doing something foolish (accidentally pointing his weapon at another Marine), stupid (fooling around with the battalion commander's fifteen-year-old daughter), or weak (falling asleep while on watch), he becomes an outcast.

Being an outcast is much worse than being a boot. Seniors may pick on boots, but they also watch out for them, like a protective older brother who won't let anyone else thrash his siblings. Nobody likes an outcast. Boots and outcasts do shit details and working parties. Shit details and working parties occur sev-

---

* In truth, anyone reporting to a new unit is a "boot" for a few weeks or months. However, junior Marines would not call a staff NCO or officer a boot to his face unless they had decided they liked the Marine and wanted to tease him about his status within the unit.

eral times a day, whenever the platoon sergeant or company gunny either needs Marines to go do something or is in a particularly sadistic mood. Marines who piss them off are given duties of carrying ammunition, fetching MREs, standing the early morning hours of watch, or—worst of all—cleaning out the burn shitters.

Above the boots and outcasts are the lance corporals. Being a lance corporal is like being caught in a real-life version of William Golding's *Lord of the Flies*. Boots survive by doing what they are told. Lance corporals excel through alpha male characteristics of strength, cleverness, skill, and force of personality. Lance corporals who possess greater leadership ability—which is a fancy way of saying that they can inspire, persuade, or threaten other lance corporals into doing what they tell them—are promoted into more senior positions, such as SAW gunners. The strongest among them became team leaders. They are given omnipotent power by the gods of the Marine Corps over the lives of three other Marines.

Among the leaders, the pecking order within the three fire teams of an infantry squad is rigid. The 3rd Fire Team leader, while junior to the 2nd Team leader, is senior to the other SAW gunners. However, he can only boss them around to a point. If the junior grunts are getting harassed too much, their own team leader will step in and tell his fellow team leader to knock it off. A slightly different dynamic happens on a squad level. Squad leaders will rarely let other squad leaders give orders to their Marines. This would be perceived as weakness, and the Marines would not respect their own squad leader. The exceptions to this rule are boots, who were usually considered platoon property regardless of their squad.

Most platoon commanders expect their platoon sergeants to handle the minutiae of gear accountability and minor disciplinary infractions while they shoulder the "big picture" issues of officer politics and tactical problem solving. A point of pride for any good platoon sergeant is to handle discipline problems in the unit without the platoon commander's knowledge. If the pair trusts each other, the platoon sergeant will eventually tell his lieutenant what happened, knowing the story of the Marine who crashed his truck or got into a losing barfight or owed several thousand dollars on his delinquent credit card would soon come to the officer's attention anyway. But no platoon sergeant worth his salt will let anyone speak to his Marines without prior knowledge or approval. Doing so would mean two things: he would look weak to his peers, and his platoon would be on a one-way express straight to the skyline.

Sometimes higher commanders consider an entire platoon, company, or even battalion to be an outcast unit. This happens when units either fail to accomplish their mission, have Marines who repeatedly get in trouble, or display some pattern of behavior not in accordance with what the commander expects. A problem unit is "on the skyline." This expression comes from the way Marines are trained to climb over an obstacle. They are taught to keep a low profile: being on the skyline, absent cover and concealment, is wrong and could get a person killed.

No unit wants to be on the skyline. Their commanders closely scrutinize them to decipher the exact reason behind their flawed performance. They are assigned more working parties, shit details, or other unpleasant tasks. They are not trusted to handle exciting and difficult assignments. Marines from stronger units with higher morale and better reputations pick on them.

Every Marine spends at least some time as a boot. Every unit—from squads to regiments—spends at least a few days on the skyline. The test of the individual Marine and unit leader comes when they are the boots or outcasts or their units are on the skyline. Can they bounce back? Can they fix themselves? Nobody asks these questions unless the unit or Marine is skylined.

After he left Bangor for the Thundering Third of 3/4, Cpl Brian Zmudzinski had the kind of platoon commander who kept his men off the skyline. After Zmudzinski had served with 3rd Platoon, Kilo Company, 3/4, the corporal said that Lt Fredrick Stokes was "a tactical and common sense genius." No officer could have ever received a higher accolade than establishing that reputation with his men. On the other hand, Zmudzinski said the platoon sergeant was a pushover who had no control over the platoon and little backbone in combat. Consequently, Stokes relied on the strength of his squad leaders to get the job done.

For Lieutenant Stokes, they were willing to die trying.

When Cpl Dan Amaya deployed in January 2003 with Lieutenant Stokes and Kilo 3/4 for the attack into Iraq to topple Saddam Hussein's regime, he succeeded as a leader by striking an expert balance between Order and Disorder, applying the strengths derived from both cultures in each unique situation. Amaya had the serial numbers for his squad's weapon, radio, and night-vision devices written into a little green notebook (Order). Through experience and training, he instinctively recognized where to deploy his fire teams if an ambush happened (Disorder). He knew how to request a resupply of water or food from his platoon sergeant or company gunny. But he also possessed the ingenuity, resourcefulness, and mental agility necessary to find any source of water or food available to survive in the unforgiving terrain. Amaya punished his Marines when he deemed necessary so that no one questioned his authority. At the same time, he also covered up minor infractions, protecting those in his charge from high-level retribution, so none questioned his loyalty.

In September 2003, Cpl Brian Zmudzinski left Bangor and reported to Twentynine Palms, a remote Marine base in the southern California desert three hours east of Los Angeles informally known as the Stumps. The corporal felt impotent because he had missed OIF I, which, at that time, was "the war." Zmudzinski was assigned to 3/4, which was one of only four battalions permanently stationed at the Stumps.

Duty in Twentynine Palms is a mixed blessing. A barren land of scrub, desert flowers, and live fire ranges with names like Quackenbush and Lava Lake, Twentynine Palms is also the largest training area in the Marine Corps. Throughout the 1990s, Marine infantry battalions from across the country rotated through a month-long training exercise where they learned to choreograph the ballet of mortars, artillery, bombs, and bullets that military experts call combined arms. "We use Twentynine Palms to perfect our combined-arms synergy," said the officers. "The Stumps might be a dirty, nasty rat hole, but it's the best place in the world to blow shit up," said the sergeants.

Lt Fredrick Stokes, 3rd Platoon commander, Kilo 3/4, had learned early to make friends in every section of the battalion. Muscular, intense, and admired, Stokes had buddies he could count on in administration, intelligence, operations, communications, and especially supply. Marine leaders learn to develop a Godfather-like habit of informally doling out favors and accepting them in return.

Stokes had made one such arrangement with the administrative Marines of 3/4. Quietly, they would alert him whenever a new corporal, sergeant, or staff sergeant was checking into Kilo. Before he arrived at the company area, Stokes would walk down, ask the new Marine a few questions and observe his response.

Lieutenant Stokes looked for the best he could find to lead his platoon.

After his informal interview, Stokes liked Zmudzinski. "He was intelligent, straightforward, and courteous." The lieutenant knew the company first sergeant would like him too. Stokes told a couple of his Marines to help Zmudzinski with his pack and sea bags, and then conferred with the first sergeant. A few minutes later, Kilo's newest corporal was assigned to 3rd Platoon.

After reporting to Kilo 3/4, Zmudzinski walked into the three-story concrete barracks. The first person he saw was Cpl Dan Amaya, who had an extra rack in his room and invited Zmudzinski to take it. Friends from their days at Bangor, Zmudzinski and Amaya were now roommates and platoon mates.

Amaya carried a lot of weight in the platoon. He used his leverage to help ease Zmudzinski's transition into the unit. 3/4 had bragging rights as the battalion that had reached Baghdad on April 9, 2003, flagging down a tank recovery vehicle and pulling down Saddam Hussein's statue in Firdous Square while the world watched. Anyone who hadn't seen combat with them was viewed circumspectly. With Zmudzinski, Amaya's word was enough. "When Dan Amaya said someone was a good guy, it meant something," Zmudzinski said.

But Zmudzinski also proved to the platoon why he was worthy of Amaya's good opinion. When he checked in, Kilo Company was in the middle of their last combined-arms exercise before deployment. Viewed as the bar exam for an infantry unit, grunts often spent months preparing for the event.* Zmudzinski had nothing beyond his training at Bangor and his skills as a corporal. Coolly, he led his squad through maneuvers at Range 400,

---

* Beginning in 2005, a new culminating event for units deploying to Iraq evolved. Called Mojave Viper, the training exercise was designed from lessons learned fighting the insurgency in the Al Anbar Province.

a complex live fire problem that challenges leaders of all ranks. Underneath his quiet demeanor, Zmudzinski had that mixture of courage, brilliance, and moxie that Marines call "leadership ability" and that writer Tom Wolfe once called "the right stuff."

As Marines like Soudan, Zmudzinski, and Amaya advanced in rank and learned to fuse the polar opposites of Order and Disorder together, they discovered a type of sober, focused stoicism that characterizes those who pursue the Spartan Way. As corporals, they were the stalwart laity, responsible for passing the tenets of the Way to those under their charge, guiding them in finding balance. An absence of discipline and rigor—or the presence of inane Orderly edicts—could easily drive the warrior into a dangerous Disorderly insanity.

In the Iraq they were heading to, insanity would be present in spades.

Market Street

After Dusty Soudan joined the Corps, he and Krista, his high school girlfriend, broke up and got back together twice. Eventually Krista moved from their hometown of Girard, Pennsylvania, to Silverdale, Washington. The couple lived together in an apartment while Soudan was at Bangor. By the time Krista came out to Washington, they were both certain that marriage would only be a matter of time—a mere ceremony that would formalize what had already taken place in their hearts.

Their nuptials would have to wait. Dusty was leaving Bangor, deploying to go after those "camel jockeys" the sergeant major had hollered about. In the meantime, they decided Krista would move back to Girard and wait for Dusty while he went to Iraq.

Soudan joined Lima 3/7 in January 2003, just a few days before his new battalion, whose motto was The Cutting Edge, sharpened their blades and deployed to Kuwait. He was assigned as a fire team leader to Lt Isaac Moore's 1st Platoon. Moore, who grew up in Wasilla, Alaska, had shot his first caribou at a young age. Moore was relaxed around men, stress, and guns. His Marines, including Soudan, felt comfortable with his command. Moore eventually became one of the lieutenants that the Marines in Lima 3/7 used as their standard for measuring the performance of other junior officers.

The three weeks of war in the spring of 2003 were a blur to Soudan. The closer they got to Baghdad, the more intense the fighting became. One day in early April, Soudan's fire team was near a military complex outside Iraq's capital city. Manning an observation post, the team was detached about 200 yards forward of their platoon. Suddenly, two dozen uniformed Iraqi soldiers approached. Their AK-47s and RPGs were at the ready. Soudan and his fire team engaged. The Iraqi platoon returned fire.

After calling for backup, Soudan continued fighting the Iraqis with just five Marines: three from his fire team and a pair of machine gunners that had gone forward with them. By the time Lieutenant Moore arrived, Soudan's team had already decimated the Iraqi platoon. Using classic maneuver tactics, Moore took over. The lieutenant set up two squads as a base of fire and used his remaining squad in a flanking attack. The Iraqi platoon was destroyed.

Cpl James Lis, another friend of Soudan's from Bangor, was the squad leader that led the charge into the Iraqi flank. During the attack, an Iraqi grenade exploded next to Lis's left ear, leaving him with a minor shrapnel wound. With the flank complete, Moore called up his remaining squads. As the Marines consolidated their new position, a single Iraqi soldier had survived by building a rampart with the bodies of his dead comrades. The Iraqi continued to fight.

Soudan jumped over a brick wall and was running forward into the attack. Suddenly, Lis, who was in front of Soudan and still bleeding from his wound, turned around, shoving Soudan back towards the wall. "Get down! Grenade!"

Soudan and his squad leader, Sgt Tim Wolkow, bounded back over the wall, following Lis. The grenade exploded. Thanks to Lis's warning, no one was injured.

That firefight marked the only major combat Soudan participated in during OIF I. The fight had turned out just like it was supposed to: the bad guys were all dead; the good guys were bloodied, but alive. Combat with the Marine Corps, it seemed, was always a winning proposition. Soudan liked it. As Sir Winston Churchill once said, "There's nothing quite as exhilarating as being shot at and missed."

In May 2003, after the intensity and chaos, life relaxed for Soudan. Instead of holing up in secure bases and pining for the next flight home, 3/7, 3/4, and the other infantry battalions fanned out in southern Iraq and worked to regain the Shiite's trust. Battalion commanders became ad hoc potentates. In the southern Iraqi cities of Karbala, Babil, Najaf, Hillah, Diwaniyah, and Samawah, Marines presented an air of authority. They formed town councils, identified trustworthy citizens, held local elections, sent their men on patrols, trained town policemen, responded to local complaints, evicted corrupt mayors, restored running water, fixed the energy grid, and rebuilt sewer systems. After May 1, the Blue Diamond did not sustain a single combat-related casualty for the rest of the year.

At the time, many casual observers dismissed this fact. Conventional wisdom said that the Shiites—who had been brutalized for decades under Saddam—would embrace the Americans. Nevertheless, the Shiites still resented the American abandonment after Operation Desert Storm. In 1991, U.S. operatives encouraged the Shiites to mutiny against Hussein, and then abandoned them to a bloody fate. Thousands were tortured, raped, and killed—all because of American policies. The potential for guerilla violence remained strong.

Beyond the planning in 2002, no specific postwar structure had been crafted by higher headquarters for the Marines to utilize. They were on their own. The Coalition Provisional Authority (CPA) provided little assistance.* Instead, the Marines used initiative, perseverance, and common sense. Squad leaders acted on instinct to determine whom they could and couldn't trust.

In the summer of 2003, events in southern Iraq were largely benign. The men shed their body armor and Kevlar helmets when patrolling, projecting a peaceful image. Soudan's patrols in Karbala often ended at a local Iraqi restaurant, where Marines were offered a free meal and several glasses of *chai*, Iraqi tea. Marines took advantage of the Shiite joy at Saddam's removal by demonstrating an ability to measurably improve the lives of more than 10 million people. Months later, when Polish, Spanish, and Ukrainian troops patrolled Shiite cities like Diwaniyah, they were often asked, "When are the Marines coming back?"

In Baghdad and central Iraq, this did not happen. The Sunni heartland, equally ripe with grudges and furious with the loss of power and prestige, tipped toward rebellion. Any question of whether or not a long-term guerrilla war would ensue was answered when the CPA announced the disbanding of the Iraqi Army, a move that many American generals strongly opposed.

The Army's 82nd Airborne Division had been tasked with mollifying the wild west of Al Anbar Province. They handled

---

* According to Marines, CPA stood for Can't Produce Anything. David Phillips's *Losing Iraq* and Larry Diamond's *Squandered Victory* address the tragedies and missed opportunities involving the CPA.

their assignment with a fraction of the troops that the Marines brought when they relieved them in February 2004.* The covert supply routes that sustained the insurgency in Baghdad and elsewhere originated primarily in Syria and ran straight through the 82nd's territory. When planning commenced in October 2003 for the return to Iraq, the Network chattered that Marines were being sent back in to fix the Army's mistakes.

On this point, the Network was wrong. Despite the postwar momentum in April 2003, stabilizing Al Anbar was a task no military unit in Iraq—Marine or Army—was fully equipped to handle. However, the constant emphasis Marine units placed on building trust with local Iraqi citizens immediately after the war helped prevent the southern region from "going guerrilla." The accidental shootings of unarmed civilians in Mosul and Fallujah soon after the fall of Saddam did not help soldiers keep their tenuous grip on what remained of loyalty or favor towards their liberators.

While 3/7 was in southern Iraq, Soudan had a chance to make a name for himself as a squad leader. After 3/7 returned to Twentynine Palms, Soudan impressed battalion leaders enough to win a meritorious promotion to sergeant. The competition hinged on a question-and-answer session with a panel of senior enlisted men. A final subjective vote was required. Soudan and another squad leader had tied. They both had near-perfect scores on marksmanship and physical fitness tests. Soudan's stoic bearing during the Q&A won the promotion, but both Marines were viewed as two of the battalion's best.

The other Marine was Cpl Peter "Link" Milinkovic.

---

* Even with the personnel increase, many Marines still felt they were undermanned for their mission in Al Anbar.

Three days after his foray into the mosque with his best friend Link, Sgt Dusty Soudan thought he was starting to get a feel for the town of Husaybah (pronounced "Whoose-EYE-ba"). Although the Marine base took an erratic pounding from enemy mortars, 3rd Platoon had not yet been directly attacked. At the time, Soudan and Link thought that perhaps their brazen placement of the posters might have made the Muj think twice about confronting the Marines in direct combat.

On the afternoon of April 8, 2004, Soudan, Link, and the rest of 3rd Platoon, Lima Company 3/7, stepped off on a patrol down Market Street in Husaybah. Since becoming the platoon sergeant two weeks earlier, Soudan had conducted a couple of patrols around the town. He had worked through countless scenarios, immediate action drills, and rehearsals. Other than the mortars, the men hadn't seen much action. It wasn't quite as peaceful as southern Iraq, but they thought it might get there soon.

Soudan had taught his Marines what to do if he went down. He had learned the job of men two levels above and below him. He had wrestled with the shoot/don't shoot scenarios that were the necessary constraints of the rules of engagement in guerrilla war. Tactically, he was ready to be a platoon sergeant. But tactics is only part of the equation. Could he lead forty men instead of twelve? On Market Street, he would find out.

The patrol on Market Street was a routine sweep through Husaybah, a town of three square miles with several hundred multi-story concrete buildings, a grid of dusty streets, and at least two mosques. The Marines maintained a small outpost on the northwest corner of town. The base was manned by Lima, a platoon from Kilo, a detachment from Recon, and a section of the combined anti-armor team (CAAT) platoon. The CAAT vehicles carried machine guns and bore heavy, thick armor plates. The entire detachment at Husaybah: 250–300 Marines.

Soudan's platoon commander, 2nd Lieutenant Benatz, had taken the psyops—psychological operations—truck on the patrol. At certain times, psyops trucks would play loud heavy metal music or even taunt the Muj with Arab swear words. This particular psyops unit had a different task. They were broadcasting a phone number in Arabic for locals to call if they wanted to rat out insurgents to Marines. Since Lima Company had arrived in March, whenever the psyops truck had gone out on patrol, it took heavy fire. The Muj wanted to send their own message.

That day, 3rd Platoon planned to patrol the northern area of town. 2nd Squad headed straight down Market Street, which ran east from the Marine base for nearly a mile. 1st Squad walked one street above Market, and 3rd Squad patrolled one street below. Because of the street activity and presence of obstacles, the Marines could see only the other men in their squad. The squad leaders coordinated their movements with the platoon leadership over Motorola radios the unit had purchased earlier in the year. This allowed them to "maintain situational awareness," meaning they could tell each other what the hell was going on.

Market Street was busy; improvised explosive devices (IEDs) could be hidden anywhere. The sullen, gawking crowds demonstrated a silent hostility toward the Marines. Despite the reaction, the patrol's task to put out the message about the phone hotline remained. Because of this, it made sense to take the platoon down the road with the most people. Which was Market Street.

Soldiers from the 82nd had said that the boulevard was dangerous. Because of this, both Soudan and Benatz went with 2nd Squad, who would be walking down Market. They wanted their Marines to see them leading from the front. Both were concerned about their perception among their men.

Soudan had been the platoon sergeant for only two weeks. His predecessor, a staff sergeant, had been relieved of command for punching a junior Marine who refused to obey an order. The staff sergeant also had a confrontational relationship with Lieutenant Benatz, whose authority he constantly undermined. Consequently, Benatz often went directly to his squad leaders, bypassing the platoon sergeant to get things done.

Normally, a platoon sergeant is a seasoned veteran on his second or third enlistment. Soudan was transferred from 2nd Platoon and given the job of leading 3rd on March 27, 2004, his twenty-second birthday. He had been a Marine for three years, and had earned a meritorious promotion to sergeant, narrowly beating Link, one of his closest friends. But Link had been in 3rd Platoon for a couple of years, and was accustomed to the new platoon commander's style. He was also the 1st Squad leader, which made him one of the lieutenant's confidants.

Having fought in Iraq in 2003, Soudan thought he was battle-hardened. However, nothing in his training or experience could fully prepare him for the violence, chaos, and fury that Lima and the Muj would unleash on each other over the next two weeks. What his training did was help him think. He did simple things under difficult conditions. He did what Marines do.

That was Dusty Soudan's favorite motivational phrase: "Let's go do what Marines do," and he used it constantly. Small unit leaders have catch phrases or other quirks of individualism that endear them to the men they lead. Before they step off on patrol, they utter movie quotes from Mel Gibson's *Braveheart* ("At least we don't get dressed up for nuthin'"), Nicolas Cage's *Con Air* ("I'm gonna go save the fuckin' day"), or Vin Diesel's *XXX* ("I live for this shit!").

And Marines are only half joking—they really do live for this shit. Grunts take pride in enduring more hardship, adversity, and pain than the contemptible "pogues" that populate the rear areas. In an infantry platoon, it is perfectly acceptable to refer to your closest friend as "bitch," "asshole," "fuckstick," or any number of profanities. The worst insult one grunt can hurl at another is to call him a "pogue."

The word "pogue" was originally the acronym POAG, meaning persons other than actual grunts. A pogue is not necessarily a non-grunt. Infantrymen hold other jobs in high respect so long as they are "hard." Like the "rear-echelon motherfuckers" of an earlier era, pogue is a contrasting term used to describe a man or woman in uniform ensconced in an easier, softer, weaker life.

Classifying a pogue is a matter of perspective as much as job description. To infantry Marines in Al Anbar, Iraq, anyone living at Camp Fallujah, Al Asad, or Camp Taqaddam (known as TQ) is a pogue. Personnel deployed anywhere in Al Anbar—who risked mortar, rocket, or IED attacks every day—think people stationed in Kuwait are pogues. Anyone in the searing, windy dust of the Middle East believes those who are serving their tour in the comforts of the United States are pogues. And many in the military think those who have never worn a uniform are the ultimate pogues.

As events would illustrate, Soudan was no pogue. Twenty minutes into the patrol down Market Street, Soudan was conferring with Benatz when he noticed a piece of plywood leaning upright. The plywood was placed in the middle of the road. Something was propping it up. Did the Muj put an IED there? Would the hajjis tip them off?*

Seeing debris and litter on a street in Iraq was hardly unique. Most roadsides were covered with garbage: stripped MREs, man-

---

* Muj and hajji represent two very different slang terms referring to Iraqis or Arabs in general. A Muj is an insurgent or militant, and never good. Hajji means Iraqi civilian, as in "Hey, that hajji just smiled at me" or "Let's go eat hajji food today." The Marines tried to win the hearts and minds of hajjis while killing every Muj they could find. Separating Muj from hajji was the hard part.

gled crates, and twisted metal. Urine and feces mixed freely with rotting vegetables and rancid sacks of moldy rice, producing the effect of overheated vomit. At times, steady trade winds dissipated the pungent scent.

Soudan sensed the item looked suspicious. Plywood, animal carcasses, and rice sacks were among the objects the Muj used to conceal an IED. Barely three weeks into their deployment, 3rd Platoon had already discovered several IEDs throughout Husaybah. Thus far, they had managed to find a couple of them using an unconventional, dangerous, and effective technique: kick the IED.

The procedure was simple. When the unit noticed an object that appeared to be hiding an IED, a Marine would walk up and kick it. If his foot hit metal, the unit would cordon the area and call in an explosive ordnance disposal team (the bomb squad). In 2004, Marines in Husaybah and other parts of Iraq discovered IEDs by walking around town kicking things, not by using sensor teams or bomb-sniffing dogs. Sometimes the kick disabled the remote detonation mechanism of IEDs. Sometimes it didn't.

What drove young Marines to kick at objects that might explode and kill them on impact? One reason was their devotion to the Spartan Way. The Spartan king Leonidas, who died with his men at Thermopylae, sacrificing himself for the sake of his country's independence and way of life, was once asked to name the supreme warrior virtue, from which all other virtues derived. "Contempt for death," he replied.

Finding IEDs was also a tangible demonstration of progress. Discovery of a roadside bomb brought a measure of glory, valor, and respect; they had, like a firefighter, rescued the innocent. But more importantly, discovering an IED meant they had probably saved another grunt's life.

Soudan approached the plywood. He was standing about eight feet away.

BOOM!!!

Everything went black. Soudan was hurled backward. His M-16A2 rifle flew out of his hands. An instant later, Soudan saw a flash of orange.

Then he heard the concussion blast, the sound of combustible material and gas releasing thousands of pieces of hot metal in nanoseconds, unleashing impersonal fury on anything within a twenty-, thirty-, or forty-yard radius.

Soudan flew through the air and landed on his back. He got up, trying to regain discipline and composure. Shrapnel from the blast had cut the black sling that kept the rifle attached to his body. He realized his weapon was missing. Blinded and unable to hear anything other than a loud ringing, Soudan's first instinct was to find his weapon.

Scientists have observed that humans respond to threats to their survival in one of two ways: either they fight with all the energy they can muster, or they flee from the danger. This is called the "sympathetic fight or flight" response. Soudan wanted to fight something . . . anything . . . *right fucking now.*

Corporal Mejia, Soudan's 3rd Squad leader, was one block south of Soudan, towards the rear of the formation. Mejia ran up. He grabbed Soudan and shook him.

"Hey, sergeant, you okay? Are you hit?"

Soudan looked down. A piece of metal had grazed his face. He quickly checked his chest and groin. Mejia noticed two cuts on Soudan's right hand. They were pieces of embedded shrapnel.

"I'm fine. Don't worry about me." Soudan knew that Mejia had other things to think about. "What's happened? Any other casualties?"

"The lieutenant's hit!" Corporal Lightfoot, the 2nd Squad leader, was yelling so Soudan could hear; the explosion had left the sergeant temporarily deaf. Shrapnel had sliced open a vein in the platoon commander's leg, missing his femoral artery by inches. Lieutenant Benatz was excited and jabbered orders incoherently.

"We've got casualties! We've got casualties!" Marines in 2nd Squad were screaming. In addition to Lieutenant Benatz, Lance Corporal Dial had been hit in the face. Both were bleeding profusely.

Benatz got on the radio and called back to base. His company commander, Capt Richard J. Gannon II, answered the call. Gannon had heard the explosion and knew the patrol might have taken casualties. As Benatz writhed in pain, he finished the MEDEVAC call, and then handed the radio over to Soudan to follow up on the details.

Gannon had a standing company policy that all units would immediately evacuate their wounded, no matter how benign the injury. Soudan didn't mention to Gannon that he had been hit. He wasn't about to leave the platoon without any leadership in the middle of their first heavy contact on a patrol. Regardless of Gannon's edict, Soudan knew two things had to happen: the lieutenant needed immediate medical attention, and 3rd Platoon needed their platoon sergeant.

"You okay to take this, Sergeant Soudan?" the lieutenant asked. By now the Navy corpsman that was stationed with the Marines, "Doc" Tivy Matthews, had staunched the flow of blood from the lieutenant's leg.[*] Despite this, both Benatz and Soudan knew that he still needed to go back.

---

[*] Regardless of rank, all Navy medical personnel stationed with Marines are known as "Doc."

"No problem, sir. It's just the rest of the patrol. I can finish it out." There was no other option. Soudan had to step up.

Because the explosion was close to the base, the medical evacuation (MEDEVAC) happened quickly. Marines from Lieutenant Moore's CAAT platoon drove their steel-laden humvees out to the site, recovered the wounded, and returned to the base. 2nd Squad remained stationary in a security halt, ready to repel an ambush if it came. The event took less than five minutes.

Sergeant Soudan called Captain Gannon. "Lima Six, this is Lima Three. We are all accounted for and continuing the patrol."

"Roger, Lima Three." Gannon's voice was smooth, even, and crisp. His Marines always said he never lost his cool. They loved him for that.

When the IED detonated, 1st and 3rd Squads had also halted, waiting to see if the platoon needed them for support. Now Soudan called them, talking directly to his squad leaders over their Motorola radios. He told them what happened,and that he would be in charge of the patrol.

The patrol stepped off. They were heading east, farther away from base camp.

Three minutes passed.

BOOM!!!

From the sound of the explosion, Soudan knew this latest IED had hit south, on the street 3rd Squad was patrolling. He tried calling Corporal Mejia, his 3rd Squad leader, over the Motorola. No response. Soudan grabbed Doc Matthews and ran west several blocks, looking for an alleyway to cut south to get to 3rd Squad.

At that moment, Corporal Lightfoot, 2nd Squad leader, called Soudan on the Motorola. "We've found another one." This IED hadn't detonated. Yet.

The Muj used dozens of methods to set off IEDs. They would rig the charge to a cellular telephone or low-frequency radio, transmitting a signal, phone call, or even text message to ignite the charge. Although they attempted several frequency-jamming solutions, the Marines decided their best defense against the IED was to find the bombs before the Muj turned them loose. This meant patrolling. And psyops truck escorting.

Lightfoot told his squad to set security, keeping both Iraqis and Americans out of the IED danger zone. The Iraqis on the street were silent. Many had already started leaving the *suq*, or town square.

Soudan called Link, his 1st Squad leader, and told him to halt. In the absence of orders, 1st Squad had continued heading east. Soudan thought the platoon was getting too dispersed, so he stopped them.

Running south, Soudan and Doc Matthews found a route through a graveyard and linked up with 3rd Squad. The unit was in shambles. Three Marines hit. Bad. All from the same fire team. Only the team leader, LCpl Derek Brown, had emerged unscathed. With one of his three teams wiped out, Mejia had one team setting security and the other treating the casualties.

Arriving at the scene, Soudan looked at LCpl Chris Wasser and knew right away that he wouldn't make it. A native of Ottawa, Kansas, whose first day of boot camp had been September 11, 2001, Wasser had been walking next to an oilcan that concealed an artillery shell. When it exploded, the steel cylinder had magnified the effects of the blast, making it even more lethal. When Soudan found him, Lance Corporal Wasser was missing all of his fingers. All that remained of both hands were bloody stumps. Body fluids gushed out of his chest wound. His hair was gone. His face was gashed and disfigured. His lungs were fighting a losing battle. His eyes were rolling back into their sockets. By the time the rescue vehicle brought him back on base, Christopher B. Wasser had already died.

The other two casualties were also critical. PFC Luis Vega was screaming. His tibia and fibula were mangled. Two fingers from his hand were gone. Pfc Kevin Rumely was missing most of an artery. Soudan could see his femur.

Doc Matthews started with Rumely. Having just patched up Lieutenant Benatz, Doc stabilized his second leg wound in minutes. He gave Rumely a shot of morphine before turning his attention to Vega. While Matthews was working on him, Rumely had been surprisingly calm. Now, with the morphine, Rumely sounded downright chipper.

"Sergeant Soudan, is my dick still there?"

Soudan laughed. The same thought had flashed through his mind a few minutes before.

"You're fine, Rumely." Soudan thought it was ironic that all Marines had the same one-track mind.

By now, the streets were empty. Iraqis had melted into their homes. Late afternoon slipped into dusk. Still intending to complete their psyops mission and routine sweep, the Marines planned to continue the patrol route after handling the MEDEVAC. Soudan got on the radio and began the nine-line. Again, Gannon took the call.

Right then, a firefight erupted to the south. A different Lima unit, 1st Platoon, was under attack. Before 3rd Platoon had stepped off, Lieutenant Benatz had mentioned that 1st Platoon would be patrolling to the south. 1st Platoon had moved in the central area of Husaybah, only a few blocks away from Soudan.

Led by Lieutenant Ruge, 1st Platoon was taking AK-47 and RPG fire. Soudan ordered his squads to push out their security perimeter and then hold fast. The ambush sounded close, and Soudan didn't want his men to be caught off guard or to accidentally shoot their fellow Marines.

"Lima Three, it's Lima Six. I'm standing by for your nineline. Send it whenever you're ready."

The sound of Gannon's steady voice once again gave Soudan confidence. The men of Lima admired their skipper. While in Husaybah, Gannon believed that his most important duty was to walk at least one patrol each day with his men. He didn't do it to watch over their shoulder. Rather, Gannon thought his presence would bolster the spirits of those he led. It worked. His men would have followed him into hell.

As it turned out, that was exactly what they did. The Marine base in the town of Husaybah was located nearly forty miles from the battalion headquarters in Al Qaim. Under most circumstances, infantry Marines would be thrilled. Most grunts conform to Order when they have to, but at heart they are rugged individualists who want to be away from higher authority. A squad, platoon, company, or battalion is not viewed as well led unless the commander is chomping at the bit for the freedom to make his own decisions—and maybe find a little Disorder in the process.

Husaybah was no lark away from the flagpole. When the Marines had arrived a month before, the camp didn't even exist. The men had built it from scratch, using a few empty single-story concrete buildings as their command posts and fortifying the ramparts with layers of sandbags and Hesco barriers.* By this time, Marines were enduring a daily barrage of mortar and rocket attacks, some of which appeared to originate from the Syrian side

---

* Hesco barriers are large cylinders made of coarse fabric and wire that are planted into the ground and filled with dirt. They are useful for stopping shrapnel and other debris from explosions.

of the border. Many of the Marines felt exposed in Indian country, too far from the cavalry and the larger fort at Al Qaim.

As Soudan called in the nine-line, he noticed his Marines—who were supposed to be maintaining security—were staring at their dead and wounded comrades.

"Stop looking at me! Get your eyes outboard. Watch out for an ambush," the twenty-two-year old growled at the other boymen within earshot. He knew what they were feeling, but he couldn't let them dwell on it. Not now, while they were still in the thick of the fight. Stay alert; stay alive. Complacency kills.

Twenty minutes later—a seeming eternity—Gannon called Soudan and told him the ambulance was coming out to pick up the casualties. The 1st Platoon commander, Lieutenant Ruge, had sent a squad, led by Lance Corporal Sweeney, and a corpsman. Sweeney's squad was supposed to assist Soudan with the casualties and tie 1st and 3rd Platoons together so the units wouldn't ambush each other while 1st Platoon was handling their firefight.

While they were on their way, Sweeney's squad from 1st Platoon discovered a fourth IED—an artillery shell coated with an adhesive and wrapped with glass, nails, and steel ball bearings. When Soudan was told about this new IED, he called Link, his 1st Squad leader, and ordered him to bring his squad down south. He wanted 1st Squad to cordon off the area so Sweeney's squad could help Soudan with 3rd Squad's casualties and return to 1st Platoon's firefight. Meanwhile, Corporal Lightfoot's 2nd Squad was occupied maintaining security on the other unexploded IED.

Link called Soudan. "We're on our way."

Ten seconds passed.

BOOM!!!

Link's squad.

"Sergeant Soudan! We've got casualties!" The number of IEDs they had hit brought the ever-cool Link close to panic. They had no idea what else was out there. Link's tone quivered over the Motorola.

"Calm down, Link. Stay cool." Soudan channeled the confidence Captain Gannon's smooth radio voice had brought him. "Just take a breath and get me a SITREP when you're ready."

Link sorted things out. A couple of Marines had nicks and scratches, but only Pfc David Palmer had a serious injury. Palmer had shrapnel in the back of his neck. The metal had penetrated his Kevlar helmet and pierced the base of his skull.

"How is he?" Soudan asked.

"Not too bad." Link had calmed down. "Not urgent. Maybe a priority."

"Can you get him down here?" Soudan didn't want the company's ambulance running all over this IED-infested neighborhood.

"Roger. I'll run him down to your pos. We're on our way."

Link's squad ran south with their injured and made it to Soudan and 3rd Squad without further incident. Link dropped off Palmer and then left with his squad to relieve Sweeney's squad—the unit from 1st Platoon—on IED security. By now, the firefight involving 1st Platoon had stopped.

The ambulance arrived for the third time, picking up the casualties and returning to the base. Things were quiet. The psyops vehicle had left. Nobody was moving. They were all waiting for the explosive ordnance disposal team, or EOD.

Night had fallen. The Marines were pissed. While they were waiting for the bomb squad to drive down from Al Qaim, the Muj were probably busy sneaking around the town dropping off more gift-wrapped packages. They hated being stuck out on the road.

Noise erupted to the south. 1st Platoon was engaged in another firefight.

With 3rd Platoon decimated and guarding unexploded bombs, Captain Gannon told CAAT—Lieutenant Moore's anti-armor platoon—to get back out and support 1st Platoon in their latest firefight. Half of Gannon's strength was now committed out in Husaybah. Although Gannon wanted to leave the base, he trusted the lieutenant to stabilize a situation that was spiraling out of control. Moore had commanded then-Corporal Soudan's 2nd Platoon during OIF I, and the battalion commander had chosen him to run CAAT. This gave the lieutenant tougher vehicles, heavier weapons, and more Marines. All would prove useful in Husaybah.

Moore linked up with Soudan first. 3rd Platoon was stuck, immobilized by the requirement to guard the IEDs. The EOD team from Al Qaim would not arrive for another hour. Soudan needed to know what was happening down south. He left Link in charge and headed out on foot with Lieutenant Moore and two other Marines from CAAT. They intended to do a leaders recon.

As Soudan and Moore ran further south, they glimpsed Iraqi men—civilians—carrying guns and darting between buildings. The men didn't shoot at them, so Soudan and Moore didn't engage. At that point, they were unwilling to risk hitting an innocent with a stray round. *First, do no harm.* The hajjis moved quickly, in and out of shadows, maintaining good cover and concealment. Soudan and Moore moved swiftly toward 1st Platoon, waiting and watching for a chance to attack. For the moment, all sides had decided to hold their fire.

By the time Soudan and Moore found Lieutenant Ruge, the 1st Platoon commander, the firefight had subsided again. Since Ruge's platoon looked okay, the pair of commanders—seasoned and rookie—ran back to Link. Since the firefight had stopped, Moore left with CAAT, going back to the base.

After the long wait, EOD finally arrived, but they took another two hours to dispose of the IEDs. The bomb technicians would send out a remote-controlled robotic device that probed the same unexploded bombs the grunts had just kicked. The robot would analyze the object, set a charge, and perform other mechanical calculations that allowed the EOD team to blow things up from relative safety. This was certainly the smart way to do business.

Unfortunately, this method took a great deal of time—so much time that three months later, the men from Lima carried satchel charges when they went on patrol so they could destroy IEDs themselves. At the beginning of their deployment, satchel charges were not an option. The battalion commander, LtCol Matthew Lopez, had thought hand-carried explosives would be an unnecessary escalation of force. Events in Husaybah would soon change his opinion.

While the EOD robot maneuvered and whirred and crunched and chipped, night had fallen. A team from Recon moved out to establish an observation post on the northeastern corner of town. The Recon Marines fell under a separate chain of command, but they talked with Soudan and coordinated their movements with him. They planned to move a few blocks north and east of Soudan, over to what had been the Ba'ath Party headquarters building.

BOOM!!!

Two blocks away from Soudan, an IED hit the Recon team. The unit fired two red-star clusters in the air. A red-star cluster is a portable pyrotechnic that comes wrapped in an aluminum cylinder about a foot long and two inches wide. The fireworks are offered in several different colors. Pyrotechnics are used as signaling devices. That day, red meant the team had an emergency.

Three Recon Marines were wounded. They called their platoon commander, and a couple of humvees with Recon members drove out, loaded up the bloodied men, and brought them back to the base. Soudan never found out exactly what type of wounds the Recon Marines sustained, he just knew none of them were killed—at least not that day, by that particular IED.

Around 11 P.M., EOD finished its work, disposing of the IEDs with explosions that injured nobody. 1st Platoon had returned to base. 3rd Platoon had been on patrol for seven hours. As they moved back towards the Marine outpost, a platoon from Kilo under Gannon's command left for a night patrol. By this time, almost every Marine stationed at Husaybah had been out in the town at least once in the past twelve hours. As Soudan walked his men west down Market Street, the platoon from Kilo patrolled east. They were on a road they called Trash Street, which was a few blocks north of Market.

BOOM!!!

The blast marked the fifth IED to explode during a seven-hour period. This latest missive from the Muj was off the mark. The Kilo platoon took no casualties.

Soudan felt relieved that the last two IEDs had not hit 3rd Platoon. Each squad in his unit had been attacked. 3rd Squad had lost an entire team. Lieutenant Benatz was gone, evacuated to a hospital. Wasser was dead. But at least the message from the psyops vehicle had gotten out to the town of Husaybah. Maybe someone would call and turn in some Muj bastard.

At midnight, Soudan made his report to Gannon. Fifteen minutes later, an exhausted Soudan left the company office to go to sleep. As he walked back to the foldout green cot that was his home, Soudan's pale blue eyes met the gaze of GySgt Sandor

Vegh. Officially, Vegh was the second-highest enlisted man in Lima Company. As the company gunnery sergeant, Vegh was responsible for Lima's logistics, ensuring the unit has all the ammunition, MREs, water, and other supplies it needs. But Lima's first sergeant, the senior enlisted man in the company, was from the aviation branch of the Marine Corps. The first sergeant knew little about ground combat. Marines respected the first sergeant's rank, but they rallied around Vegh's experience.

Vegh had fought as a sniper with 2/7 during Operation Desert Storm. One of Vegh's platoon mates, Anthony Swofford, offered a brief sketch of him in the book *Jarhead*.* A Christian family man, Vegh did not smoke, drink, swear, look at pornography, or chew tobacco. However, Vegh loved being in combat. He especially loved leading and mentoring his men in the thick of it.

Vegh often talked Soudan's ear off. In fact, Vegh never yelled at his Marines when they did something wrong. He would pull them aside, set them down, and lecture them. This happened routinely during mortar barrages. As enemy missiles rained into the base, Vegh would be discussing some arcane point of morale with his subjects and continue without even flinching. His lectures often rambled for an hour, and Soudan found himself wishing for a quick ass-chewing just so he could get back to the business of running his platoon.

That night, Vegh had no lecture for Soudan. Their eyes met. Vegh nodded. Soudan had stepped up. He had demonstrated leadership amidst insanity and held the platoon together when it counted most. He had been patient and tenacious. His judgment had restrained the men's fury at their loss, forced them to keep their discipline and composure, and prevented the patrol from

---

* According to Soudan, Vegh strongly disputes Swofford's characterization of him.

descending into a bloodbath or debacle. Lima Company's newest platoon commander had done what Marines do.

Soudan thought it couldn't get any worse than hitting three IEDs on one patrol.

He was wrong.

CHAPTER 3

The Snake Pit

In seven days, God created the heavens and the earth.
On the eighth day, God created hell.
Then came the convoys . . .

—*Port-A-John graffiti at an American base*
in Kuwait, February 2004

During OIF I, while Cpl Dan Amaya and Sgt Dusty Soudan were in Iraq toppling Saddam Hussein's regime, Cpl Craig Atkins, a fire team leader with Fox Company 2/4, was at a Marine base called Camp Hansen in Okinawa, Japan. Thin and of other-wise average stature, Atkins spoke with a heavy southern Indiana twang and was prone to unconventional idiomatic expressions. "Fellas, it's hotter'n a coon's eye today."

Craig Atkins is from St. Anthony, Indiana, a village in Dubois (say "Dew-Boys") County. Located about two hours north of Louisville, Kentucky, St. Anthony is a freewheeling outdoorsman's paradise. They work hard: each Monday morning, most of the town is up before 6 A.M., headed for the sawmill, farm, or cabinet factory. They play hard: on Saturday night, half the population might close out Arnie's Tavern for a few Buds or Busch Lights.

The next morning, they atone by attending mass at St. Anthony's Church, the town's only house of worship.

Arnie's is not open on Sundays, but home brew is always available for the thirsty. In-house alcoholic beverages are popular in the rural regions of southern Indiana. Rhubarb and pumpkin wine are often chased with a corn-and-malt blended beer. Self-sufficiency, fierce independence, and rugged individualism are their mottos and creeds. We are proud, strong, and free. Don't tread on us.

Most villagers own several dozen acres, or have a parent or uncle who does. On any evening in Dubois County, the cracks of .22 rifles and 12-gauge shotguns are as common as fireflies. Men are out hunting deer, rabbit, or squirrel. Squirrel and dumplings are a favorite in St. Anthony. The tender meat goes down well with home brew.

Gordon and Bev Atkins always knew their oldest son, Craig, would join the military. What they did not foresee was the galvanizing effect his decision—combined with the 9/11 terrorist attacks—would have on their two younger boys, Garrett and Mitch. Craig had planned to put in only four years before returning to St. Anthony and opening up a woodworking shop. Things turned out much differently.

Craig Atkins had spent his youth collecting guns, mowing lawns, and delivering newspapers. During summers, he apprenticed as a woodworker and welder. His high school, Forest Park, included 400 students from five other towns just like St. Anthony. After considering a career as a Marine maintenance technician, Craig enlisted in the summer of 2001 as an infantryman.

After completing boot camp and the School of Infantry, Atkins was sent to 2/4, the battalion also called the Magnificent Bastards. In August 2002, Atkins and his battalion went to Camp

Hansen, a garrison on the Japanese prefecture of Okinawa. Camp Hansen, and the island of Okinawa, is an infantryman's purgatory. Marines call it the Rock, a casual reference to the Alcatraz-like cabin fever the island induces. Battalions rotate through six-month tours as an American talisman warding off any potential Chinese or North Korean demons. They perform the air contingency mission, which requires them to remain on various levels of alert. They also train in ocean swimming on the beaches of Kin and Oura Wan. The scout swimmers of 2/4 were confident in their water skills. The swimmers included Craig Atkins and his friend and squad leader, Cpl Dustin Schrage, a tall, tanned and wide-grinning Marine from Florida.

Away from home but with little to do, the Magnificent Bastards tromped back and forth through the island's central and northern training areas. Offended by the sixty-year American presence on their home, local Okinawan politicians, citizens, and farmers took offense to the slightest of infractions. Time-honored traditions of rowdy off-duty Marine behavior had a way of becoming sticky international incidents. Consequently, the Magnificent Bastards were often banned from relaxing outside the gates. They responded like caged animals, becoming bored and despondent and getting into even more trouble.

In January 2003, on the verge of wrapping up their six-month deployment to Camp Hansen, Atkins, along with the rest of 2/4, was ordered to remain in Okinawa instead of deploying to the Kuwaiti desert. Atkins returned from Okinawa during the summer. Like Zmudzinski, Atkins was angry that he had missed the war.

A few weeks later, Atkins met a girl while at China Beach, a karaoke bar north of Camp Pendleton that Marines frequented. In the quintessentially romantic form of coupling that draws opposites together, the good ol' country boy became twitterpated with a starlet. Deborah Edwards is a violinist, performer, and theater/drama major with long straight brown hair, hazel eyes, and a cherubic face. Years before her China Beach encounter with Atkins, Deb had moved from New York to California to become an actress. After becoming disillusioned with Hollywood, she settled in San Clemente and taught music. Having grown up in a suburb near Detroit, Deb had never imagined that she would fall in love with a Marine who had held his first gun before learning to walk.

Craig Atkins and 2/4 were excited when they finally got the call for their February 2004 deployment to Ramadi, Iraq. At last! Our chance to get some! Deb smiled, feigning enthusiasm as her man scampered off for adventures. She put on her brave face, waving goodbye as she sent Craig and his buddies off to a mystique she only knew from television, newspapers, and the Internet.

After arriving in March 2004 at Ali Al Salem International Airport in Kuwait, the Magnificent Bastards were shuttled to Camp Victory, a holding area where they would make final preparations for their convoy north. The Marines stowed their gear in white circus-style Bedouin tents filled with green military cots and enjoyed the last decent food they would eat for several months.

A couple of days after entering Kuwait, 2/4 received a pep talk from the 1st Marine Division's commanding general: Maj-Gen James N. "Mad Dog" Mattis, who has short gray hair, blue eyes, and bulldog-like jowls that bracket his dimpled chin. Mattis looks like a warrior in his mid-fifties should: wrinkled and weathered skin, eyes alert, mind sharp. He carries himself with an air of dignity, intellect, and confidence that causes him to appear much taller than his height, which is slightly over five and a half feet.

James N. Mattis—Jim to his friends—was born and raised in Richland, Washington, a small town located in the central Tri-Cities area adjacent to the Columbia River. When Mattis was growing up, he found Richland's expansive Pacific prairie a wide, free place to hunt, fish, and ramble at will. Mattis's uncle served with the American Red Cross and was attached to the 2nd Marine Division in the Pacific theater during World War II. As the second of three sons, Jim Mattis and his older brother Tom grew up listening to stories of their uncle's Hemingway-like exploits.

Jim Mattis attended Columbia High School and graduated in 1968. In a 2001 article in the town's newspaper, Mattis's teachers remembered him as "studious, serious, and direct." The general has different memories. "I nearly missed graduation because I was drunk," he confessed. In high school, the future Marine was the team manager of the junior varsity and varsity basketball teams. When asked about his youth, however, Mattis recalled other extracurricular pursuits—"swimming in the Columbia River, drinking surreptitiously, and chasing the ladies"—with much greater vividness and enthusiasm.

In 1966, Jim's brother Tom enlisted as a Marine, becoming the first of the Mattis brothers to join the Corps. Tom later served in Vietnam with 1/12, an artillery battalion. Emotionally galvanized by his older brother's service, Mattis followed his lead in 1969, attending Central Washington University on a Marine ROTC program. He was commissioned a second lieutenant in 1972.

While in college, Mattis would often skip class, hitchhiking on the road and backpacking like a beatnik throughout the Palouse Hills of southeastern Washington. "I graduated in three and a half years because I was bored," he said. "I had a natural curiosity about life. Eventually, that became very helpful as a military officer charged with taking people off to war."

That Kerouac-like curiosity expressed itself most in Jim Mattis's love for reading. Because the Mattis family did not have a television, the future general read hundreds of books during his youth. Mattis eventually compiled a personal library that one observer estimated at "over 7,000." When asked what previous experiences helped shape his strategy during OIF II, the general had a simple reply: "My study of war and the human condition."*

The Marines of Blue Diamond liked to say that their unmarried commanding general was a sergeant who happened to wear stars. Like the fabled LtGen Lewis B. "Chesty" Puller, the earthy Mattis succeeded in making corporals and sergeants believe he saw the world just like they did. In both OIF I and II, Mattis was known through nicknames and call signs. His radio call sign was Chaos—a reference to his penchant for Disorder—but the grunts of Blue Diamond called him Mad Dog.

Each time a unit from the 1st Marine Division arrived into or departed from Iraq, Major General Mattis flew from his headquarters in Ramadi to address them. He wanted to personally explain to his Marines what he expected of them. "A general must never allow rank or authority to divest him of the responsibility of having a close relationship with his troops," Mattis said.

When talking in his relaxed, even, staccato cadence, the general's tone was gentle but firm, decisive but open, courteous yet filled with compelling authority. Mattis spoke with a slight lisp; particularly when lowering his voice to make a point. In any other man, this quality would be considered effeminate. For Mattis, it worked the opposite: this small speech impediment human-

* Mattis himself lost count of how many books he owned. "I gave away most of my books to libraries over a six year period," he said. "I would pack up to move and have 10,000 pounds of books. The rest of my household effects only amounted to 2,000 pounds."

ized him, making his words and presence that much more genuine and credible.

Back in Kuwait with Atkins and 2/4, Mad Dog Mattis walked in front of the battalion and began. "I sure am glad that you Magnificent Bastards could join us for this round back into the desert. Going to war last year without you was like only having one leg in an ass-kicking contest."

The Marines cheered, ooh-rahing at their general with authenticity rather than false motivation.

Despite their preference for fighting, Mattis made it clear to the men that he didn't want them maintaining an aggressive, antagonistic posture. He reviewed the three Blue Diamond mottos—first, do no harm; no better friend; no worse enemy—and then expounded on them. "We will stay patient one hour longer, one day longer, one week longer than the enemy expects us to," the general said.

"You fine young men are the key to this fight, especially you corporals and sergeants. Our country is counting on us even as our enemies watch and calculate. They are hoping that America does not have warriors strong enough to withstand discomfort and danger. I want you to prove our enemies wrong. You are going to write history, my fine young Marines and sailors, so write it well. I feel sorry for every sonofabitch back home who doesn't have a chance to serve with you.

"Keep faith in your fellow Marines, and keep your spirits up," Mattis finished, turning to leave. "Remember that we aren't coming here to fight. We want to help give the Iraqi people a better future." Mattis paused. "However, if some bastard tries to take you out, I want you guys to attack hell and drink the devil's liquor."

Energized, the Marines jumped to their feet with cheers before the sergeant major could even call them to attention. The devil's liquor sounded pretty good to them. Especially if Mad Dog Mattis was buying the first round.

Cpl Craig Atkins's first mission in the Root of All was common to almost every soldier, sailor, or Marine who went to Iraq in early 2004. When the Marines and the Army changed hands in western Iraq, each new unit of Marines had to drive all their equipment up from Kuwait. This involved a two- or three-day convoy from a base camp somewhere in Kuwait to their new home in central Iraq. For most of the men in 2/4, including Atkins, this was their first view of the fabled cradle of civilization.

Planning for the convoy was a formal, professional affair. Marines wrote an order, conducted intelligence research, performed route reconnaissance, tuned up their vehicles, checked their radios, and rehearsed numerous events. The morning they left Kuwait for Iraq, they conducted a convoy brief, checked the radios again, had a short pep talk, and did more rehearsals, jumping in and out of the back of 7-tons. After test-firing all weapons, it was finally go-time.

For the Magnificent Bastards, like all grunts, establishing a combat mindset—a Spartan attitude of contempt for death—is as important as the rehearsals and weapons testing. In the popular HBO series *Band of Brothers*, Lt. Ronald Speirs talks to Private Blythe, a soldier who cowered in a trench during an enemy attack. Speirs says, "We're all scared. You hid in that ditch because you think there's still hope. But Blythe, the only hope you have is to accept the fact that you're already dead. The sooner you accept that, the sooner you'll be able to function as a soldier is supposed to function." Approach life stoically, says the Spartan Way, and consider yourself dead already.

By accepting that life is fleeting and that death may come at any moment, Spartan followers cease to dwell on it. They can be either brutal or compassionate. They are ready to attack and kill, or to defend and protect, as the situation dictates. They expend their mental, emotional, and psychological resources engaged in life. They don't fret over the hereafter or the condition of their bodies or souls.* Most Marines are far too busy cleaning their weapons or talking to their men or rehearsing squad tactics or checking on batteries for their radios or jacking off or giving a patrol order or sharpening their K-bar or going for a run or writing their mom or wife or girlfriend or doing a million other things besides spending one iota of thought on something as mundane and foolish and boring as whether or not they will die. They accept that death is. And then they get on with living.

Marines learn to think this way from the moment they enter the Corps. Death is spoken of humorously and euphemistically. "Keep your body down on that low crawl," the drill instructor screams, "or you'll take one between the running lights." "Don't forget the atropine injector," the bio-terrorism weapons specialist intones, "or you'll be slobberin' all over and doin' the funky chicken." "Watch out for those IEDs in rice sacks," the patrol leader mutters to his squad, "they can really ruin your day."

Armed with his combat mindset and led by his squad leader, Cpl Dustin Schrage, Atkins jumped into the rear of their 7-ton. The 7-ton is a new version of the venerable 5-ton truck that has served American supply convoys since World War II. The more

---

* This does not pertain to their penis, which grunts fret over constantly. To a grunt, the loss of one's manhood would represent a fate far worse than death.

modern behemoth is essentially a camouflaged, souped-up version of a monster truck. The bed of the truck has bench seats. The 7-ton can run over just about anything. Marines like that.

Sitting near Atkins was LCpl Justin Oliver, who manned a squad automatic weapon, or SAW, which is a light machine gun. Hailing from Oswego, Illinois—a town similar in geography and temperament to St. Anthony, Indiana—Justin Oliver had been a recent addition to 2/4. Like Zmudzinski, Amaya, and Soudan, Oliver had been stationed with Marine security forces. Unlike the others, Oliver was with a small detachment in Rota, Spain. Ordinarily, this would have been an exciting and exotic duty station, but anti-American sentiment made off-base liberty rare. Disgruntled, Oliver volunteered twice for immediate transfer to a regular infantry battalion and was rejected. He wanted to go to war in Iraq. He was finally getting his wish.

It was cold in early March when Schrage, Atkins, Oliver, and the rest of 2/4 arrived at Navistar, the Kuwait-Iraq border station. The men donned green and black fleece jackets and checked their gear one last time prior to crossing the threshold. They received a warning to avoid distributing MREs and water bottles to the locals. Because Iraqi children risked injury darting into the sand-covered roads to retrieve an errant water bottle, an area Army general based in Kuwait had declared it illegal to perform such random acts of kindness.

The terrain and population varied from the southern town of Safwan all the way north to Baghdad and west to Ramadi. The main road snaked through desert sand and clay. A fresh, verdant breeze filled the air as they drove north, crossing the Euphrates and penetrating the Fertile Crescent. Throughout much of southern Iraq, beggars clad in dark *dishdashas* and black/red-and-white checkered *kheffiyahs* lined the roadsides, asking for a handout from passing vehicles with smiles and thumbs-up.

Disregarding the general's mandate, Marines tossed goodies out of their vehicles in a display of charitable goodwill. The local southern Shiite Bedouins smiled and gestured, palms on hearts. The kids yelled "Marine good! Bush good!" while waving tiny, dirty hands and giving the road warriors a thumbs-up. It seemed a positive sign. They remembered the Marines.

A water bottle from a passing convoy was a little thing—a small, minor expression of generosity toward a people or family that remained as likely to hate Americans despite accepting the gift. Nonetheless, the Marines hoped these types of gestures would go a long way towards reinforcing the perceptions Major General Mattis intended to communicate—that Marines had not come to the Root of All to oppress or inflict harm, but to help Iraqis create the conditions for security, growth, and prosperity.

On their first evening in Iraq, the convoy stayed at an American combat service station called Scania. Located along the main highway about a hundred miles south of Baghdad, Scania was a cross between a truck stop and a Dodge City frontier outpost. Columns of hundreds of oil tankers lined both sides of the road while truck drivers from all over the world whipped out mattresses, teapots, and ethnic vittles. The event was like a cattle drive, with trucks replacing horses, oil heaters substituting campfires, and smoke curling from communal *hukka* pipes instead of tobacco juice flowing into spittoons.

The next morning, the Magnificent Bastards loaded up and pushed out, anticipating explosions and firefights. The tension was palpable; they were entering the mythical Sunni Triangle for the first time. They approached a city called Iskanderiyah on the outskirts of Baghdad.[*] Traffic flowed in all directions in every

---

[*] Iskanderiyah was founded in 330 B.C. by the Macedonian conqueror Persians called Iskander—known today as Alexander the Great.

lane of the street. Cobbled out of rubble, the *suqs,* or open-air markets, blossomed like spring flowers with mercantile activity. A lone Iraqi policeman haphazardly waved at the mess.

For an American Marine driving through Iraq in 2004, any urban environment within a two-hour radius of Baghdad bore certain similarities to parts of New York City, Washington, D.C., or Los Angeles. Everybody spoke a different language. Most were also packing guns. And traffic was always at a standstill. However, the cause of traffic jams in Iraq normally involved the detonation or discovery of a car bomb, suicide attack, or IED.

As the Magnificent Bastards skirted Baghdad, they passed by a stalled Army supply convoy. The soldiers had disembarked to maintain security on their vehicles. The Marines nodded as the veterans waved them through. Children from all ages were lining the road, begging for candy, water, or anything else the Americans would part with.

Even more than candy and water, the children prized pens. Soldiers and Marines brought crayons or map markers on convoys just to entertain the kids who surrounded them if they had a lengthy breakdown. Ballpoint pens became a status symbol of sorts; Iraqi children compared ink-sticks with each other like American youngsters size up baseball cards or lunchboxes.

When begging didn't work, the kids would offer trades for things they wanted, asking to swap small Iraqi dinar notes for everything from Oreo cookies to GPS receivers. To the children, the former was more valuable than the latter. The ballistic sunglasses called Wiley X's especially drew their fancy, but the Marines refused to part with those. Many Americans in Iraq retained their eyesight after an explosion because of the protection offered by the thick plastic shades.

With only sandbags to stop shrapnel—months later, the humvees and 7-tons would receive heavy Kevlar armor to line the rear for protection—Fox 2/4 drove past Baghdad, past Fallujah, and finally arrived at the Snake Pit in Ramadi. Tucked between the Euphrates River and a man-made canal on the northwestern corner of Ramadi, the patrol base of the Snake Pit would be their home for the next seven months.

After all the hype, Lance Corporal Oliver felt let down. He and the other Marines had envisioned being attacked all the way through the Sunni Triangle. "Was that it?" Oliver said, summing up the thoughts of every other Magnificent Bastard.

That wasn't it, as Oliver would soon learn.

The Muj were lurking in Ramadi, waiting for them.

The Marines had been told Ramadi was dangerous, but their initial impressions left them confused. They had expected to be hit by IEDs on the convoy north, and they were not. The Snake Pit was not heavily fortified. Soldiers from the 82nd Airborne strolled the perimeter without gear, rifles slung over their shoulders as though nothing was happening.

Corporal Schrage's 3rd Squad, which contained Atkins and Oliver, spent the next week patrolling with the 82nd. The soldiers were thrilled to see the Marines; their presence meant the 82nd was on its way back home.

For their part, the Marines were unimpressed with the absence of discipline and complacent routine they observed from their Army counterparts. Like the rest of the battalions in Blue Diamond, 2/4 planned to patrol their areas on foot to develop more interaction with the locals. The soldiers, who remained in tanks and humvees, thought the Marines were crazy but they really didn't care. *You dumb jarheads can do whatever you want,* they said with rolling eyes. *It's your war now.*

The corporals took this in stride. The way they saw it, Army corporals and specialists had responsibilities equivalent to Marine lance corporals. Because of its small size, large enlisted population, and emphasis on decentralized decision-making, the Marine Corps holds the bar high for their corporals and sergeants—perhaps higher than other services. Many Marine squad leaders believe that their generals expect them to handle tasks equal to those of Army staff sergeants, or men two ranks their senior.

The third week of March, the 82nd Airborne returned to Fort Bragg, North Carolina, and the Marines started their new routine. Fox Company began a saturation effort. Based out of the Snake Pit, platoons spread out in their areas. They alternated routes when they could, spending as much time as possible meeting with Iraqis. They looked the hajjis in the eye, communicating through smiles and gestures. Some of the Iraqis reciprocated, offering them a cup of *chai* or a loaf of thick *hubbous* flatbread. Others turned away in disgust.

On March 21, 3rd Squad, led by Cpl Dustin Schrage, finished their first solo foot patrol. Patrols through the urban desert ghettos of Ramadi kept their adrenaline pumping. Even when nothing was happening, there was always a chance that an ambush or explosion lurked around the next date palm, white Opel sedan, or filthy alleyway.[*]

Having walked a good distance away from the Snake Pit, Schrage called for the Fox Company quick reaction force to come pick up the squad. Comprised of a handful of humvees and/or 7-tons, almost every unit patrolling in Iraq had some type of reaction force, or QRF. Led that day by Sergeant Navarro, the QRF was part taxi service and part rescue cavalry.

_____

[*] The Opel, one of the most popular vehicles in Iraq, is a German car manufactured by a subsidiary of General Motors.

The QRF arrived with four open-backed humvees, and the Marines from 3rd Squad jumped in. Sitting in the second humvee, Atkins noticed the QRF was taking the same route back to the Snake Pit the patrol had used when they went out. It was a little detail, but it gave Atkins a bad feeling. Patrols were supposed to use different routes each time they departed and entered the base. Trouble was, there were only two or three roads in and out of the Snake Pit. The enemy knew this.

Driving the third humvee was LCpl Andrew Dang of Foster City, California, a suburb of San Francisco. In high school, Dang wrestled, played varsity football, wrote for the school newspaper, and started a robotics club. Underneath his yearbook picture was a quote from the Anglo-Irish novelist Iris Murdoch that illustrated Dang's view of life: "We live in a fantasy world, a world of illusion. The great task in life is to find reality." A few weeks after the war began in 2003, Andrew Dang, looking for reality, discovered the Spartan Way and enlisted.

Officially, Lance Corporal Dang was stationed with the 1st Combat Engineer Battalion, but Dang's engineer platoon was attached to 2/4. In intense combat, an engineer's job includes, among other things, blowing holes through minefields, obstacles, or buildings. In murky guerrilla work, however, engineers often become regular grunts.

Looking back at the third humvee, Atkins heard a loud noise and gunfire. A rocket-propelled grenade, or RPG, flew through the window of the third humvee, decapitating the driver, Andrew Dang. The humvee plowed into a concrete bus stop, spilling metal shards into the faces and torsos of four men in Schrage's squad, including LCpl Justin Oliver. Also injured were Lance Corporals Cugliata and O'Geary as well as Corporal Richardson, whom the Marines had nicknamed Babe.

Immediately, the gunfire ceased. It happened that quickly.

Near the front of the convoy, Doc Jared White jumped out of his humvee and began wildly firing his 9mm pistol in the direction of the ambush. Other Marines were staring in disbelief; the corpsman was the only one shooting. If gunfire was necessary, Marines were supposed to do that. Corpsmen had other jobs. ("Doc White was always more of a Marine than a corpsman," Oliver later said.)

Cpl Dustin Schrage grabbed White and shook him. "Doc, what the hell? We need you back there. Marines are hit!"

"Corpsman up!" the four Marines echoed.

Wide-eyed, Doc White holstered his pistol and ran back to treat the wounded. All four had shrapnel and/or burn wounds, but none were seriously injured.

As Sergeant Navarro, who was in command of the QRF, called in the MEDEVAC, Corporal Schrage assessed the ambush site and posted his squad on or near buildings, walls, and other key terrain along the roadway. His Marines were impressed with his poise. Other than a couple of mortars near the Snake Pit, this patrol was 3rd Squad's first time under fire.

Corporal Schrage had shown a leader's decisiveness and fortitude. When Oliver came to after he was knocked out, all he saw was Dustin Schrage running back and forth, calmly dishing out commands. It seemed like Schrage had everything under control, that he always had the right answer. Schrage was always confident. Atkins, Oliver, and the rest of the men in 1st Platoon knew they could count on him.

Soon after their first encounter with the IED, the division chaplain, Commander Bill Devine, stopped by the Snake Pit to check on the Magnificent Bastards as he made his rounds around western Iraq. A devoted Catholic and Spartan minister, Father Devine spent most of his years as a Navy chaplain stationed with Marines. He often requested assignment with units likely to be deployed or sent into combat.*

In turn, most young Marines held the fighting padre in high esteem. Many thought Devine even looked like Mad Dog Mattis: they had the same height, physique, and gray hair, except the chaplain spoke with a Boston accent—"Lawd, bless awhr Mahrines as we send them into baht-tle." Devine smiled often; his face seemed reflexively buoyant. He had a believer's tender faith and a warrior's aggressive soul.

Along with commanders themselves, chaplains are responsible for knowing the level of esprit de corps in a unit. Beyond performing religious services, they also counsel, encourage, and motivate. During World War II, General Patton told Chaplain O'Neill to encourage a spirit of prayer within the Third Army, hoping to convince the Almighty to provide good weather for the Battle of the Bulge. After the victory, Patton awarded O'Neill a Bronze Star.

Although the Patton-like Mattis never told Devine to pray for good weather, he did employ his chaplain as an instrument of morale. Mattis asked Devine to keep an eye on the spirits of the men, injecting encouragement and fervor into units or Marines who needed it. Mattis often quoted General George Marshall, the World War II-era commander and statesman: "Military power wins battles, but spiritual power wins wars."

As the eyes and ears of the Blue Diamond, Devine flew all over Al Anbar, giving services, watering the flock, and noting

* In addition to surgeons and corpsmen, the Navy also provides religious personnel for Marines.

problems that he thought might require the general's attention. Battalions and companies had relieved the 82nd Airborne and were starting to gather into their own fiefdoms. Devine sensed that part of his job was to remind the young Marines in remote areas like the Snake Pit and Husaybah that those in higher headquarters were still looking out for them. As the relief took place during the month of March, Devine logged as many miles on helicopters and convoys as most generals.

One of the places Father Devine visited was Camp Fallujah. Known colloquially as the MEK, Camp Fallujah sprawled with concrete structures, unexploded ordnance, scrap metal, and other detritus left from twenty-plus years of uninterrupted war. MEK stands for Mujahideen-E-Khalikh, a group that seeks to replace the current Iranian regime with a Marxist-Mohammedan state. In 2002, Saddam Hussein evicted the sect from their facilities after the members of the MEK were designated as terrorists by the American government. In 2003, the U.S. evicted Hussein. By 2004, visitors to the Camp Fallujah PX could purchase T-shirts emblazoned with the MEK logo.

To many observers from the Blue Diamond, including Father Devine, no camp seemed more out of touch with their efforts than the MEK. Camp Fallujah was the sort of place where staff officers would call to complain loudly whenever their air conditioners were broken. Their tone of voice suggested that their own personal comfort was the most important thing happening in Iraq. The MEK was also legendary for its swimming pool, which was frequented by the women who populated the headquarters areas. "The MEK had a pool and girls," one infantry corporal noted, "so of course we couldn't live there."

Adding to the Camp Fallujah malaise was Kellogg, Brown, and Root. A subsidiary of Halliburton, the KBR Company had provided food distribution services for the Army during the

1990s peacekeeping missions in Bosnia and Kosovo. Sometime in early 2003, the Department of Defense finalized a contract with Halliburton to provide these services for American bases in Iraq. In addition to meals, Halliburton was also obligated to clean laundry, distribute ice, and conduct morale programs.

During the preparations for war in Iraq, the Pentagon had not planned on sending contracted civilians into a combat environment. They expected that postwar Iraq would be similar to Kosovo: secure roadways, mortar-free bases, and a small amount of leftover ethnic tension. The food service employees were Indians, Pakistanis, and Bangladeshis who were hired from a Jordanian company that subcontracted the labor. A Turkish company handled the laundry. The hodgepodge of nationalities created confusion, as well as concern about potential espionage.

The staff of KBR also organized dozens of silly activities with an eye towards rear area entertainment rather than front line combat. There was salsa night, where Marines could show up and learn their favorite Latin two-step. There was amateur poetry night, reggae night, and blues night. Like other bases in the region, Camp Fallujah was part military operation, part experiment in globalism, and part Club Babylon. To outside observers, KBR appeared to view the insurgency as a mere nuisance to their profit margin that would go away with time. To Major General Mattis and the infantrymen of the Blue Diamond, the enemy meant business and deserved their full attention.

Camp Fallujah was owned and operated by the MEF Headquarters Group (MHG), which was the type of pogue unit that grunts loved to hate. The group commander, a colonel, was a tall man with icy blue eyes. His most prominent feature was his sandy-colored eyebrows. They sprung off in long, untrimmed strands, giving his face a Doctor Strangelove appearance when he barked out edicts to his staff.

One reason the commander garnered a negative reputation was because of his obsession with hammers. When he arrived at the MHG in 2002, he wanted to instill a warrior spirit in his pogues. Infantry battalions have mottos, so he issued one for MHG—Honor, courage, commitment; Mission; Marines; Readiness. HMMR. To reinforce the motto, he displayed hammers everywhere. The commander also redesigned the unit's logo as an eagle flaring its wings while clutching a pair of hammers in its talons. The symbol was plastered throughout Camp Fallujah. It was supposed to appear regal and bold. It looked like a bird dancing the funky chicken.

But the colonel performed his duties as headquarters commandant well. The efficient functioning of myriad services at Camp Fallujah—generators, chow halls, air conditioning units, Internet cafes, Port-a-Johns, and showers—were all his responsibility. He insisted on maintaining Order at the MEK, and for this task he was well qualified. At his direction, Marines rose at 5 A.M. each day, scrounging the area for trash or anything else that would make the camp look unmilitary.

Mired in the static MHG routine was Cpl Jarod Stevens. Known mostly by his call sign of Shady, Stevens was tall, neither thin nor fat, had a round face with a square jaw, smoked, and spoke with a slow, deep voice. Shady was twenty-seven, old for a corporal. He enlisted as a communications technician for four years in the mid-nineties. After a tour with an aviation unit, he left the Corps as a sergeant during the tech boom to find greener pastures.

On 9/11, Shady Stevens was a wealthy, happily married dot-commer living in Austin. The day after the attacks, he went down to the Marine recruiting station, quit his job, and reenlisted. Because he had been out for over two years, he was demoted to lance corporal. His orders were delayed. His pay got screwed up.

The couple moved into a small apartment and struggled to pay rent. Weeks later, his wife left him.

Shady maintained an ambivalent attitude towards the Corps. He was the same age as many lieutenants and captains, and had more life experience than most of his peers. Growing up in Dallas, Shady had donned his first suit when he was seven. At that young age, he began learning the art of smooth talking, posturing, and deal making. His mom had always said he was a natural businessman.

Shady was like Red in *The Shawshank Redemption*, the classic "man who knew how to get things." His status as an informal power broker derived in part from his knowledge of cyberspace. Everyone either needed or wanted to get online. Shady traded favors, connecting email accounts in exchange for either goods or insurance. The arrangement helped him run a nice business at Camp Fallujah. He procured Cuban cigars, Iraqi dinar, and other illicit material for interested parties.

But most of his contraband trade involved alcohol. US Central Command's General Order 1-A banned "the introduction, possession, sale, transfer, manufacture or consumption of any alcoholic beverage by military personnel." Like Prohibition, the order only prevented public alcohol consumption. Searched thoroughly for weapons at the Camp Fallujah checkpoints, Iraqi workers would bring in cheap, thin "hajji whiskey" for the underground trade. Shady would lubricate the guards with a couple of free bottles or email accounts.

Like any member of an ancient global profession, Shady just wanted to give people what they needed to get by in the barren land, making a few bucks on the side. Civilian contractors who migrated back and forth from Baghdad's Green Zone often brought back high-ticket items like scotch, vodka, and bourbon. Because Shady was a computer technician for the MHG—the organization in charge of both gate guards and contractors—word got around the Lance Corporal Network that Shady had access to a ready supply.

Theoretically, senior enlisted Marines—better known as staff NCOs—are the pastors and friars of the Spartan Way. Informally, the Corps charges the staff NCOs with the duty of shepherding any who depart the Way. Officers are taught from their earliest days to learn from their staff sergeants and gunnies. A good senior enlisted Marine advises those in his unit early and often—even when they don't want it. Good gunnies might find they have few friends. Even colonels and generals are not immune from a closed-door conversation with a strong-willed sergeant major.

However, as Camp Fallujah illustrated, sometimes the staff NCO example can have the opposite effect, generating a climate of tolerance for indiscretion or deception. As a professional whiskey courtesan, Shady kept a judicious roster of clientele by catering primarily to staff NCOs and officers. He mainly sold through a mediator, and rarely kept any liquor stocked for more than a few hours. Those in need of their fix or looking for an escape would sneak away to the speakeasies of their rooms, two or three at a time, sipping and complaining about their lack of air conditioning.

When he wasn't fixing computers or running his business, Shady went on convoys. Throughout Iraq, thousands of pogues like Shady were given the collateral duty of a grunt's job: deliver supplies and gear while driving on the most dangerous roads in the world. On the one hand, running constant convoys on the streets of Iraq gave pogue units a grunt-level status. Pogues were jealous of the honor bestowed upon grunts, and they relished the chance to stare down danger and perhaps garner a good war story or two in the process. Convoys involved playing a life-size game of Russian roulette against the random ambush, booby trap, or roadside bomb. Gunners stood in turrets for hours as wind, heat, and sand filled their nostrils and skin pores.

In many ways, convoy duty served as a type of litmus test, sorting out armchair warriors from those willing to enter harm's way. Marines often volunteered to go out on convoys as a demonstration of Spartan resolve and mettle. Some lusted after the adrenaline rush. Some, however, only wanted to ride on a convoy because they thought it would be the best way to obtain the coveted combat action ribbon (CAR).

The CAR is colored with striped bands of blue, yellow, red, and white varying in thickness. For men and women choosing to make the Corps a career, the ribbon makes a statement: *I've been there. I've seen the shit. Listen to me.* For persons who scrutinize the biography of ribbons and medals emblazoned on a warrior's chest, possession of a CAR is an extremely meaningful achievement.

Many civilians consider the Purple Heart to represent a significant demonstration of valor. Those who have endured ground combat have a different perspective: a Purple Heart indicates only that the unlucky soul wound up as a human pincushion for bullets or shrapnel. If any American serviceman (or woman) was treated at an aid station for wounds sustained in a combat engagement, they were awarded a Purple Heart. For many grunts, the randomness of the horror, like that of bullets and shrapnel, made it seem like candy. The CAR, on the other hand, was viewed as meat and potatoes.

Officially, the combat action ribbon was established on February 17, 1969, as "a personal decoration awarded to members of the Navy and Marine Corps who have actively participated in ground or surface combat." Unfortunately, the CAR became watered down over the years. During Operation Desert Storm, Navy ship captains who fired Tomahawk missiles in support of offensive operations awarded their entire crews the CAR, under the justification that they "actively participated in surface combat."

This type of liberal evaluation did not sit well with Marines, who felt slighted when a grunt in a fighting hole received the same award as a chief petty officer that slept in safety aboard a ship hundreds of miles offshore. Prior to Operation Iraqi Freedom, Major General Mattis confirmed exactly what would justify an individual receiving the CAR in the Blue Diamond. Personnel must "receive and return fire" or participate in some activity directly associated with ground combat.

The renewed scrutiny caused the pendulum to swing in the opposite direction. Commanders were required to justify, via written documentation and verifiable sources, the specific occasion an individual exchanged fire. On the surface, this became a benign paperwork drill. Since after-action reports of enemy engagements are compiled regardless, commanders attached a roster of all Marines names that participated. Nonetheless, it often took several months to justify awarding a Marine a CAR. Support personnel located on camps near Fallujah and Ramadi, who received enemy fire in the form of rocket and mortar attacks hundreds of times over several months, often had to be wounded or killed to be considered for a CAR.

With supply for the CAR dwindling, demand rose exponentially, particularly among senior officers and enlisted. Other than patrolling with the grunts, the best chance for obtaining a CAR was out on a convoy. If one's convoy was "fortunate" enough to be ambushed or IEDed, then, presto, instant CAR. In the weeks after the Marines relieved the Army, senior staff officers wanted to take convoys everywhere. Eventually, they decided (or were convinced) that it was a bit irresponsible to take Marines out for a spin just for a meeting they could attend through the wonders of the video-teleconference.

In some ways, the routine of Marines like Shady out on convoys mirrored the rigors of an infantry unit. They might spend two weeks straight on the road, driving day and night, catching catnaps at rest stops located at the bases where cargo was exchanged. They lived on energy bars, soda, and Red Bull, the carbonated syrup that served as ambrosia to grunts throughout Iraq. They either ate MREs or sent a couple of boots to the chow hall to acquire food for their entire crew.

Convoys in Iraq also created similar emotions as air sorties or foot patrols: a preparation cycle, an adrenaline/anxiety rush prior to departure, and reliance on quick, decisive action in the midst of Disorder. Those who went out on convoys regularly developed a fraternity within the fraternity. Typically, the same individuals would stick together in a vehicle team: driver, gunner, and assistant. Large sandy lots where vehicles staged prior to hitting the road felt like aviation ready rooms or rifle company command posts.

Despite the media attention, however, convoy duty did not replicate front line combat. Supply convoys were not patrols; they were logistics missions designed to move gear or personnel from one place to another. They could support a fight, but they could not win one. Whether they were grunts on patrol or pogues moving gear, all Marines armed themselves to the teeth for battle. The difference was that grunts went out on patrol to make their presence known. In contrast, supply convoys simply wanted to make good time moving their gear.

Shady often saw females on his convoys. Is a woman permitted to be in combat? Combat zones are supposed to be easy to define, with clear borders, enemy and friendly uniforms, and a well-secured rear area. By this rationale, a rear area should not be a combat zone. So a female soldier, sailor, or Marine whose job is not directly related to combat should be free to be stationed in that "non-combat" region.

In any insurgent conflict such as the one in Iraq, this logic is folly. Although some places were theoretically safer than others, there was no actual rear area. At Camp Fallujah, Shady routinely took shelter alongside women in concrete, sandbagged bunkers while mortars and rockets exploded around them.

In Congress, recent legislation was introduced to legalize the use of female soldiers for certain duties "related to combat." Although various lobbies and advocacy groups thwarted the effort, rules and regulations meant nothing on the ground in Iraq. By March 2004, only a year into the Iraq war, 16 of the then-700 Coalition casualties were women (about 2.5 percent). In contrast, only 8 of the over 58,000 dead in the entire Vietnam War were female (less than 0.01 percent).

A woman can drive a humvee down an IED-stricken road every bit as well, or as poorly, as a man. The Marines of Team Lioness, who searched female Iraqis during house raids for weapons and explosives throughout western Iraq, represented an invaluable asset to warriors seeking to maintain cultural sensitivity and human dignity.* Neither gender had a monopoly on courage.

Like men, some women functioned better than others in the vague, amorphous "combat" environment of post-Saddam Iraq. Some lacked the warrior mindset and withered and panicked

---

* Team Lioness garnered a reputation for success during OIF-IIA. One year later, a group of women performing a similar mission were directly targeted by a suicide car bomb in June 2005 near Fallujah. Six died: three women and three men. Thirteen others of both genders were wounded.

under fire—but men sometimes did too. Although grunts and pogues are job descriptions, they were also mindsets that distinguished the strong and determined from the weak and craven. Women were more than capable of developing the mental and psychological fortitude required of pogues-turned-grunts.

And many of the pogues would become grunts much sooner than they had expected. On March 31, 2004, four security contractors working for Blackwater USA were hung from a bridge in Fallujah. Their corpses were mutilated, leading to public outrage.

Overnight, the orders for Blue Diamond had changed. "First, do no harm" was no longer the motto. Someone way up in the chain of command wanted revenge, and the Marines were about to switch from being the face of America's compassion to the instrument of America's wrath.

CHAPTER 4

Fallujah, Interrupted

Fallujah. Great name for a rock band.

—Lance corporal, 1st Marine Division

On April 6, 2004, Cpl Jason Howell sipped water with his Marines from 2nd Squad as they sat on a rooftop in Fallujah, tied into a defensive perimeter with the rest of 1st Platoon, Bravo Company 1/5. With a shaved head and almost zero body fat, Howell smiled as LCpl "Dirty Steve" Nunnery—a baby-faced fire team leader who spoke softly and wore thick military-issued glasses—tossed over Howell's favorite MRE, spaghetti with meatballs. Like any squad leader, Howell checked to ensure all his men received their portion before he tore his meal open with the rapture of a six-year-old on Christmas.

Jason Howell smiled a lot. It was part of his leadership style: stay optimistic in the face of adversity. When Dan Amaya and Dusty Soudan had been tearing through Iraq in the spring of 2003, a disgruntled Cpl Jason Howell had been stuck back at Bangor, Washington, guarding national strategic assets. A laid-back leader from Palmdale, California, a suburb north of Los Angeles, Howell had a grunt's enthusiasm and a surfer's way-cool-dude charisma. He had chafed against the static routine of security forces, where a brush with the law had tarnished Howell's stellar reputation.

At the time, Howell had thought he was getting a great deal. Construction workers were renovating the barracks, and NCOs were being paid to live out in town in order to free up space. Normally, only married corporals and sergeants were granted this privilege. One Saturday night in 2003, Howell kicked back a few beers with his buddies. By 1 A.M., the crowd noticed they were out of food. Howell was hungry, and Taco Bell stayed open all night. Plus, the restaurant was only two blocks away from his apartment. No problem, he thought. I'm fine to drive.

The policeman sitting outside the Taco Bell thought otherwise. Howell's breathalyzer test verified that he wasn't wasted, but well over the legal limit. Howell caught flak from both military and civilian authorities. From the Marine Corps, he was ineligible for promotion for over a year. Washington State mandated community service and three years of probation. One small craving for Taco Bell and one drink too many had jeopardized Jason's post–Marine Corps dream of the L.A. County Sheriff's Department. Howell longed for a fresh start in the real Marine Corps— an escape from this security forces crap.

When Cpl Jason Howell checked into 1/5, he was assigned to Bravo Company, 1st Platoon. His platoon sergeant was SSgt William Harrell, whose easygoing intensity was admired by his men. Harrell's approach to leading Marines clashed with that of his platoon commander, Lt Stephen Lewis. Aware of the conflict, the Bravo Company commander, Capt Jason Smith, decided to move Staff Sergeant Harrell to another platoon before the company's deployment to Iraq.

After the loss of his favorite platoon sergeant, Howell harbored bitterness toward the officer corps in general and his platoon commander, 2nd Lieutenant Lewis, in particular. Months before, Howell had felt betrayed by the officers at Bangor after his evening at Taco Bell. Although he knew his decision to drink and drive was wrong, Howell believed the punishment he received from both military and civilian authorities was excessive. Having been burned once at Bangor by the cold machinery of military justice, Howell was less likely to trust his seniors than other corporals.*

The first day of what later became known as the First Battle of Fallujah hadn't been particularly exciting, at least compared to what Howell expected out of combat. With bayonets fixed, Howell's squad had spent a frigid evening on April 5 kneeling or lying on the ground maintaining security. After eating, they cleared out buildings all night in the industrial area south of Fallujah. The buildings were padlocked with cheap steel bolts. Instead of using grenades and explosives to breach their entry into the buildings, Marines used Iraqi construction hammers. Applied with minimal force, they destroyed the cheap locks. Nobody got shot at. Nothing much happened.

Against the will of Major General Mattis, Blue Diamond had been ordered to invade Fallujah in response to the killing and mutilation of four Blackwater USA security contractors on March 31, 2004. Owned by former Navy SEAL Eric Prince, Blackwater had a high-profile contract providing security for the Coalition Provisional Authority. Jerry Zovko, Michael Teague, Wesley Batalona, and Scott Helvenston had independently decided to scout out Fallujah and had driven into an ambush.

_____

* A more colorful expression of Marine Corps discipline is "being screwed by the Big Green Weenie."

The majority of Marines saw the mercenary contractors as dangerous cowboys. They were not under orders, had no higher headquarters, and were immune to both civilian and military justice. Their actions often stirred up resentment among both Iraqis and Americans. In Fallujah, as in other parts of Iraq, when the contractors took their own initiative, the Marines would pay the price for their mistakes.

Although the brutal killings stirred American anger, the mutilations had also shocked the consciences of many Iraqis. In the Islamic tradition—as in most religions—corpse mutilations are blasphemous. Knowing that many Iraqis had also lost face in the situation, Marines sought to work with local authorities to bring the mob to justice. Commanders wanted to use the tragedy to build rapport with Iraqis and join them in a common cause of stabilizing their country.

Months later, Mattis's boss, LtGen James T. Conway reflected: "Iraqis would see a harsh reprisal as an act of vengeance. I said at the time: 'Revenge is a dish best served cold.' I dissented with military and civilian leaders in Baghdad who ordered this operation, but as a professional, I carried out my orders." Army Lt. Gen. Ricardo Sanchez, Army Gen. John Abizaid, and CPA leader L. Paul Bremer III all outranked Conway.*

Taking cover on a rooftop in the middle of Fallujah on April 6, Howell wondered if he would even fire his weapon. So much for the CO's big speech, he thought. After all, he was in stability and security operations (SASO). First, do no harm. Candy to kids. Be nice. Win hearts and minds.

Howell's company commander, Capt Jason Smith, had given the Marines a pep talk before they went into the attack: "I want

---

* For broader detail on why they overrode Conway's recommendation, see Bing West's *No True Glory: A Frontline Account of the Battle for Fallujah.*

you to think 'kill or capture,' not 'capture or kill.'" To Howell
and his fellow NCOs, the expressionless Smith was a machine.
He never cracked a smile, which made it difficult to determine if
he was satisfied or pissed off. He had a reputation of being hard
as steel, expecting his men to do *exactly* what he told them. He
was known as a controlling, demanding micromanager. In combat, he was intense and decisive and seemed to never be wrong.
"Nobody really liked Captain Smith," Howell said, "but *everyone*
respected him."

Howell was glad for the fight. He didn't want to do SASO.
Howell wanted to experience the satisfaction of killing a man
who was trying to kill him—the pure thrill of mortal combat. He
would never say it; Howell wouldn't want the men in his squad to
think he was bloodthirsty. It wasn't that he needed to sate his
palate with the taste of death. It was more than that. Deeper.
More primal.

Many men claim to have joined the Corps for one main reason: to legally kill another human being. Civilians read those
words and formulate a hasty impression: Marines are a bunch of
psychopaths. Howell wanted to be ready when the moment came.
While on guard duty in Bangor, he had read *On Killing* by former
Army Ranger and psychology professor Lt. Col. Dave Grossman,
which was required reading for infantry officers, but too deep for
many younger grunts.

Having studied the art and science of killing for several
years—analyzing death as a professional warrior, not a maniac—
Howell knew the act of killing was a societal taboo that doubled
as an intimate rite of passage into manhood. Would he piss his
pants and crack under the strain? Would he rise to the occasion
and dynamically inspire his Marines? He couldn't know until he
had been there, until he had shared the tragic drama of dealing
death. He wanted to cross a threshold, to enter a fraternity where

it was "cool not to talk about where you had been and what you had done."

At the moment, however, Howell's mind was on eating, not killing. He slipped the main meal into the plastic heating pouch and poured water in, activating the heater. Howell smiled: spaghetti with meatballs had wheat bread instead of crackers. Little things make a grunt happy.

Crack, crack, crack, crack, crack. Gunfire exploded. A pair of RPG shots whizzed past. Marines dove for cover.

Howell tossed his wheat bread aside, livid that the sanctity of spaghetti and meatballs had been violated. Mortars and rockets would have been fine, but a firefight? Now? During a chow break? Howell was so furious about leaving his favorite MRE that he almost forgot he was getting shot at. For grunts, chow time is sacred.

Corporal Howell's 2nd Squad descended from the rooftop and received the order from their platoon commander, Lieutenant Lewis, to attack (specifically: "We're gonna go fucking kill bad guys!"). Accompanied by Lt Joshua Palmer's 3rd Platoon, Howell and his men ran north across Route 10, the main east-west highway through Fallujah. Route 10 was the boundary designated to separate 1/5 from 2/1, the other battalion that had initially handled the Fallujah invasion. They heard the distinctive whiz and snap of 7.62mm rounds fired from an AK-47 accompanied by the *whoosh* of rocket-propelled grenades.

After crossing the highway and taking cover behind a series of two-story buildings, Howell looked around and saw several heavily armored humvees. This meant weapons company's anti-armor platoon was here. Strange, Howell thought. Nobody from 1/5 was supposed to be on the northern side of Route 10, and now elements of two companies had breached into 2/1's sector. *Is anyone else somewhere they shouldn't be?*

Sensing the imperative for immediate and decisive action, Howell ordered his squad to begin clearing houses. Hold! Are you covered? I've got you covered! One man in! Two man hooking! Where's the cover man? I've got the overhead! Clear? All clear! The Marines piled in and out of buildings, periodically depositing a pair of men to guard their rear or flank. As Howell ran down an alley, a Muj popped out with an RPG. He fired. The rocket skipped off the ground in front of him without exploding, then detonated a hundred meters away. Howell hugged the wall for protection.

Like a lifelike amoeba with a robotic brain, the squad instinctively morphed and reoriented, focusing on yet another brown concrete three-story house. Dirty Steve's fire team of four Marines established a tight cordon of security around the structure. Howell moved the other two teams quickly through the doorway, clearing out of the front as swiftly as possible. The area in front of the door is commonly known as the "fatal funnel" in urban combat—Marines are taught to transition rapidly from outside a structure to inside a room, moving the whole time with a cover man. Rule number one of urban warfare: don't hang out in the fatal funnel.

Howell reached the top of the staircase and found a locked wooden door. The hair raised on the back of his neck. What was on the other side? Women and children? A suicide bomber? Muj terrorists with rifles and grenades? He glanced at his cover man. They knocked with their rifle butts, yelling "*Awghf*," which means stop, but gets the general message across: "Open up, or the Marines on the other side will kill you." Nothing happened.

Howell turned around, facing away from the door, rearing up his leg to mule kick the door down. He kicked. His leg plunged all the way through the decrepit wood, leaving a gaping hole in the door. Red-faced, Howell pulled out his leg, reached through the hole, opened the door, and confirmed that the room was empty. All the Marines managed a smile.

By this time, Howell was running on nothing but adrenaline. His legs cramped. His spittle, caked around the side of his mouth, was dirty white. Dehydrated, Howell ran out of the room and up to the roof. Kneeling on the roof, he saw a flash of movement out of the corner of his eyes. An Iraqi kid put his face out of a window.

Corporal Howell had not eaten in eighteen hours or slept in thirty-six. The human brain, nerves and audiovisual centers cannot handle unlimited sleep and food deprivation. Performance eventually degrades. Instead of processing a voice command— "awghf" or any other intelligent phrase in Arabic or English—all Howell could muster was an involuntarily war cry: "AaauUUG-GHH!!!" His scream caused the child to pull the filthy curtains closed and run away.

Howell raised his weapon to shoot. Then he blinked. Clarity returned to his thoughts, and he lowered his M-16A2 rifle. In the books he read about Vietnam, they called it a "mad moment"—a time when the warrior cracks under the strain of intense combat and nearly slips into insanity. He had sworn he would never have one. He almost just did. It would not be the last time.

Howell turned his squad around, moving south along with 3rd Platoon in a massive crowd of fifty Marines. They were getting too dispersed, and it was time to head back to 1st Platoon and get his men back to their chow. They sprinted across the street, under fire the entire time.

Suddenly, Dirty Steve Nunnery saw a Muj vehicle in the open. Exposed in the middle of the street, Dirty Steve dropped to a knee and fired a grenade from his M-203.* It exploded on target.

---

* The M-203 grenade launcher fires 40mm grenades from a single-shot tube that attaches below the barrel of the M-16.

Still exposed, Dirty Steve, wearing his geeky-looking glasses, pumped his arm and looked over to Howell in celebration. "Yeah, baby!" he yelled, as though he was in a dance club, apparently ignorant of the bullets snapping around him. Howell was amazed. *That guy is the bravest sonofabitch I've ever seen,* he thought.

As they were running back to their original position, Lt Joshua Palmer stopped, motioning Howell's squad ahead of him. As 3rd Platoon commander, Palmer was not technically responsible for Howell and his men from 1st Platoon. Despite this, Palmer assumed moral authority, placing himself at risk to ensure all junior Marines in the area were accounted for. Marines of both platoons spoke highly of Palmer—he was admired as a warrior and respected throughout Bravo Company.

Less than forty-eight hours later, Palmer's life would be changed. Forever.

While pandemonium exploded to the northwest, Cpl Shady Stevens stood at a vehicle checkpoint on Route 1 south of Camp Fallujah, listening to the bedlam. On the afternoon of April 6, as Howell sprinted into the heart of the city, rumors swirled of a pending order to displace eight miles east. If told to go, the MHG wouldn't be tied into any other friendly units. Instead, Shady would be isolated with about forty-five Marines of assorted military backgrounds who had been cobbled together two days before. They would be in charge of controlling traffic in an area normally patrolled by an entire infantry company.

Shady and the pair of lance corporals under his charge, "Sky" Hawthorne and "Kid" Montcalm, were not trained for this type of independent duty. Unlike infantry companies who have a formal system of unit call signs, each individual within the MEF Head-quarters Group had their own specific moniker to use on the unsecured handheld radios they employed on convoys or around the camp. The system was awkward and a bit silly; officers from other units often scoffed at the pantheon of nicknames. However, for a group of pogues called into battle, the action proved oddly effective. Call signs became a badge of honor or alter ego, and unit cohesion developed as people invariably (if unjustifiably) took on the swagger of Viper, Maverick, or Goose.

On April 3, the day prior to the invasion, Lieutenant General Sanchez traveled from Baghdad to speak to the senior officers who would command the invasion. As the commanding general of all U.S. forces in Iraq, Sanchez told the Marines that "national prestige is at stake" regarding the Fallujah operation. After that meeting, the I MEF chief of staff, Col John Coleman, walked into the MHG operations center. He clapped a captain on the shoulder and said with a martial Georgia drawl: "Boys, General Abizaid just got out of the conference call with the Secretary of Defense and the President. Looks like we're going."

With the Blue Diamond spread out over thousands of square miles, Mattis did not want the operation, called Vigilant Resolve, to suck out all the resources—both material and spiritual—from his command. With a limited number of infantry battalions and nearly a third of all of Iraq to police, Mattis needed other units to participate in some capacity. He wanted a few extra vehicle checkpoints on the two main highways east of Fallujah oriented towards Baghdad. Contingents from the Navy's construction battalions—commonly known as Seabees—and the Marine combat service support battalions pitched in. As a last resort, the division called their higher command, the MEF, who dispatched a hasty coalition from MHG, including Shady, into the chaotic fight.

To establish the position, the Marines emplaced rolls of concertina wire and concrete obstacles known as Jersey and Texas barriers.* The barriers were transported on flatbed trailers and lifted by cranes. The trailers and cranes were owned and operated by local Iraqis. Because their location was closest to Baghdad and farthest from Fallujah, authorities wanted this position to be well fortified and visually intimidating. At the time, the Marines of MHG were not aware that during his rule, Saddam Hussein had arbitrarily closed highways prior to a purge or massacre.

Accounting for the unique driving habits of motorists in Iraq—vehicles often drove in the same direction on both sides of the highway—the MHG placed five-foot concrete Texas barriers across the entire road. The Iraqis who owned the flatbed trailers carried the barriers out into the highway and operated the cranes to maneuver them into position. They worked for a construction company that MHG had hired to perform contract labor at Camp Fallujah. These men had arrived to work that day expecting to be performing menial duties (such as, perhaps, spying) inside the relatively safe confines of the camp. They had not expected to be dragooned into constructing a defensive position for American forces. They were not happy.

Traffic was heavy the morning of April 5. The Marines processed hundreds of vehicles through both checkpoints. Hundreds more turned around on their own, traveling on dusty trails to avoid the inconvenience of being searched and/or detained by the Americans. Their orders were to search civilian vehicles leaving Fallujah, and not permit any westbound traffic from Baghdad to enter the city.

---

* Concrete barriers come in three basic sizes: Jersey (2 feet), Texas (5 feet), and Alaska (8 feet).

Shady was the driver for Capt Bill Anderson, an infantry officer on staff with the MHG. Anderson's previous duty station had
been at Bangor, where he had worked with Dusty Soudan, Jason
Howell, Brian Zmudzinski, and Daniel Amaya. Shady's captain
was an intense, combative perfectionist. In Shady's view, he was
focused on simple things: doing his job and taking care of his
Marines. Despite the fact that he refused to touch alcohol in the
war zone, Shady liked and trusted him. Anderson was now
responsible for running the checkpoint.

Shady watched the vehicles as his captain chatted with Iraqis
through a pidgin of Arabic and English. The traffic from Baghdad consisted of pickup trucks carrying produce from markets,
commercial high-wheeled Mercedes tractor-trailers, and sedans
jammed with college-age urbanites road-tripping to Syria, Jordan, and Lebanon to party for the Thursday-Friday Iraqi weekend. The five-day workweek runs from Saturday to Wednesday in
Iraq; Friday is the holy day. Secular Iraqis dressed in designer
European clothes claimed to be heading west to find a club
scene in Amman, Beirut, or Damascus where they wouldn't have
to concern themselves with mortars, IEDs, and car bombs while
they got their groove on.

This demonstrated the distinctive character of Fallujah in
contrast to Baghdad. The word *fallujah* means "green land" in
Arabic, a reference to the town's proximity to the fertile soil near
the Euphrates. Fallujah is known as the city of mosques, and
green and gold minarets paint the skyline of this anarchic settle-
ment of 300,000.

A rough, xenophobic town occupied by people described by
urban Iraqis in words equivalent to the American "redneck,"
Fallujah is to Baghdad as West Virginia is to the District of
Columbia. Many of Saddam Hussein's senior officers from the
Iraqi Army and Ba'ath Party regime lived in the *Al-Askari* (The

Officers) neighborhood in Fallujah. Both major highways heading west out of Baghdad—Routes 1 and 10—run into the city. The roads cross at the Fallujah cloverleaf, which had become the most contested intersection in all of western Iraq. All traffic heading into Baghdad from eastern Syria and Jordan has to pass through the cloverleaf.

Shutting down the cloverleaf made perfect tactical sense since the intersection was the lifeline into Fallujah. However, most trade goods were trucked into Iraq from either the west—Syria and Jordan—or the north from Turkey, through Kurdistan. The Kurds placed a tax on imports and exports, which was one of the methods they had used over the past decade to develop the politically autonomous region of Kurdistan within Iraq. With the cloverleaf closed, Iraqis importing grain, rice, and other basic foodstuffs from the west—or exporting world-famous Iraqi dates—were locked down, their supply lines cut. Iraq's businessmen, urbanites, and technocrats—the keys to building a stable, prosperous, and free nation—were livid at this encroachment on their liberties.

The night before, the frigid weather had surprised everyone except Master Sergeant Nunez, a field messman-cum-grunt who, according to Shady, had muttered to Anderson, "Sir, I think we should take the cold weather gear out with us." The captain had reacted strongly against his suggestion; he had seen Marines cocoon inside their "snivel gear" during training, and he didn't want his warriors more worried about their comfort than maintaining security. That night, the MHG interpreter, or "terp," Abdul*, shivered with disbelief, "It's never been this damn cold here in April!"

Despite the fact that Abdul did not hold a formal leadership billet, as a terp, he was an influential member of MHG's ad hoc

---

* Abdul is a pseudonym.

company. Often, terps became de facto intelligence analysts, making split-second decisions and advising the commander whether or not a person was trustworthy based on cultural factors of dress, gestures, and speech patterns few Americans could recognize.

At the checkpoint, Abdul behaved as though he were an officer, observing the Marine Corps tradition of refusing to eat until all the troops were fed. When mortars came in, he was calm under fire. He willingly sacrificed his own sleep for the sake of operational demands. Most of all, Abdul seemed to have a sixth sense when it came to interpreting situations and events.

In mid-afternoon on April 5, reports drifted in from vehicles coming from Baghdad of a "large group of men dressed in black coming to attack the Marines." A few days earlier, in addition to the Fallujah chaos, Muqtada al-Sadr's Mahdi Army had started an uprising in the Shiite south. Shady glanced at Abdul, who waved his hand.

"Don't worry about it. Those guys are just trying to scare you. They are full of shit." No waves of raving black-dressed hajjis materialized. That evening at sunset, a local shepherd drove up on a tractor. The shepherd motioned for an Arabic speaker. Abdul went with several other Marines to analyze the situation. When he returned, Abdul said the position would take mortar fire within five minutes. A few moments later, three mortars impacted 100 meters away, barely detonating in the soft sand and causing no damage. Shady was impressed with Abdul's prognostication.

After the mortar attack, the area remained silent. Marines were unable to confirm the identity of the attackers, who had probably driven away seconds after they fired the rounds. The night passed uneventfully, and April 6 dawned. All was quiet. There was no traffic. By noon, only a small number of vehicles had trickled in.

Shady thought the silence felt ominous.

Back home on the rooftop where he had started the morning, Howell set security while his squad scarfed down their MREs, standing watch so his Marines could eat first. When a grunt is in the field, "home" is defined as the place a Marine leaves his pack. The pack normally contains the basic necessities of survival for every lance corporal: food, water, shelter, ammo, and the latest issue of *Maxim.*

Sated at last with spaghetti and meatballs, Howell scanned the twilight horizon. He heard a pop, immediately followed by a violent, whistling *whoosh* that came out of nowhere. A 122mm rocket had just been fired at his building.

Rockets induce a different type of fear than a routine mortar. A rocket wails with a noise that seems animate, an explosive projectile with a built-in rebel yell. A person who has heard the scream of a 122mm rocket near his or her vicinity never forgets the violence of the sound. The distinctive whine reverberates like a jet engine, as opposed to the more common *thud* or *chhrummp* of a mortar explosion.

The sunset had hearkened the end of the day's fighting. Both sides were drained. Tonight it seemed the Muj weren't interested in martyrdom. After being awake for two straight days, the men needed a break.

Howell's team leaders wrote out the fire watch on their pocket-sized green memorandum pads, which were disintegrating from their sweat. The term "fire watch" is routine garrison-speak for a Marine assigned the job of staying awake and guarding gear at night while a unit trains in the field. During combat, fire watch took on a whole new meaning.

As thirty mile-an-hour winds whipped the mercury well below freezing, Howell curled himself into a ball, a feral, exhausted creature. Marines were filthy and unshaven. They had packed light for combat, not carrying their hygiene gear or sleep systems. Howell shivered, bundling up in his flak jacket for warmth. In the corner of the roof, a pair of Marines wrapped their arms and legs around each other, spooning to retain body heat. Any trace of homophobia the grunts harbored had fled.

Howell longed for his sleep system, which, from his perspective, was one of the smartest things Pentagon supply gurus had purchased in decades. The sleep system is a Gore-Tex waterproof bivy sack, a thin green-colored sleeping bag, and a thicker black bag. Zippers and snaps allow users to mix-and-match. In cold climates, Marines use all three bags. In warmer environs, grunts often sleep with nothing but the bivy sack and a thin green blanket called a poncho liner.*

Small-unit leaders throughout the Marine Corps often spent inordinate time considering which combination to order their troops to bring. Black bag? Green bag with bivy? All three? Rebellious grunts seeking to lighten their pack took it upon themselves to modify the platoon sergeant's orders, thinking they could tough it out with just the lighter green bag while the other pussies in the platoon lugged the bulky black sack. Their buddies ridiculed them for their insouciance when the weather turned cold.

It started raining. Someone yelled: "If it ain't raining, we ain't training!" Marines hooted off in the distance—the adverse

---

* Poncho liners were designed to line the interior of the plastic rain slickers used during Vietnam. Today's Marines rarely use either article of gear for their intended purpose: the poncho is normally used as a hasty type of tent, and the liner as a blanket. Marines lacking a sleep system often lash the two items together, forming a "Ranger roll."

weather seemed to increase morale rather than dampen it. Grunts have a perverse love for misery, and unlike Muj and rockets, at least rain was a familiar adversary.

Of course it's raining, Howell chuckled, *why wouldn't it? Only Marine grunts would come to the Iraqi desert and get rained on,* he thought, amused by the irony of it all as he rested his Kevlar helmet on a rock and drifted into a grimy, cold sleep.

"Hey, sir, you'd better get over here. XO's on the hook. He says we've been ordered to displace east," Shady deadpanned.

Shady thought it had to be a joke. Until two hours ago, April 6 had been a dull day. Around noon, the MHG executive officer, LtCol David Pere, came out to talk to Captain Anderson. Headquarters was concerned about the road situation. Maps indicated a possible bypass through a village about seven miles east that civilian traffic could be routed through. Shady, Anderson, the XO, Abdul, and twenty other Marines left to take a look.

Unbeknownst to any of them, the attack into Fallujah was becoming a major international incident. Furious at being spurned from consultations prior to the attack, the Iraqi Governing Council had threatened to disband. With the Coalition on the verge of breaking, the Americans needed to illustrate that Fallujah was not isolated. Lieutenant General Conway, who was receiving pressure from Washington via Sanchez, wanted to find a way for normal Iraqis to navigate the roads while the Marines wrapped up the operation. Moving the checkpoint east might satisfy the powers in Baghdad and buy Mad Dog Mattis and the Blue Diamond enough time to finish the job in Fallujah.

Shady, Anderson, and the others drove east along Route 1 away from the checkpoint, turning north into a village near an area called Nasser Wa Salaam (Arabic for "victory and peace"). The villagers glared as they drove through the dusty one-story hovels. The few children present spat in the direction of their vehicles. They saw no women, only young, angry Iraqi men. The Marines waved and smiled. The Iraqis did not.

The road had meandered out of the village and across several sand dunes before abruptly ending in front of a wide irrigation canal. Across the canal was the bypass. The map missed this obstacle. They drove back through the village quickly, on high alert. The men had mostly disappeared. Bad sign. This was often a prelude to an ambush or IED.

All six vehicles returned to the checkpoint without incident. The officers conferred. The bypass clearly did not exist. Displacing the checkpoint bordered on lunacy. They agreed that no sound tactical argument could be made for moving a ragtag bunch of untrained pogues eight miles away from the nearest friendly unit, right outside of a hostile village.

Confused, Anderson glanced at Shady. "Are you sure he said 'displace'?"

"That's what he said." Shady couldn't believe it.

The captain took the radio. "Say again, over?"

"You need to displace immediately. I say again, immediately." Pere paused. He knew the checkpoint would be an inviting target. "I'll get a FAC* out there as soon as I can. By the way," he added, "this came straight from the top."

What Pere didn't tell Anderson was that the same authorities in Baghdad who had shoved the Fallujah invasion down their throats were about to mandate an even more foolish action. They wanted the Marines to stop. A very small part of the effort

---

* Forward Air Controller. A FAC is a pilot responsible for coordinating air assets from a stationary ground location. Pere ensured the captain would have an individual dedicated to obtaining aircraft if necessary.

to let the grunts finish their attack was to create a bypass route for all civilian traffic around Fallujah. Which was what the MHG was supposed to do.

Meanwhile, Mattis was livid. His entire battle plan for dealing with Al Anbar—building up a base of support among the local villagers on the outskirts of the city in order to avoid using the military as the main effort—had been swept aside by officials whose decisions did not appear to be influenced by the opinions of their ground commanders. The next day, as the assault became a siege, Mattis commented to his staff on the historical parallel he saw unfolding in Fallujah.

In 1683, an Ottoman Pasha called Kara Mustapha attacked Vienna with a force of 140,000. Rather than invade, the Pasha laid siege to 11,000 Viennese who were attempting to cut off their supplies and starve them into submission. The town held out for two months as relief armies gathered from across Europe, eventually defeating what had been a sizable Ottoman force. In his own memoirs, Napoleon referenced this tactical error. When Mattis halted the offensive, he said, quoting Napoleon, "Next time we set out to take Vienna—we fucking take Vienna."

As the late afternoon of April 6 marched on, Shady knew nothing of the delicate negotiations senior Marine generals—including Mattis—had pursued in an effort to finish the Fallujah operation. What he did know was that Captain Anderson had less than three hours of daylight left to tear down the current position, displace, and establish a new site in front of a hostile village. They also needed to move the Jersey and Texas barriers on flatbed trailers driven by restless contracted Iraqis. Knowing their countrymen were in full revolt against the Americans, the men were on the verge of mutiny and required significant cajoling—almost at gunpoint—to finish the day's labor.

Shady watched as Anderson bribed the Iraqis, loaded up the Marines, and drove seven miles east. When they arrived, the scene was a mess. About thirty of the headquarters Marines had jumped from the back of their 7-tons and knelt behind a guardrail, shoulder to shoulder, weapons pointed towards the village. They looked like they were at the Battle of Gettysburg preparing for Pickett's Charge.

To Shady, Anderson had a frustrating habit of expecting him to fix certain problems simply because he was an older NCO. Fortunately, Shady knew how to posture well; he could act like he knew what he was doing. When Anderson saw the Marines bunched up behind the guardrail, he called Shady over, chewed his ass, and then told him to handle it. *Now.*

It had been years since Shady had any infantry training. As a Marine, he had been a communications expert, computer technician, and humvee driver. He had never been a grunt. He had never been shot at. Nevertheless, Shady barked orders at the Marines, dispersing them into a wide perimeter so they did not display such an inviting target. For the moment, his captain was satisfied.

The village next to the new checkpoint location was bracketed by an open meadow and a large grove of date palms. Farther down, there was an overpass where the captain had posted a pair of humvees. The cranes unloaded the Jersey and Texas barriers onto the road. Shady pulled the humvee perpendicular to a Texas barrier, forming their command post on the highway.

As sunset approached, the FAC arrived and conferred with the captain. Maj Jamie Cox, an AH-1 Cobra pilot stationed at Camp Fallujah as a staff officer, was universally known by his call sign, Boner. Shady liked aviators. They had laid-back attitudes, cool call signs, and a reputation for drinking. Anderson was exactly the opposite.

But that night, both the aviator and the grunt were all business. Boner and the captain reviewed their plans for the evening. Anderson had wanted to take a patrol into the village with Abdul to explain the reason the Marines were there. After the Pickett's Charge debacle, he decided against it. There was nothing left to do besides cover their sectors, watch for vehicles, build their positions and wait out the night.

Thunk. A small pop echoed half a mile behind the date palms.

Shady sat down on the edge of the Texas barrier next to the humvee, where his favorite lucky charm, the boar's tooth, was taped on the front of the windshield. He was chatting with Master Sergeant Nunez, a gunny, and a lance corporal. He had an MRE in his hand. Beef stew. His favorite.

BOOM!

The mortars impacted immediately at sunset. One round landed about ten meters away from Shady. Shrapnel cut the back of his hand and sliced through his beef stew, spilling the contents onto his uniform.

Shady crouched behind the Texas barrier, attempting to take cover. Screams. Boner was down in the middle of the road, his trousers shredded. Nunez ran out, grabbed the major, and dragged him back to the Texas barrier.

BOOM! BOOM!

Two more rounds hit. More screams. A combat service support battalion had been assisting MHG with constructing the checkpoint. One of their Marines was also wounded.

Shady ran over to Anderson. He was moving slowly and reaching for the radio.

"Grab your first aid kit," the captain growled.

Shady looked up. Blood was trickling down Anderson's neck, spilling onto his flak jacket and boots. A piece of shrapnel was stuck in his jaw. Behind him, Boner was still screaming.

This is not good, Shady thought. Normally, Shady preferred the absence of officers. This was different. Both of these guys seemed to know what they were doing, and they had both been hit at the same time.

A common admonition to officers is: "Don't get killed, it's bad for your men's morale." When leaders are evacuated or wounded, it affects the tempo and rhythm of a unit. Marines look to the NCOs, whether pogue or grunt, to provide direction amidst uncertainty.

Although wounded, the officers weren't planning on going anywhere. As his legs were being bandaged, Boner was on his satellite phone calling for air support from any unit that would answer. Anderson was on the radio, calling in a MEDEVAC for the other wounded Marine. Shady stuffed a gauze bandage on the captain's face, and then changed it out again when it became soaked with blood.

Five minutes had passed since the mortar attack. As Boner stabilized, Anderson worsened. "I need some water," he said. Then his face turned white, and he passed out, going into shock.

Shady and a gunnery sergeant named McMichael caught the captain before he slammed into the ground. A female corpsman, Doc Lobenberg, ran over to Anderson. She wiped off the blood. It appeared the puncture wound wasn't that big. Still, he'd have to go back and get checked out. Captain Anderson woke up and got angry when he realized the Marines were carrying him away.

"I've gotta stay," the captain said, slurring his words.

"Sir, we're taking you back," Shady said, enjoying giving Anderson orders now that he knew he would be okay. "Boner and I will take care of this."

Boner looked up, wondering who the hell this corporal was. Obviously, he must be a grunt, since he planned on "taking care of this."

With Anderson gone and an angry Abdul standing next to him, carrying an M-16, Shady looked at Boner. "I'm taking some Marines out on a patrol." Shady's tone suggested violence.

Boner paused. In an instant, he had gone from being the FAC—an advisor—to the ranking officer in charge of a disparate band of Marines. At that moment, most of the Marines at the checkpoint didn't even know each other's units, much less their names.

Boner may have been a helicopter pilot, but he instinctively knew that something didn't sound right. It smelled like rage or bloodlust. Years of experience sizing up trash-talking aviators had given Boner his own sixth sense when someone was posturing.

"Let's hold off on that patrol for now Shady," Boner said. Shady looked around. Gunny McMichael stood nearby, nodding in agreement. Shady backed down.

Later that night, another lieutenant and a major from the MHG came out to the checkpoint to assist Boner. At least twice more, the checkpoint was attacked with AK-47 fire from the village. The Marines responded with a massive volume of lead that silenced the shooters. No other Marines were hit.

Early the next morning, MHG was ordered to abandon the checkpoint. Shady drove back with Boner and the rest of the MHG Marines. Even after they moved their position, they had only observed three Iraqi vehicles. There was no civilian traffic on the road. The bypass idea had been futile.

Even if the bypass for civilian traffic had worked, it wouldn't have mattered. The Battle of Fallujah was taking a major strategic shift. The warriors were being ordered out. Politicians had decided it was time to step in.

CHAPTER 5

The Little Things That Kill

To err is human. To forgive is divine.
Neither is Marine Corps policy.

—Popular USMC bumper sticker

On April 7, as the attack into Fallujah ground to a halt, the unfortunate timing of a simultaneous revolt in Baghdad within the Shiite community compounded the Disorder happening in the city of mosques. Muqtada al-Sadr—a street-savvy, Shiite demagogue whose father was a revered cleric—leveraged the Fallujah frenzy into another uprising. Wearing what Marines referred to as black pajamas, Muqtada's Shiite followers denounced the Coalition attack on Fallujah, the Iraqi Governing Council, and anything associated with America. Muqtada issued what was, effectively, a declaration of war. Marines were told that anyone dressed in black pajamas should be shot on sight.

Although Muqtada's Shiite rebellion was eventually suppressed, the political damage was done. As pictures of bloodied women and children tumbled out of Fallujah, leaders around the world condemned the American actions. The Iraqi Governing Council—a symbolic, if impotent, representation of Iraqi sovereignty—threatened to disband. Rumors flew that British prime minister Tony Blair had informed President Bush that he would withdraw from the Coalition if the offensive was not halted.

The next day, over 100 miles west of Fallujah, Cpl Dan Amaya and Cpl Brian Zmudzinski, 1st and 3rd Squad leaders of 3rd Platoon, Kilo 3/4, were taking a walk. It was 4 A.M. on April 8. To the west of Amaya and Zmudzinski, Lieutenant Benatz, Sgt Dusty Soudan, and 3rd Platoon, Lima 3/7, were waking up on the border outpost of Husaybah and getting ready for the final rehearsals for their patrol down Market Street.

Operation Vigilant Resolve had become a political lightning rod. What had been a mission to attack the city and find the insurgents had devolved into a siege. Regardless of what would happen next, Major General Mattis needed reinforcements. With both 1/5 and 2/1 heavily engaged, the general called on the Thundering Third of 3/4 to support the ground activity. By this time, ground activity in Fallujah might have meant anything: attack, siege, or amorphous cease-fire.

Amaya and Zmudzinski were joking with Cpl Matt O'Brien, a Marine from 2nd Platoon. They were like schoolboys at recess. We're going to the action, baby! Zmudzinski was especially excited. Although he had earned respect, the laconic, quiet Marine from Wisconsin was still the only corporal in the platoon who lacked a combat action ribbon.

Kilo 3/4 was stationed at Haditha Dam, not far from Al Asad Air Base. Completed in 1987, Haditha was the second largest of Iraq's eight hydroelectric dams. In 2004, it provided an electrical output of 675 megawatts. Without the dam, the fledgling Iraqi power grid would be destroyed. With Capt Morgan Savage in command, Kilo 3/4 had relieved a detachment of Azerbaijanis a few weeks earlier and taken control of the dam. As a leader of men who enjoyed whiskey and violence, Captain Morgan Savage was well named.

For Marines in the spring of 2004, Haditha was the Marriott of western Iraq.* Guarded by a joint Azerbaijani-Marine effort, the breezes across the wide Euphrates kept the temperature ten degrees cooler than anywhere else in the region. Absent the sting of wind and sand, the surrounding terrain was almost lush.

The Marines from Kilo had a lot of down time when they weren't on post. Zmudzinski and Amaya became company champions at the card game of spades. They had an unfair advantage: the pair had trained for months during hours of boredom while on guard duty at Bangor.

As they waited to board the 7-tons bound for Fallujah, Amaya and O'Brien tossed grotesque jibes back and forth. "Ya know, O'Brien," Amaya said, "I keep looking at you and thinking . . . you just ain't gonna make it."

"You bitch," O'Brien said.

"Seriously, man," Amaya continued. "You're so dog ugly, a bullet to the face would be an improvement."

"Go fuck yourself." They all laughed.

The trio indulged each other with morbid humor for a few more minutes, then shook hands and said their goodbyes. They packed their squads and platoons onto 7-tons and humvees, and then departed for their convoy east.

The cities, bases, and landmarks flew past as they meandered towards Camp Fallujah. Haqlaniyah. Al Asad. Hit (pronounced

---

* This did not last. In 2005, Haditha became a hotspot for mortars and IEDs. On August 3, 2005, fourteen Marines from Lima 3/25 and one interpreter were killed in their amtrack from a monstrous IED, which was one of the largest single-event casualties that Marines sustained during this period of the Iraq war.

"heat"). Ramadi. Habbiniyah. Saqlawiyah. The Fallujah Clover-leaf. Four hours after departure, they pulled into the MEK. The first thing they saw was a sign that said: Welcome To Camp Fallu-jah. It was emblazoned with the MHG funky chicken.

Battalions of amtracks, tanks, supply vehicles, and light armored trucks had arrived from everywhere. Although they still thought of them as pogues, the grunts agreed that MHG was good at building and sustaining supply camps. As white circus tents and plywood outhouses proliferated like cherry blossoms in the Washington springtime, Camp Fallujah bloomed from a headquarters outpost of 4,000 to an international media spot-light. Within a few days after the Fallujah siege began, the MEK population had tripled to over 12,000—almost half of all Marine forces stationed in Iraq. Instead of sitting on the periphery of a dwindling enemy, Camp Fallujah was suddenly at the center of what was perceived as the most important fight in theater.

Twenty minutes after arriving at the MEK, Captain Savage was told to take out Kilo and reinforce the cloverleaf.

Quickly, Lieutenant Stokes called over his squad leaders, issu-ing them a terse combat order: "We're going to the cloverleaf."

The Fallujah cloverleaf, where routes 1 (north-south) and 10 (east-west) intersect, was designed like any highway on/off ramp system in the United States. The feeder roads were lined with mosques and three-story concrete buildings instead of gas stations and strip malls. The ramps were a mixture of dirt and asphalt. When the cloverleaf was open to regular traffic, the on/off ramps became two-way streets.

East of the cloverleaf was a hospital handled by a volunteer group from Jordan. Several hundred Iraqis were protesting at the hospital. They were restricted from their homes in Fallujah. They were very angry. Kilo had been asked to provide a show of force to quell the disturbance, in support of 1/5's Charlie Company.

The cloverleaf intersection formed a quadrant. Savage took 1st and 2nd Platoons into the northeast, and Stokes went southeast with 3rd Platoon.

Stokes told his squad leaders—Amaya, Zmudzinski, and a corporal named Osborne (called Ozzy)—to get across the road and establish security. They would lie down on the ground and face their weapons towards the city of Fallujah.

Zmudzinski and his squad jumped off the 7-ton. They were hyped up, fully expecting a firefight, ambush, or attack. Marines from Charlie 1/5—men who had been fighting for several days— were relaxed. *What the hell are these new guys doing?* the grunts from Charlie thought.

3rd Platoon ran to the edge of the road, ready to get some.

Nothing happened.

An hour went by. Silence. What the hell *are* we doing?

Lieutenant Stokes ran off and talked to Captain Savage, who was talking to the battalion commander, who was talking to the regimental commander. Much to the grunt's annoyance, the big minds were meeting for a long time.

"Hey, corporal, what the fuck is going on?" LCpl Marcus Ward said. Ward was one of Zmudzinski's fire team leaders. A veteran of OIF I, Ward had an arrogant streak and occasionally challenged Zmudzinski's authority in the squad. When they first met, Brian hated him. In Iraq, they became close friends.

"Shut up, Ward. Watch your sectors." Zmudzinski had no idea what the fuck was going on.

Two mortar rounds exploded several dozen meters away, causing no damage.

Ward glanced at Zmudzinski and smiled. "Congratulations, corporal. You just got your combat action ribbon."

For Cpl Jason Howell, April 8 was a bad day.

Regardless of what the politicians were saying, as far as Bravo 1/5 was concerned, the Battle of Fallujah was still in full swing. Although the Marines had complied with the order to cease offensive operations, the Muj inside the city had missed the memo. As Marines dug in for the siege, the rest of Iraq seemed to explode.

Earlier that day, four bridges had been destroyed on a main supply route, leaving bases around Camp Fallujah cut off. Two days before in Ramadi—not far from the Snake Pit—Echo 2/4 had lost a dozen men to a vicious and well-coordinated ambush. The casualties included a platoon commander, platoon sergeant, and squad leader.* In Husaybah on the Syrian border, Sgt. Dusty Soudan's platoon from Lima 3/7 was hit with multiple IEDs on their patrol—and things were about to get much worse.

Howell did not know any of this. What he did know was that Josh Palmer and William Harrell, two charismatic leaders of Bravo Company, were dead. Grunts know the dozen staff NCOs and junior officers of their company by name; within a rifle company, these men comprise an unofficial tribal council. Bravo's 3rd Platoon commander, Lt Josh Palmer, was shot three times in the side while throwing a grenade into a door. His wounds proved fatal. A few days before, Palmer had sent an urgent email home requesting candy—for Iraqi children.

---

* In August 2004, the *Philadelphia Inquirer* ran an entire series on Echo Company 2/4 that included a detailed account of the ambush. The Marines killed from the April 6 attack were: Pfcs Benjamin Carman, Christopher Cobb, Deryk Hallal, Ryan Jerabek, and Christopher Mabry; Lance Corporals Marcus Cherry, Kyle Crowley, Travis Layfield, and Anthony Roberts; SSgt Allan Walker; and 2ndLt John Wroblewski. Navy Corpsman Fernando Mendez-Aceves was killed while trying to save Staff Sergeant Walker's life.

SSgt William Harrell, the machine-gun section leader from weapons platoon, had been Howell's platoon sergeant when he first arrived to 1/5.* Prior to the deployment, Harrell had been moved to weapons. Staff Sergeant Harrell had a reputation for looking out for his corporals and sergeants, letting them do their jobs without imposing his own Order (or Disorder) upon them. "Harrell was hard and professional, but he also had that 'fuck-the-bullshit' vibe. He was cool. We would have followed him anywhere," Howell said.

Howell and his squad were on a rooftop in central Fallujah. The weather was warming after the earlier cold. The roof was sticky with a blackish tar-asphalt that the wind had mixed with sand.

The day before, their squad had been shooting back and forth at a house. Suddenly, white flags had appeared. A group of men ran out from the buildings, covered by women and children. They turned and ran west, deeper into the city. Angry at the absence of legitimate targets, the Marines held their fire.

As they took cover on the roof, searching for targets, mortars came in. They got closer. They impacted on the ground, about fifty meters from Howell and his rooftop. The Muj were obviously targeting them. Howell thought it was time to move.

Bravo was in an awkward position. They had attacked deep into the southeastern corner of Fallujah when they were ordered to halt their offensive. Although tied into Alpha Company on their left flank, Bravo was a few blocks north and west. On April 8, Bravo was the Marine unit farthest into the city. Since first pla-

---

* In addition to three rifle platoons, an infantry company also has a "weapons" platoon. With fifty to sixty Marines, weapons platoons include machine gunners (0331), mortarmen (0341), and anti-tank assaultmen (0351).

toon was holding down the far right flank, Capt Jason Smith had told Howell's platoon commander, Lieutenant Lewis, to secure it at all costs. If the flank collapsed, the position of the entire company—and battalion—would become precarious and exposed.

Generally speaking, the candor of the Marine Corps is a refreshing aspect of the Spartan Way. While Marines must respect the chain of command, junior men are also expected—even encouraged—to "wave the bullshit flag" when they see a problem. Outside observers would be aghast at witnessing the temerity of a lance corporal or sergeant approaching a general and saying, "Sir, this is all fucked up," while explaining what should be done to fix it. This boldness breeds confidence that the creeds of the Spartan Way have been passed on to yet another generation of initiative-taking warriors.

At this particular moment, however, Lieutenant Lewis wasn't in the mood for candor. He had seized a position, and his orders were to secure it. His squad leader had suddenly become a lousy team player.

"Sir, can I take a fire team and find another building?" Howell asked, his first thoughts towards protecting his men while still accomplishing the mission.

Lewis called Smith. "Bravo Six, this is Bravo One. I'd like to move off this rooftop."

As taught in the Marine Basic Officer Course, one of the primary lessons of military leadership is the concept of Commander's Intent. When Smith had ordered Lewis to hold his position, he could have cared less which building he was on, so long as the flank didn't collapse. That was his Commander's Intent: hold the flank. 2nd Lieutenant Lewis had the freedom to choose any course of action he wanted, provided he accomplished the overall Intent.

Taking the call from Lewis, Smith thought his platoon commander wanted to withdraw his position, which would have been catastrophic. Smith had no idea that Lewis was calling him asking for permission to move from one rooftop to another. This was the type of decision Smith would have trusted any of his platoon commanders to make without his guidance, so long as they were meeting his overall Intent.

Lewis, listening to Smith on the other end of the radio, looked back at Howell. "Negative," 2nd Lieutenant Lewis said to Howell. "We have to hold our position."

Another mortar landed nearby. Howell was getting pissed. "Sir, *we have to get the fuck off this roof!*"

"Corporal Howell—" 2nd Lieutenant Lewis cut him off, pulling rank.

Howell dropped all professional courtesy. "Sir, this is a fucked up position. They know we're here." *Chruuump!* "We are bunched up on this roof. If we stay here, Marines in my squad will die. We can still hold our sectors from another building." *Chruuump!* "We need to get out of here *now!*" *CHRUUUMP!!!*

Realizing he had to make his own command decision, Lieutenant Lewis finally relented. "Fine, Howell. Get a fire team and go take a look."

Howell ran towards another building. The squad and platoon fanned out, dispersing across the urban terrain. Enemy mortars continued targeting the original location. For the moment, no one in Howell's squad was wounded.

At Camp Fallujah, all of 3/4 bivouacked in white circus-style tents with wooden floorboards placed in a square-mile sandlot at the southern end of the fortress. They formed a battalion perimeter around the tents and put Marines on watch. Brick and concrete walls surrounded the battalion, where Marines from a reserve infantry company, India 3/24, were posted as sentries.

The night of April 9, Captain Savage was loading up his humvee in preparation for Kilo 3/4's imminent attack into Fallujah when—*Boom!*—mortars landed near the MEK. They were close, but did not land inside the camp.

Suddenly, gunshots rang out.

"We're taking fire!"

Hundreds of Marines ran out of their tents and established a perimeter, preparing to repulse the attack. In the confusion, some of Kilo's men wound up exchanging gunfire with 3/4's H & S Company, as well as Marines from 2/2, a battalion located on the other side of the camp. Attempting to quell the action were the sentries from India 3/24, who were furiously calling for their own quick reaction force to calm everybody down.

About a minute later, the gunfire ceased. Apparently, Camp Fallujah had been taking fire from an Army convoy passing outside the camp. The mortars had spooked the soldiers on the convoy, and they had opened up on the phantom insurgents they thought they saw near the explosion. Despite the cacophony, no one had gotten shot.

The Marines laughed. Even though the humvees and 7-tons were now littered with bullet holes, the excitement had been a good stress release. Marines have a funny way of blowing off steam.

Captain Savage wasn't laughing. This was *his* company . . . these men were *his* responsibility. With rounds flying over his humvee, he had run toward the tents to wake up his Marines. In the process, he had tripped over something. As things calmed down, he felt a twinge of pain in his right leg but didn't think anything of it.

Over the next two hours, Captain Savage and the other company commanders confirmed that everyone was okay, issued final orders, and tied up all the loose ends for the attack. Before major operations, company commanders run through as many mental checklists as a bride planning her wedding. Batteries for radios? Rifle ammo? Communication frequencies? Machine-gun ammo? MREs? Hand grenades? More rifle ammo? Water? Pyrotechnics? Tow straps? First aid kits?

Finally, at about 2 A.M., Captain Savage fell asleep next to his humvee. He had been buzzing with caffeine, nicotine, and no-doze pills. In the frenzy of preparation, adrenaline and chemicals masked the pain he should have felt.

Savage awoke the morning of April 10, surprised to discover that he was unable to move his leg. He looked down and saw that his trousers were covered in blood. He dropped his pants and found his right quadriceps ripped open, the muscle flapping down and nearly exposing the bone. When he had tripped during the intramural firefight, the nick Savage had received was actually his leg ramming through a piece of steel rebar that was serving as a makeshift tent stake.

Savage thirsted to lead his Marines into the heart of the Disorder in Fallujah. Fate denied him the opportunity. For the next two hours, Captain Savage languished in a field hospital. Doped up from medicine, Savage nevertheless called a lieutenant to pick him up and bring him back to the battalion. Eight days later he got his company back, having listened to the events in Fallujah over the radio. "It was as painful to me as losing my father," Savage said.

With the company commander gone, Capt Timothy Walker, a staff officer from the battalion, arrived to lead Kilo in the attack. The Marines of Kilo liked Walker, but they looked to familiar faces like Lieutenant Stokes to make decisions and issue orders. As a veteran of OIF I, Stokes was esteemed for his maturity, bearing, and combat experience. Eyes were on him to get the job done.

Later that morning, 3rd Platoon assembled on Route 1 north of the Cloverleaf, preparing to attack into the northeast corner of Fallujah. 3/4 had an elaborate plan to sweep all the way through Fallujah, and Kilo's mission was to get a foothold into the town. Zmudzinski's 3rd Squad was the base unit for 3rd Platoon. Amaya's 1st Squad was on his left; Ozzy and 2nd Squad were on his right. Stokes decided to stay with Zmudzinski's squad.

Lieutenant Stokes was a man of few words. He had trained his platoon time and again to guide off each other's movements, using a technique called the Base Unit Concept. If Zmudzinski's 3rd Squad was moving, Amaya and Ozzy would cover, and then catch up. If Zmudzinski's squad stopped, they stopped. All Stokes had to do was control Zmudzinski, whose 3rd Squad was the Base Unit. Everything else would take care of itself.

Zmudzinski thought the attack felt surreal. Full of adrenaline, Marines yelled out every time they saw something. Machine gunners sporadically fired down the street. Psyops vehicles were blaring out a message: *Marines are here to find the terrorists and bring them to justice. Stay in your homes, and follow their orders. You will be safe.*

Amaya, Zmudzinski, and Ozzy were conductors orchestrating a symphony of violence. With the accordion-like affect of movement, Marines would bunch up and then spread out. Their biggest challenge was not getting too far apart. At first, they didn't have much enemy contact.

To the left of 3rd, the mortarmen attached to 1st Platoon wanted to get into the fight. Marines thought they saw a muzzle flash from a nearby building on the edge of the road. First Platoon's mortar team fired at the building with white phosphorous rounds. Commonly known as Willie Pete, white phosphorous is practically impossible to extinguish when on fire—the modern equivalent of a medieval catapult.

When 1st Platoon's mortarmen fired the Willie Pete, they did not account for the wind, which was blowing hard from the west toward the Marines at the cloverleaf. The Willie Pete rounds began booming and hissing near 3rd Platoon Marines.

"Kilo One, this is Kilo Three," Stokes called back. "Goddammit! You're gonna get my men killed if you pull that shit again!" 1st Platoon stopped firing Willie Pete.

Finally, Stokes looked over at Zmudzinski. Not one to mince words, Stokes delivered his orders to Zmudzinski short and sweet.

Stokes pointed. "I want that house."

"You got it, sir."

Zmudzinski took his squad from the road and bounded up through a series of steep dirt mounds. With machine guns covering their approach, they ran up to the door, which was locked. They set an explosive charge and blew up the door. Zmudzinski and his squad cleared the building. All secure. Zmudzinski put a team on the rooftop to cover the platoon's movement. They had not taken any fire, and they had their foothold in Fallujah.

The platoon sergeant was floating behind, bounding along with whatever team was bringing up the rear. Months before, the Marines of 3rd had tagged their platoon sergeant as weak. Captain Savage, who had his own concerns as well, had given Lieutenant Stokes a chance to replace him.

Stokes decided against it. Like an ace poker player, the lieutenant wanted to work with the hand he was dealt. As long as the platoon sergeant stayed out of his way and let the squad leaders do their jobs, Stokes would keep him.

3rd Platoon was kicking down doors and clearing houses at a rapid rate. They ran into a problem. The battalion was supposed to be advancing online, moving from house to house to ensure all occupants were clear. However, units were speeding up or slowing down at their own rates. Some squads and platoons were bogged down in a long search or in-house firefight. Others, like 3rd Platoon, were encountering no resistance. This meant some houses weren't being searched, leaving gaps in the line. Confused Iraqi civilians were wandering through areas that, in theory, had already been secured.

The Marines in 3rd were getting tired, but not as tired as the men from 2nd. Despite the protests of their NCOs, including Amaya's friend Cpl Matt O'Brien, the 2nd Platoon commander had ordered his Marines to carry their daypacks into the attack. This added twenty to thirty pounds to the grunt's normal load of forty to sixty pounds.* The mules of 2nd were moving slowly, and 3rd was constantly waiting for them to catch up. Eventually, the 2nd Platoon squad leaders staged a small mutiny and cached their daypacks inside a random building.

When the Marines searched a house and found it occupied, they evicted the homeowners and dispatched them towards the headquarters units following behind them. Before the deployment, Zmudzinski was one of a handful of Marines to attend a month-long Arabic class at Camp Pendleton. Theoretically, this

---

* Marines were issued both a large and small pack for use in combat. Designed for carrying a two- or three-day survival load, the small pack is called a daypack. Although the Marines certainly needed some extra gear, only an absolute minimum of weight should be carried into an urban blitz like Fallujah. The problem could be solved by staging the packs with a gunny or platoon sergeant to bring up from the rear lines in a vehicle.

should have enabled him to communicate with the families as he evicted them from their homes. That didn't happen. All he could say was *"awghf"* before pointing a gun at them and directing them with hand gestures back to the rear. He was too busy leading the attack.

To their left, both 1st and 2nd Platoon received sporadic fire from ambulances marked with a red crescent. The ambulances had been ferrying food and medicine into the city. They were resupplying the men fighting the Marines. Later that night, 2nd Platoon destroyed a pair of vehicles that appeared suspicious.

And so it went. Zmudzinski's squad progressed, doing the work of urban war. Run up to a building. Set security. "Breecher up!" Slap an explosive charge on the door. Blow up the door. Clear the building. See a possible enemy bunker. Take a shoulder-fired rocket shot. Destroy the bunker. See a possible enemy bus. Another rocket shot. Destroy the bus. Minimal enemy resistance. Not much shooting on either side. Nobody killed or wounded. They were making good progress.

By the early part of the afternoon, Stokes pulled each squad into a house. "You got 'em," the lieutenant said to his squad leaders. The implicit message in those three words—understood by every infantry unit leader—was that the Marines needed a break. 3rd Squad spent about an hour eating, drinking, and recharging for the next fight.

Given what was about to happen, the break was well timed.

Corporal Howell had found his new rooftop. It was a "sweet" position: good cover and concealment, solid observation of the main highway, and enough room to spread out his entire squad.

Howell's biggest problem with the first rooftop (other than the fact that it was being directly targeted by mortars) was the small size. His squad was bunched up and unable to disperse.

Like the accordion effect, dispersion is another constant infantry balancing act. A squad leader wants his men spread out far enough so that no single mortar, grenade, or IED can take them all out, but not so far away that he loses control. Howell was happy with the new roof. It was small enough that he knew where everyone was, but large enough so that if the Muj snuck in a lucky mortar shot, it would hit only one or two Marines instead of five or six.

Before Howell could run back to Lieutenant Lewis, he heard the crack of sniper rounds and the telltale reports of an M-240G machine gun. The rounds were coming at him. The military term for fratricide—deaths caused by friendly weapons—is blue-on-blue. Howell and his team ran into the staircase, calling over their radio, "We're taking blue-on-blue!"

A Marine sniper on a nearby rooftop saw what was happening, ran to his radio, and called off the machine guns. Soon, the firing stopped. For most grunts, their worst nightmare is not that they will die, but that they might accidentally do something to cause the death of other Marines. Or the loss of a certain part of their anatomy.

More mortar rounds impacted. Howell's corpsman, Doc Perkins, always seemed to be next to him when the mortars came in. After the attack, Howell and Perkins looked wide-eyed at each other . . . and laughed. Howell's motto: "Everyday I found something to smile about, even in Fallujah. Anytime I could get a smile, I rocked it."

From squad leader to commander in chief, humor has long been one of the most valuable remedies to the horrors of war in a military leader's kit bag. Although few doctrinal manuals mention the significance of humor, the strength gained from a well-timed chuckle sustains a warrior's spirit in a way that MREs never can. During the bleakest period of the Civil War, President Abraham Lincoln called humor "an emollient that saved me much friction and distress."

In July 1864, when Fort Stevens in Washington, D.C., was under attack, President Lincoln went to observe the battle. Standing up on a parapet—as bullets whizzed past—Lincoln's stovepipe hat made an inviting target. After a medical officer standing five feet away was wounded, a twenty-three-year-old captain, Oliver Wendell Holmes, Jr., tackled Lincoln, shouting, "Get down you damned fool!" President Lincoln obediently remained behind cover, and Captain Holmes was convinced his career was over.

Leaving Fort Stevens after the victory, the commander in chief walked over to his young officer. "Goodbye, Captain Holmes. I am glad to see you know how to talk to civilians." At a more somber moment when the war was going badly, President Lincoln was asked why he often joked when confronting sorrow. He quietly replied, "I laugh because I must not cry."*

Satisfied with his reconnaissance, Howell ran back to the original position, verified the coordinates with the lieutenant, and took his squad up on the roof. Mortars had been detonating so often for the past two days that Howell and his Marines had become numb to their sound. They dug into tar-covered shin-

---

* At Fort Stevens, Abraham Lincoln became the only American President to ever expose himself to enemy fire while serving as commander in chief. Of his visit to the front lines, Lincoln said, "The Commander-in-Chief of the Army must never show any cowardice in the presence of his soldiers, however he may feel." Capt. Oliver Wendell Holmes, Jr., later became an influential justice of the U.S. Supreme Court.

gles, hiding from the barrage until it stopped. So when a mortar landed directly on their rooftop, Howell knew it was close, but he couldn't tell exactly *how* close. They all sounded the same.

Then he heard the screaming.

Howell looked over and saw Pfc Matthew Brennan writhing. "Doc Perkins, get over here! Brennan's hit!"

The entire squad ran over, abandoning their sectors in their passion to help their fellow Marine. Howell saw that the left side of Brennan's flak jacket was shredded. One of Howell's team leaders grabbed him. "We're getting too bunched up, corporal. We need to get some Marines back on security."

Good point, Howell thought. *That's why he's one of my team leaders.*

Another Marine ran up screaming. "My face is burning!"

Howell and Doc Perkins checked him out. They couldn't find anything. A small piece of shrapnel might have singed his neck. The Marine kept screaming, insisting that he had been hit. Howell and the corpsman exchanged glances. *Is this dude for real?*

While Lieutenant Lewis called in the MEDEVAC, Howell talked to his wounded Marine. "You're gonna be fine, Brennan," he said, talking to him to keep him awake. Brennan had shrapnel wounds in his left side, above his kidney. Howell and the Doc each grabbed an arm, carrying Brennan as his pants dropped down to his ankles, dragging ignominiously behind him.

"Will they send me to the hot nurses at the MEK?"

"Absolutely, Brennan." Howell wasn't worried about him anymore.

Back at the MEK, Shady was arguing with Captain Anderson. "Sir, I don't want a goddamn Purple Heart."

"I didn't want one either," the captain snapped back. A piece of gauze was taped to the side of his face. "But orders are orders. You were treated for wounds sustained under enemy fire. You're getting one whether you like it or not."

"The beef stew took more damage than my hand." Shady carried the copy of *Gates of Fire* that Anderson had given him for emotional leverage to make his point—the Spartans were stingy with their distribution of prizes for valor. The corporal knew if he was awarded a Purple Heart, he would be perceived as a pogue trying to take advantage of his minor wound. He didn't want that stereotype. Not only was it not his style, it would be bad for his business. He had done his job. Wasn't that enough?

"MREs don't rate medals. Look at it this way," the captain explained. "Sometimes the Corps screws up and punishes you when someone else deserves it. And sometimes you don't get the recognition you should for a job well done. But sometimes the Corps rewards you instead. I know you don't believe you rate the honor of that award. And maybe you don't. Other guys went through a lot more to wear it than you did. But just shut up and take it. What's on your chest doesn't really matter. What's in your heart does."

Capt Jason Smith, who was making the rounds from platoon to platoon in Bravo 1/5, made his way out to the right flank. A concerned Lieutenant Lewis carefully briefed Captain Smith on his new rooftop positions. Lewis expected Smith to be angry that he had usurped his authority, but he was prepared to justify his actions.

"You're still holding the flank, aren't you?" Smith asked.

"Yes, sir." Lewis said.

Smith just nodded. "Good work, Lewis." The captain had known nothing of the conflict with Howell about the rooftop, or Lewis's dilemma in making the decision to move. All he knew was his lieutenant had secured the flank. Lewis had met the Commander's Intent.

Recharged, Corporal Zmudzinski's 3rd Squad continued their urban attack. LCpl J. D. Smith, a SAW gunner, approached the door of a house. An Iraqi man ran out the door with his hands up, moving past the squad.

Smith brushed past the Iraqi. Carrying his machine gun like a rifle, he ran into the entryway. Zmudzinski heard the distinct crack of an AK-47.

Zmudzinski ran out of another house and saw Smith stumbling out, bleeding from the hand, face, and shoulder. His SAW was gone. Fragments from the weapon were splattered all over his body.

Zmudzinski yelled for a corpsman and began working on the MEDEVAC. After the corpsman said that Smith would be okay, the corporal didn't give him much thought. Zmudzinski realized that clearing this house was going to be a problem. Smith hadn't taken more than two steps into the doorway when he had been hit. Also, Smith's SAW was somewhere inside. Broken or not, a machine gun would be valuable to the enemy.

Stokes showed up and immediately understood that securing the house would take his entire platoon. He pulled his squad leaders in for a quick conference. "Amaya and Ozzy, I want you to cordon off the house."

What Stokes didn't know at the time was that several other structures behind this building were connected with basement tunnels. The Muj—at this point, every adult male in Fallujah was assumed to be a Muj—were scampering like rodents from building to building. They were not shooting but observing, watching the Marines establish the cordon to see if they could find a gap in their position. For the moment, they couldn't.

Stokes called up an M-240G machine gun and ordered several hundred rounds dumped into the concrete. The Muj sporadically fired back. The concrete was thick, providing the enemy inside with good cover.

Stokes looked hard at Zmudzinski. "I need that SAW back."

Zmudzinski nodded. He took a team up and they stacked against the wall, next to the door. "Frag out!" They threw a grenade in, which exploded, blackening the long entryway with smoke. As they turned to run in the door, AK-47 rounds zipped past their bodies.

The entryway was a long, narrow corridor, pitch black and twenty meters in length. In these situations, urban combat doctrine called for "flooding": pushing several Marines through the so-called fatal funnel to gain a foothold in the house. Obviously, the doctrine said, the first few Marines would be shot.

Additionally, pre-OIF urban combat training had often used models where a house contained a small entryway that hooked into a room. A long, narrow hallway was any attacker's nightmare. It was not simply a fatal funnel; it was a fatal tornado.

Zmudzinski and Lance Corporals Hoyt and McNeil were lying flat on their bellies in the entryway and trying to low-crawl towards the hallway. They couldn't see anything. A large pillar was in the middle of the entryway. Zmudzinski and Hoyt squeezed behind it. McNeil, who had grabbed an AK-47, was spraying the hallway with rounds through a window.* The bullets ricocheted around the room, bouncing near Zmudzinski and Hoyt. Blue-on-blue.

Zmudzinski and Hoyt crawled out and tried the drill again. Frag out. Boom. Smoke. Going in blind. Enemy AK-47 fire. Long hallway. Can't make it. Back out.

Zmudzinski went back to Stokes and described what had happened. Stokes nodded, and then called up a pair of light shoulder-fired rockets. They fired. The shots bounced harmlessly off the concrete.

Stokes had some tear gas grenades with him. "Let's try to gas them out." The Marines put on their gas masks. Stokes ran up to a roof of another building with a team of snipers. Zmudzinski took his team below. They flung the tear gas grenades in through the windows. The entrenched enemy fired back.

Next, they tried a satchel charge. The platoon demolitions expert, Lance Corporal Nelson, rigged a box-shaped package of explosives with a time fuse. They threw it in. The explosion turned the front of the house into a pile of concrete rubble. But the hallway of the fortress remained intact. Again, the Muj fired back at the Marines, letting them know they were still alive and ready to fight.

Stokes got on the radio. "Kilo Six this is Kilo Three. Can we get an air strike?"

---

* The AK-47 fires a larger caliber round (7.62mm) than the M-16 (5.56mm). Although far less accurate, the larger round goes through thicker walls. Additionally, the AK-47 is an automatic weapon, firing a stream of bullets like a machine gun. Many grunt platoons had at least a couple of men carrying AKs.

By April 10, the offensive for the Battle of Fallujah had technically halted. Because of the claims of heavy civilian casualties made on international television, politics surrounded requests for air strikes. "Negative, Kilo 3."*

The sun was starting to go down. Kilo had been fighting all day. Stokes pulled his men back into a safe house and tied his platoon into the rest of the company.

As night fell, silence enveloped the city. Both sides were at a disadvantage. The Marines did not know the terrain, and the enemy could not move freely. Nobody fought at night. Both Marines and Muj dug in, resupplied, and hoped that God would be with them tomorrow.

The next day was Easter Sunday.

---

* Months later, Mattis explained that air strikes were turned down because Marines were so close to the target that they were in danger of becoming collateral damage themselves. "Politics had nothing to do with it," he said. "There were simply too many other Marines nearby."

CHAPTER 6

Martyrs

mar·tyr—
(1) a person who voluntarily suffers death as
the penalty for refusing to renounce a religion
(2) victim; especially: a great or constant sufferer

Bev Atkins, the mother of Cpl Craig Atkins from Fox 2/4, has blond hair, blue eyes, and a direct, no-nonsense manner. Of average build, Bev carries herself with a certain strength developed from growing up on a farm in Indiana, marrying a motorcycle rider, and raising a trio of boys.

On April 6, when Jason Howell and the rest of Bravo 1/5 were attacking into Fallujah, Bev was in southern Indiana working as a manager of a medical office and having a fairly normal day. In between chores, she was reading and sending messages back and forth on the Magnificent Bastards' chat room. Everyone on the chat room was feeling relieved that 2/4 was nowhere near Fallujah.

Chat rooms for military families are domestic versions of the Lance Corporal Network. Parents, spouses, and friends of deployed Marines thought of their unit-level chat rooms as a second home. The befriending, storytelling, consoling, explaining, and rumor swapping made them feel connected to the broader picture; regardless of their politics, they became a sort of coalition. *At least somebody else out there knows what I'm going through.* The Marines may have volunteered, but most of these civilians felt conscripted into the worst duty of all: waiting.

Bev went home with a sense of uncertainty gnawing at her. She turned on the television. "Twelve Marines Dead in Ramadi," the Fox News banner headline read.

Twelve Marines. Dead. Ramadi. Seeing it on the screen, calmly intoned by the announcer as a cover story with an appropriately somber face just before commenting on the impending Michael Jackson trial, made Bev feel the same panicked sensation of anger and survival mechanisms that Marines do. Fight or flight.

Although she couldn't fight, at least she could be ready. If Craig was wounded the Marines would call, and—if it was worse—they would come to her door. Because the Atkins home had dial-up internet, she couldn't use her computer. At that moment, Bev thought it was important to keep the phone free for a call she didn't want to receive.

Bev called Deb Edwards, Craig's girlfriend in California, on her cell phone. Had she heard the news? Deb had. Did she know anything else? Deb didn't, only what was on TV. They shared a moment of encouragement, affirmation, and love. Bev hung up.

Then the doorbell rang.

Bev jumped.

She steeled herself, took a deep breath, and opened the door. *I have to be strong,* she thought. *No tears.*

It was her neighbor Joyce.

Bev exhaled, making a mental note to tell everyone in St. Anthony never to use her doorbell. Friends and neighbors could knock or just walk in, but don't ever ring that damn bell.

Joyce had seen the news and thought Bev could use the company. To keep the Atkins' phone line free, Bev went over to Joyce's house and used her internet to check the 2/4 website. From the chat room, Bev learned that Echo Company's 1st Platoon had taken a catastrophic loss. A dozen men were hit, including the platoon commander and platoon sergeant, in a well-coordinated enemy ambush involving over fifty Iraqis and/or Mujahideen.

Bev woke up at 4:30 A.M. the next day to check the website. Sheila Cobb, an Echo Company mom, had left a post to say she had lost her only son. Bev went to work, reading the website all day for any other news. There was nothing.

That night, Bev came home and walked into the garage. Gordon had returned from his job at the sawmill and had already cooked dinner, which was normal. They had already eaten in the garage, which was also normal. The garage was the geographic hub of social life in the Atkins family. Assisted by a few of his buddies, Gordon had designed and built it himself. He installed a full bathroom, kitchen, and internal drain (the drainage helped with quick cleanup of deer, raccoons, and squirrels). In addition to fully stocked kitchen cabinets, the garage had a truck, a four-wheeler, a motorcycle, a refrigerator, a freezer, a card table and aluminum countertops. Everyone hung out there.

Bev opened the fridge and cracked open a beer. Her eyes were stuck on Craig's picture on the door as she sipped, leaning against the counter, lost in thought.

Fourteen-year-old Mitch walked over to Bev. Mitch was a freshman in high school and would soon become a star on the Forest

Park High School wrestling team. He put an arm around Bev. "Mom, are you gonna get drunk when Craig gets home?"

Bev was a good Catholic, but she was no teetotaler. However, reining in the antics of her rowdy men had made her more conservative with time.

Stone-faced, Bev stared down Mitch. The freshman winced, preparing for a lecture and reprimand.

"Baby doll," Bev said, "when your brother comes back from that hell, we're all getting drunk."

Fifty meters and an entire civilization from 3rd Platoon, Kilo 3/4, and Cpl Dan Amaya, Muhammad sat in a house that was being attacked by Marines. He wore baggy black pants, white running shoes, a tan long-sleeve shirt, and a vest stuffed with AK-47 magazines. In his pocket was a Quran. Underneath his red-checkered *kheffiyah*, Muhammad had started growing a beard. In the tunnel beneath him was a stack of rocket-propelled grenades.

At the moment, Muhammad and several other young Arab men were trying to kill the Marines of 3rd Platoon, Kilo 3/4. They were the Muj.*

Who was Muhammad? What did he want? Why was—and is— he violently resisting the appeal for a civil society in the Root of All? Why is he still killing America's sons and daughters after they came halfway around the world to liberate him from an evil tyrant?

Through the most technologically advanced surveillance equipment in the world and elaborate schemes of human intelli-

---

* Most insurgents adopted a *nom de guerre* when interviewed by reporters. In accounts of journalists, including Zaki Chehab, Nir Rosen, and Patrick Graham, the name of the Prophet appears to have been a favored pseudonym.

gence, the Marines eavesdropped and scrutinized, struggling to sort friend from foe. They learned that Muhammad is a man of many faces. Sometimes, he is a fanatic whose aim is to violently purge his holy land from all forms of Western influence. He might be a sexually repressed single man or a father of many children with one or multiple wives. He is everything from a hardened mercenary to a poor farmer defending his village. He comes from dozens of movements—from the Ba'ath Party to Zarqawi's Al-Qaeda in Iraq. Some of these factions have blood feuds with each other but conveniently set them aside to assuage the criminal, social, or political rationales of their war against the Americans.

In his chronicle *Inside the Resistance: The Iraqi Insurgency and the Future of the Middle East*, Lebanese journalist Zaki Chehab embedded with the enemies of Marines to hear their testimonies in their own words. Although much of Chehab's work articulates what the insurgents view as their grievances—the occupation and exploitation of their land and resources by foreigners being used by the Israelis—he also provides intriguing information from men who claim to be involved in the Zarqawi network. This evidence supports the theory that even before the 2003 American invasion, Iraq was becoming the next terrorist training camp.

According to Chehab's published interviews with Iraqi militants in both Fallujah and Ramadi, the Zarqawi network began planning their agenda of terror in Iraq shortly after the post–9/11 American attack into Afghanistan. In the fall of 2001, Zarqawi allegedly fled to Iran, where he came under pressure from Iranian authorities. Without contacting Saddam Hussein, Zarqawi fled across the border and found refuge in a remote area of the Iraqi Kurdish mountains. The men in Zarqawi's network told Chehab that they had established a safe route through Iran that could be used to smuggle equipment and personnel from

Afghanistan. By the fall of 2002, the Al Qaeda Underground Railroad was running full steam—from Afghanistan, through Iran, and into a northern Iraqi hideout.

Marine surveillance revealed that in cities like Fallujah, Ramadi, and Husaybah, Muhammad seemed more reminiscent of a crime boss like Pablo Escobar or Al Capone than a political renegade such as Che Guevara or Ho Chi Minh. When the Marines discovered insurgent lairs, they often found heroin, cocaine, and pure opium next to weapons, money, and torture chambers. Like corrupt medieval church officials, many Sunni sheikhs in western Iraq gorged themselves on the profits of war as they preached *jihad* from their mosque pulpits each Friday at the weekly communal prayers.

But guerrilla wars are rarely that simple. For every Iraqi who fought for the Zarqawi criminal syndicate, there were dozens who fought for reasons of practicality, survival, or honor. Most insurgent rhetoric centered on the imperative of fighting to redeem the dignity of their homeland. "Did you see *Braveheart?*" one militant asked reporter Patrick Graham during the April 2004 Battle of Fallujah. "They throw out the British and the corrupt nobles. It is about hope. The people in the movie want freedom, and so do we. In the movie, the problems start because the British invade and take the beautiful women and hurt the people. Because of the hard times, they gather weapons and get rid of the spies and traitors, isn't that right?"[*]

Muhammad dropped mortars or set IEDs because the money was good, and he needed it. He spied on American bases, maintaining ties with both sides and straddling the fence, hoping the deception would keep him alive. He fought because he was

_____
[*] See Patrick Graham, "Beyond Fallujah," *Harper's Magazine,* June 2004.

affronted by violations of home and property. He struck back at Marines to avenge the death of loved ones.

When asked for their views on the war in Iraq, the most popular quote among young Marines is, "We're killing them over there instead of over here." And in the case of Zarqawi and his Al Qaeda henchmen, not to mention the Sunni sheikhs and mafiosos, all evidence suggests this is true.

But mixed in with the Zarqawis and the sheikhs are also delusional freedom fighters, aggrieved relatives of the victimized, and poor Iraqis trying to feed their families. They might be emotional fanatics, but they might also have legitimate complaints.

Although the imperative to win the wars they fight remained straightforward for followers of the Spartan Way, victory often seemed elusive as they struggled to salvage the Root of All. Fighting is what Spartans do. Winning, the goal of fighting, takes sacrifice. But that doesn't make the sacrificing less tragic.

Especially for those left behind.

Halfway across the world in Odessa, Texas, Kacey Carpenter left for Easter services. Just as she did every day, Kacey drove to First Baptist Church thinking about her son, Dan Amaya. When she talked to him a week ago at 4 A.M., he had been laughing. "So I decided to give my favorite mom a wake up call," Dan said.

"Your favorite?" she smiled, savoring the sound of his voice.

"Well, I guess you're in the top ten."

Dan said he was fine, but that he had some work to do and wasn't sure when he could call again. "I love you guys."

"Love you, Danny Boy." Kacey held the phone to her ear after he hung up, hoping to feel that much more connected. She called him by his nickname, humming the Irish tune "Oh, Danny Boy" she had sung to him during his childhood.

Danny's voice still echoed in her head a week later, as she sat through the Easter service at First Baptist Church in Odessa with her husband, David. It was a beautiful celebration of the Resurrection and the Eternal Life. She glanced around at the women in spring colors, adorned with pink and yellow bonnets.

After church, she waved, smiled and chatted. Everybody asked about Danny. "Tell him we miss him!" "Tell him we're proud of him!" "Tell him to kill bin Laden and hurry back home!"

David and Kacey Carpenter waved to their friends and drove home, smiling at the conversation, buoyed by the Resurrection, and contemplating the Easter feast Kacey was getting ready to prepare.

The Carpenters had a house in Odessa on a corner lot. Their house had a carport. They pulled their car under the carport and walked into their house through the side door, oblivious to the government vehicle that was parked near their front porch.

Nobody had really slept. They all tried to, but Amaya, Zmudzinski, and Ozzy were all on edge. They were set up on a rooftop across the street from Muhammad's house. All night, they had been harassed by random sniper fire. But they had good cover in their positions. Everyone made it through the night unscathed.

On Easter morning in Fallujah, there was no salvation for Marines, only work. Corporal Amaya's 1st Squad started the day off with a couple of attempts to get into the house. Stack. Frag out! *Bang.* Flood the room. Black hallway. Back out again. Failure. 3rd Platoon was pissed.

Finally, Lance Corporal Nelson had enough. The platoon demo expert, Nelson grabbed another Marine and a pair of rocket launchers. They stacked about fifteen rockets between them and volleyed the rounds into the building.

The barrage worked. The fortress collapsed. The Marines cheered.

When the insurgent the Marines called Muhammad saw the Americans firing the rockets, he jumped into the tunnel carrying his AK-47 and ran. He was faster than the Americans, not because he was in better physical condition, but because he was carrying less weight. Wearing western clothes and traditional Arab headgear, Muhammad carried less than fifteen pounds of ammunition, along with his rifle and Quran. Even without packs, the Marines were laden with armor, equipment, and heavy weapons that weighed over forty-five pounds. They could not match Muhammad for speed.

He had lost the RPG stash, but no matter. There was no time for them. The building he was in crashed to the ground. The Marines had destroyed it.

Surrounded by dust from the explosion, Muhammad and another Muj ran out of the tunnel, took new positions, and prepared to defend the second house.

At first, 3rd Platoon thought it was over. Everyone ooh-rahed, slapping Nelson on the back. "Ooh-rah, Nelson!" they bellowed. "Get some, baby!!!"

Then they started taking fire from the next house.

Supported by covering fire from Zmudzinski's squad, Amaya's squad ran past the rubble and stacked on a concrete fence that surrounded the structure. There was an opening in the fence that entered into a dusty courtyard. From his vantage point on the roof, Corporal Zmudzinski could hear gunfire and see movement. Amaya's squad was past the fence and preparing to make entry on the house. A Marine named Shellabarger was on point. Stokes was not far behind them.

Mounted on Corporal Amaya's rifle was a Visible Light Illuminator (VLI). Essentially a high-powered flashlight, the VLI was used to search darkened and dusty rooms when clearing houses. In April 2004, not every grunt had a VLI on their weapon. Amaya had one. Shellabarger did not.

Shellabarger entered the house, followed by Amaya and the rest of 1st Squad. The Marines heard more gunfire.

As the Americans attacked into the house, Muhammad and his friend fled down the long axis of the hallway and made their way back into the last room.

The Mujahideen took cover. Muhammad knelt down in a corner. The American Marines were outside. They waited.

Led by Amaya, 1st Squad had gained a foothold. The enemy had not secured the hallway and the Marines poured in, flowing like water from room to room. Shellabarger was on point as they stacked outside the final room. Hoyt was behind Shellabarger. Lieutenant Stokes was not far behind.

The building was dark and dusty from the barrage of rockets, grenades, and debris. The Marines knew someone was in there. They just didn't know who or what. It was difficult to see.

Suddenly, Amaya grabbed Shellabarger. "Switch with me. I've got a VLI and you don't."

Shellabarger paused. He was carrying a SAW, the same kind of weapon that Smith had when he was shot the day before. The VLI did not mount onto the SAW.

By the book, a squad leader is not supposed to be the first man in a room. But Amaya had gear that he believed would kill the enemy better, with precision. Shellabarger could have just poked his machine gun around the corner and blindly pulled the trigger. Later, he wished he had.

But what if innocent children were in the room? Yesterday, when they were clearing houses, they had found dozens of non-combatants walking around. Marines might throw satchel charges, fire rockets, or call in air strikes that cause massive devastation, but an infantryman was instructed to *never* blindly pull a trigger. It's paradoxical, but true. A grunt is trained to see everything before he kills it.

Now the point man in the stack, Amaya glanced back at Shellabarger and Hoyt, wheeled, and ran into the room with his flashlight-equipped rifle in his shoulder.

The moment that Cpl Dan Amaya spun his body from left to right into the room, the pair of Muj hiding inside fired. Bullets struck the right side of Amaya's body. He was hit in the leg, rib, and the back of his neck, just underneath his Kevlar helmet and above the collar of his flak.

Amaya crumpled, bleeding and falling back unconscious onto Shellabarger and Hoyt. Shellabarger yelled out, reaching his SAW around the corner and emptying rounds into the room as he tried to do first aid on his squad leader. "Corpsman up!"

The Marines never knew if they got the two men who hit Amaya. At that point, they were frantically focused on saving their squad leader's life, willing to exchange the foothold they had gained if necessary. Dan the Man had seemed invincible. The glue of the platoon. And now he was down.

Hoyt and Shellabarger carried him out, followed by the rest of 1st Squad. Stokes met up with them. Zmudzinski looked at Amaya. His face was white. The corpsman could not find a pulse.

A pair of Marines wearing their dress blues walked up to the front door of David and Kacey Carpenter's house. They wore white hats, white gloves, dark navy blue tops with medals and ribbons, and blue trousers with a stripe the color of blood. They rang the doorbell.

David Carpenter, Dan Amaya's stepfather, walked over to the foyer. "Who that could be at this time on Easter?"

Kacey knew.

"Don't answer it!" she screamed.

David opened the door and saw the Marines. For an instant, he thought they were Dan's friends. He was about to open his mouth and tell them Dan's not home right now, he's over in Iraq, but he should be back later this summer. You boys can come visit him then.

Then David saw their somber look. And then he knew.

He closed the door.

David walked back and looked at Kacey, who was sitting down sobbing. He opened the door again, inviting the men into their home. One was a gunnery sergeant; the other was a captain. They were in their early to mid thirties. David could see the tears in their eyes.

"We don't want to be saying this," one of the Marines said in a measured tone. "However, on behalf of the President, and the Commandant of the Marine Corps, we regret to inform you that your son . . ."

"Not Dan," Kacey mourned into David, who held her to his chest as she fell apart, screaming. "Not Dan!"

CHAPTER 7

Bad Karmah

Before, it was about hearts and minds.
Now it's about two in the heart and one in the mind.

—*PFC Chris Ferguson, 2/4*

When the Marines had down time in Fallujah, they loved Lamasil cream.

Sitting in an abandoned warehouse somewhere in the southeastern corner of Fallujah on the afternoon of April 13, Cpl Jason Howell and the other Marines from 1st Platoon, Bravo 1/5, lathered Lamasil over their chafed waists, crotches, and feet as they heated their MREs. Rubbed raw from the constant movement of combat, the young Marines used the cream to soothe the red splotches of peeling skin, blistering feet, and pus-stained sores that had developed on their bodies where the friction built up from gear and clothing. The sores were as painful as bullets and shrapnel. Believing others in their company, platoon, or squad needed medical attention more than they did—and fearing they might be evacuated and forced to leave their units—Marines often refused to have these types of minor wounds examined by their corpsmen.

What they did instead was self-medicate. Since black market alcohol was not accessible to the grunt units, Motrin, caffeine, and nicotine were the most popular drugs. "Vitamin M" was passed out like candy as the main remedy for the aches and pains of combat. Coffee and soda supplemented the steady diet of Red Bull.

When the sounds of battle receded in Fallujah, Marines across the city would hear echoes of the telltale slap of a man's index and middle finger rebounding against a can of Copenhagen, Kodiak, or Skoal as he flicked his wrist. The slapping loosened the moist wintergreen-flavored tobacco slivers so the young addicted infantrymen could take a pinch. In the early 1980s, after marijuana and cocaine abuse was rooted out, smokeless tobacco—better known as dip—became the most popular drug in the military. Wives pleaded in vain with their husbands to break the toxic habit, to no avail. In garrison, company offices were littered with half-filled bottles or cans of dip spit.

Resting with Howell was Cpl Bob Dawson, who was from New Yawk, complete with thick accent. Dawson was 3rd Squad leader in 1st Platoon, and Howell's best friend. The pair fed off of each other through competition and mutual respect. Their company commander, Capt Jason Smith, later said they were the two best squad leaders in Bravo.

In preparation for his breakfast of processed Jalapeño cheese and crackers, Cpl Bob Dawson had removed his dip from the pouch inside his mouth between his gum and lower lip. It had been a good dip. Many of the Marines' dip cans had dried out, which made the tobacco lose flavor and led to an unsatisfactory dipping experience. This last one had been flavorful and wet. Dawson was happy.

For two days, Howell and Dawson's squads had been back-clearing houses to prevent any Mujahideen from infiltrating their lines. Although they hadn't done too much shooting, the constant pounding had numbed their feet to the point that walking was arduous.

As they continued the tedium of back-clearing, the Marines had started to lose their focus. "They would stop doing basic stuff—searching for the enemy, assessing the terrain, keeping their weapons up," Howell said. "I would have to yell at them to keep doing the littlest things that had seemed easy in training. We were more fatigued than we had been in our lives."

Howell also had to yell at his Marines to knock off their souvenir hunt, which they constantly engaged in under the auspices of "intelligence gathering." Although regulations prevented Marines and soldiers from exporting weapons or ammunition, knives, *kheffiyahs*, *dishdashas*, and Saddam-related paraphernalia often found their way into the grunt's seabags or packs. Even though Marines couldn't bring back the weapons, they still took all the AKs they could find.

Howell and Dawson had each grabbed an extra case of MREs and were using them as makeshift chairs as they prepared their breakfast. That morning, they had spent eight hours back-clearing several blocks.

"You'll never guess who just started smoking," Howell said to Dawson as he took a bite from his fudge brownie.

"Who?" Dawson was enjoying the moment of company gossip.

"Lieutenant Ayres." Because they had lived together for months, grunts knew each other's personal habits more intimately than those of their own families. The more senior in rank, the closer the smallest detail was scrutinized. Lt Chris Ayres, 2nd Platoon commander, was a well-liked former enlisted Marine from Texas—"a hell of a motivator"—whom the men had never seen smoke.

"No shit? Ayres?"

"Yeah," Howell said. "I had a house cordoned. We had security set; I was bringing out AKs and talking to hajji families. And there's Ayres chain smoking."

"Damn."

"His hands were shaking and his eyes were wide. He was kind of strung out. I was busting his balls, asking him when he started smoking. We both laughed about it. Then he went back to doing his thing."

"Must've been cool to see him."

In his bestseller *The Tipping Point: How Little Things Can Make a Big Difference*, Malcolm Gladwell observed that most human beings develop strong attachments to a maximum of 150 people, which is about the size of an infantry company. Each group of 150 men is replete with heroes and villains, chiefs and indians, leaders and losers. Each has strong opinions about the quality of their commanders, or lack thereof. Stories, a constant ritual of any grunt's life, affected morale; the buzz on the Lance Corporal Network mattered as much as chow, air conditioning, and mail.

Suddenly, a disheveled Lieutenant Lewis ran into the warehouse, interrupting Howell and Dawson's meal. Lewis's flak jacket was half open, and his gear hung from his body in Disorderly fashion.

"Get your gear! Second's in trouble! We gotta go!!!"

Howell and Dawson met his frenzy with blank stares. They weren't in the mood for this crap. Especially Howell, who was still mad at Lewis for ignoring him about the house and the rooftop. They had just seen 2nd Platoon a few hours ago during the back-clearing. They *couldn't* be in that much trouble. Howell decided that Lewis was spazzing out and the whole thing was, in Howell's view, probably some weird officer overreaction.

"Let's go! Now!" Lewis called, running out of the warehouse to find Captain Smith.

Unenthusiastically, Howell and Dawson roused their squads for immediate action. With the ease of a man tying his shoes, Howell tossed on his flak jacket and helmet, grabbed his M-16 and threaded the black three-point sling over his shoulder, leaving the rifle slung across his chest. His squad radio was clipped to his flak jacket, along with his M-16 magazines and night vision devices. His cheap, flimsy green military-issued CamelBak, which was only half-full of water, hung on his shoulders like a pack.

"Okay, so what's this about?" Dawson asked.

"Didn't you hear, Bob?" Howell said. "'Second's in trouble! We gotta go!!!'" Howell mimicked, mocking the lieutenant's frenzy as he donned his gear. They both laughed.

A few minutes later, Howell and Dawson weren't laughing.

After Cpl Dan Amaya was killed on April 11, Kilo Company had continued the fight, securing the house where Amaya had died. That night, after fighting their way through several other houses, they were relieved by India Company and sent back to Camp Fallujah for a day of rest.

Although Amaya's death had been a blow to the entire platoon, Stokes and Zmudzinski took it especially hard. Many have said that combat command is the loneliest job on the battlefield. No commander feels that sentiment more acutely than after the death of his finest warriors. Lieutenant Stokes had lost his best squad leader, the platoon had lost one of their best Marines, and Cpl Brian Zmudzinski had lost his best friend.

After a day of rest and recuperation, April 13 was spent doing rehearsals and battle drills for the next day's mission in Karmah. Supposedly, Kilo 3/4 was conducting a presence patrol. In reality they went out looking for a fight.

Many of the Muj from Fallujah had dispersed throughout the countryside, and Mattis wanted them hunted down and destroyed. 3/4's Karmah operation was designed to, in Captain Savage's words, "kick up the hornet's nest." Hobbling on his ailing leg, Captain Savage helped plan as much as he could, making his presence known to the Marines despite feeling humiliated by his absence from the Fallujah battle.

Attached to Kilo was a platoon of Iraqi Special Forces. Known commonly among the Marines as Shahwanis after the name of their leader, the Iraqi Special Forces were organized by Mohammed Shahwani, an anti-Saddam general presumably loyal to the Americans. Disgruntled with the disbanding of the Iraqi Army, Shahwani gathered several Iraqi officers and offered his (mercenary?) services exclusively to the Marine Corps. Like Marines, whose fraternal ties are central to their Spartan foundation, Shahwanis were loyal to those they personally knew had demonstrated courage in battle.[*]

The term "special forces" conjures up mental pictures of elite warriors parachuting, diving, and performing extreme feats of physical endurance. The Iraqi Special Forces—Shahwanis—were not this kind of unit. Many were overweight and slow. They wore ratty clothing and stank from rashes and disease. However, they

---

[*] Shahwani participated in an unsuccessful 1996 coup attempt to overthrow Saddam Hussein. Interim Iraqi prime minister Ayad Allawi also participated in the same plot.

were mostly veterans who had seen several campaigns. They stayed calm and steady under fire. A platoon of Shahwanis was more like a gang of forty-year-old staff sergeants.

"*Shaku maku*," Zmudzinski said to a large man with a mustache, helping him onto the 7-ton. *What's up?*

The man smiled. "Ahh, *teschki Arabi?*" *You speak Arabic?*

"*Arabi shuei*," Zmudzinski replied, offering him a cigarette. *I speak a little.*

"*Shukran.*" The Shahwani grinned, patting his AK-47 and gesturing expansively, ready to conquer the entire world now that he had sided with his powerful Marine brethren. *Thank you.*

"*Afwan.*" Despite his month-long Arabic course, that was about as far as Zmudzinski could get. *You're welcome.*

Zmudzinski flipped up the tailgate to the 7-ton and latched it tight, smiling at the Shahwanis and hoping they would shoot in the proper direction: away from his Marines. Accompanied by a Disorder soundtrack of Metallica and Jimi Hendrix courtesy of the psyops vehicles, Zmudzinski, Ozzy, and Corporal Garcia (who had taken over Amaya's 1st Squad) loaded into 7-tons and pushed out at 4 A.M. on April 14 to clean out Karmah.

The convoy should have taken only twenty minutes. As the vehicles approached the outskirts of Karmah, they ran into several obstacles that might have been IEDs. Just to be on the safe side, Marines blew them up, leaving them in flames. Unfortunately, they did not warn the 7-ton drivers, who were wearing night-vision devices. The resultant light from the flames caused their night-vision devices to turn white, blinding them.

Because of the light flash, one of the drivers plunged his 7-ton into the water, pitching Ozzy's entire squad—2nd Squad—into the stream. Although no one was killed, several Marines were injured. As they dove back into the water to retrieve their weapons and the other missing gear, hypothermia also afflicted them.

With two teams in 1st Squad assisting 2nd Squad's recovery efforts, Zmudzinski took his 3rd Squad north along with the remaining members of 1st Squad and secured his first objective, an abandoned gas station. On site with him were the Shahwanis and a section of light armored vehicles. Angled several hundred yards in front of the gas station was a mosque.

The original plan called for Ozzy's squad to cordon the mosque while the Shahwanis went in to search, clear, and—if necessary—detain. It was supposed to be a swift operation that would generate momentum. As morning dawned, 3rd Platoon had been split. Half the men were by the river, and half were at the gas station. Lieutenant Stokes and his platoon sergeant were driving back and forth, reorganizing and coordinating.

As morning progressed, Zmudzinski and friends began taking sustained mortar and sniper fire. Compounding the problem was the actual terrain Zmudzinski occupied: a gas station. Abandoned or not, flammable material was still buried somewhere amidst the decaying concrete. Zmudzinski felt very uncomfortable.

The location was not the only cause of Zmudzinski's anxiety. His squad and the attachments were holding the far right flank of Kilo's line. Several hundred meters away was the downed 7-ton in the canal. To their left, 2nd Platoon was attacking into the city, and 1st Platoon held the far left flank. None of the units appeared to have working communications. Without coordination, the whole thing seemed chaotic and dangerous. Zmudzinski had no idea what was happening to his left or what, if anything, he should be doing to support the other Marines.

Eventually 2nd Platoon held up their attack near a water tower, where they were pinned down by enemy fire. While his platoon sergeant coordinated the MEDEVAC for the injured Marines from the 7-ton, Stokes drove over to Zmudzinski's position to check things out. Accompanying Stokes was the battalion sergeant major, Dave Howell.* He had served with Recon during much of his career, and his posture was relaxed and mellow. When the humvee pulled up, bullets were snapping. Stokes and Howell walked over to their Marines as if taking a summer stroll.

The Marines at the gas station were in a firefight with a growing number of Iraqis at the mosque. Both Marines and Shahwanis were shooting back. With the Shahwanis firing AK-47s, the sounds of incoming and outgoing fire intermingled, making the Marines feel surrounded by enemy fire. Everyone was happy to see the Shahwanis remaining calm as they fought their countrymen. They would occasionally pause, throwing a smile and thumbs-up to the younger Marines, as if to say: *Relax, fellas . . . we've seen this stuff plenty of times. This is just another day at the office.*

The mosque had become, in Zmudzinski's words, "a haven for bad shit." Marines were engaging the hajjis/Muj with gunfire and rockets, and the enemy was raining down mortars all around the gas station. Expecting to see his request denied, Stokes called in an air strike. For whatever reason, the higher-ups approved it. Ten minutes later, a pair of F/A-18s swooped in, dropped their bombs, and destroyed the mosque. Again, both Marines and Shahwanis cheered.

Then all hell broke loose.

After the mosque was destroyed, the entire town seemed to swarm like ants towards the direction of the now-desecrated house of religion. Formerly neutral Iraqis instantly became enemy combatants. They ran, exposed, towards the Marines,

---

* SgtMaj Dave Howell of 3/4 was not related to Cpl Jason Howell of Bravo 1/5.

blindly firing their AK-47s. Their lack of infantry skills worked to the Marines' advantage. As the Iraqis sprinted toward them without cover, the Marines killed dozens of assailants.

Stokes led Zmudzinski's squad away from the gas station and attacked forward into the town. He wanted to pin down the enemy and call for indirect fire—artillery, mortars, anything. They set up on a rooftop near a palm grove, tossing up cans of 5.56 ammunition and quickly reloading their magazines. Just as Zmudzinski and Stokes got onto the rooftop, an RPG exploded next to them, destroying a date palm and scattering debris across the house.

Suddenly, grenades exploded nearby. They were being fired from the opposite direction. They were American Mark-19s.[*]

Blue-on-blue.

Stokes had called in his position as he moved forward, but somebody hadn't gotten the word. In the confusion, the shadowy figures maneuvering on the rooftop were assumed to be the enemy. 3rd Squad, 3rd Platoon, was being targeted by other Marines who were hungry to kill hajjis, or Muj, or whatever they called them at this point.

Unable to raise the unit firing the Mk-19s on the radio, the Marines pulled back to the gas station. Soon, they heard the unmistakable scream-whiz-bang of artillery rounds flying over their heads and impacting throughout the town. One of the higher-ups—either the company or battalion commander—had requested the barrage. Apparently the decision-makers were in a generous mood; having already approved the air strike they saw no need to hesitate in using firepower.

_____

[*] A Mark-19 is a vehicle-mounted grenade launcher. The Mk-19 fires the same size projectiles (40mm) as the M-203 grenade launcher that is mounted underneath a fire team leader's M-16 rifle.

After the artillery attack, smoke poured from the rubble of Karmah. The gunfire subsided. The Shahwanis nodded approvingly, pleased not to be on the receiving end of the violence. They thanked God for their good fortune. They would live to fight again another day, *inshallah*. For Iraqis—like any devout monotheists—things always happened *inshallah*, or *God willing*.

By now it was late afternoon. Kilo's 1st Platoon had been preparing to take down the police station when the Marines got orders to leave and return to the MEK. Instead of continuing with the security/seizure/attack of Karmah, the Marines and Shahwanis boarded their vehicles and left.

One week later, on April 23, Kilo returned for another sweep through Karmah. The remaining locals were friendly, smiling and waving and thumbs-upping. Nobody attacked the Marines. Soon enough, the attacks would return again to Karmah, but for the moment all was quiet.

"I'm not really sure what we accomplished on our sweep," Zmudzinski later reflected. "It started out as a presence patrol, but it turned into an attack. We killed a lot of people. Then we left. In Fallujah and Karmah, we kept taking ground and giving it back. That sucked."

Zmudzinski pondered the mosque destruction. "On the other hand, I suppose if the mission was to make our presence known . . ."

Back in Fallujah, Lt Stephen Lewis of Bravo 1/5 had not been exaggerating with his frantic gestures. 2nd Platoon was in trouble, and they did need immediate help. In the southwestern corner of the city, a volley of RPGs had disabled an amphibious assault vehicle—"amtrack"—carrying the platoon commander, platoon sergeant, and an entire squad of Marines. They had been moving forward from friendly lines to ambush the Muj, and had rolled into a counter-ambush. The amtrack was on fire and Lieutenant Ayres, 2nd Platoon commander, was missing half of his right leg.

As LCpl Mathew Puckett drove his amtrack away from the ambush, another volley of machine gun fire killed one of the amtrack's crewmen, Cpl Kevin Kolm. Unable to turn the amtrack around because of the narrow streets, Puckett drove west and south—deeper into the enemy-held portions of Fallujah—while attempting to find an escape route.

By the time Lance Corporal Puckett found a road heading back towards friendly lines, it was too late. Damaged by RPGs, the massive diesel engine quit about 100 meters from the turn. Taking refuge in an abandoned house, the men from 2nd Platoon were surrounded by "at least 300" angry Mujahideen. "It seemed like there were 900," the platoon sergeant, SSgt Ismael Sagredo, later said. As the squad fought to save Lieutenant Ayres's life, they were running low on ammunition and in danger of being overrun. Their fortification was becoming their Alamo.

Still pissed off about missing chow, Corporal Howell's 2nd Squad and Corporal Dawson's 3rd Squad ran west into the Mujahideen-controlled portion of Fallujah. 1st Squad was back at the warehouse on post. That was the first sign of foreboding. "In Iraq, whenever something went wrong, my squad and Dawson's squad were in the middle of it, and 1st Squad was somewhere else," Howell said.

Farther to the west, all they could hear was gunfire. They ran toward it, linking up with one of the squads from 2nd Platoon that had been left behind when the platoon commander's amtrack was ambushed. By this point, 2nd had been fighting without reinforcements for hours. "They're coming from everywhere!" the exhausted 2nd Platoon Marines called out to Howell and Dawson.

While Lieutenant Lewis got on the radio to coordinate their next move, Howell's and Dawson's squads were stacked up against a building, waiting. Waiting. Waiting some more. Bullets snapped. It seemed like hours, but it was only minutes.

Corporal Howell always seemed to have a war movie stuck in his head. That day, he was thinking about *Blackhawk Down*. The platoon had left the warehouse with nothing more than the ammunition and water on their bodies. Like the Rangers in Mogadishu, they were trying to rescue comrades who had been cut off in an urban area swarming with Muslim fanatics. Like in Mogadishu, there were hundreds of militants bent on killing them. Howell didn't want to be in this movie. But he was.

Capt Jason Smith, Bravo's company commander, had been meeting with the battalion staff in a soda factory about a mile behind the main lines when 2nd Platoon was attacked. 1/5 dispatched its quick reaction force as a rescue convoy with a section of tanks in tow. The rescue convoy took off towards the last known position of the track, which was the same area where 1st Platoon was now pinned down. Smith jumped into the convoy.

Back at the house, about 150 meters away from where the battalion thought he was, Sagredo and the squad had been dragging Ayres from room to room, trying to protect him from the RPGs that were penetrating the interior. "I felt like they were trying to mop up the floor with me," Ayres said.*

Running low on supplies and with increasing numbers of wounded Marines, Sagredo had been able to maintain sporadic communications with other Bravo units. Unfortunately for

---

* See Ross W. Simpson, "Fallujah: A Four-Letter Word," *Leatherneck*, 2005.

Sagredo, he needed to find an area without concrete obstructions so his antenna could maintain reception. Like a dead zone for a cellular telephone, the concrete fortifications in the house that offered protection also prevented him from calling in the cavalry. Sagredo and his radio operator climbed up to the roof and tried to set up their antenna when a Muj combatant hurled three grenades at him.

Finally, the pair set up the radio in an exposed position outside in the courtyard. At last, Sagredo had a good signal. "We are in a house and in danger of being overrun. Our amtrack is on fire," Sagredo told Lt Jon McGaughey, Bravo's executive officer. "Bravo Two Actual is an urgent casualty." Despite the blood loss, Ayres was still holding on. The RPG had missed his femoral artery.

However, in addition to Ayres's leg, the RPG had destroyed his GPS and map. Sagredo didn't know exactly where they were.

"Our house is about 150 meters south of the burning vehicle," Sagredo said to McGaughey.

The executive officer never got that transmission. Suddenly, three RPGs exploded above Sagredo and his radio operator, cutting short his conversation with headquarters. They withdrew from the courtyard and pulled back into the house. Ammunition was almost gone. Hundreds of Mujahideen swarmed outside. Things looked grim. The motto for both sides had become Make Peace or Die. And neither party was waving a surrender flag.

"Okay, Marines," Sagredo said. "No more suppressive fire." Marines train to use a barrage of bullets from machine guns and rifles to keep their enemy's head down while another unit flanks them. The Muj had reversed the tables on Sagredo's men and put them on the defensive. "Only fire two rounds at a time," Sagredo continued. "And only fire when you have a clear shot." This was the modern-day equivalent of the famous command at the Battle of Bunker Hill: "Don't fire until you see the whites of their eyes."

Several of the men checked their bayonets. They couldn't hold out on bullets much longer, and they were determined to die fighting. They would take as many of the goddamned Muj with them as they possibly could, which, of course, was the same thing the Muj were thinking about the Americans as they approached their own martyrdom.

Back at 1st Platoon's position, which was north of the downed track, Corporals Howell and Dawson were starting to lose their bearings. The two squads had been moving from house to house as a platoon when they became dispersed by enemy fire. LCpl "Dirty Steve" Nunnery was in front of the squad and Howell was towards the rear. As Howell was about to jump over the concrete wall, an RPG slammed into it. Howell briefly lost his rifle, and his corpsman, Doc Mark Perkins, was scratched in the face from shrapnel ("It looked like a bad shaving cut," Howell later said).

The result was that 1st Platoon occupied two houses, but each group didn't know where the other was. Lieutenant Lewis, Dirty Steve, and most of Howell's squad were in one house. In the other was Howell, one of his Marines, and Dawson's squad. Adding to the confusion were the Mujahideen, who seemed to be attacking from every direction.

In an effort to figure out what was going on, Howell and Dawson kept poking their heads above the three-foot concrete parapet on the rooftop. Simply looking out over the roof took courage. Each time a Marine stuck his head above the rampart, it looked like a mushroom and made an obvious target on the roof's skyline. The corporals knew that if their Marines did not see them exposing themselves to the firefight, there was no chance they could order their men to do the same.

Mounted on Howell's rifle was an Advanced Combat Optical Gunsight (ACOG). The sight equipped Marines with a magnified optic that allowed them to engage the enemy with an accuracy approaching the level of trained snipers. According to Major General Mattis, "The ACOG mounted on the M-16 has been the biggest improvement in lethality for the Marine infantryman since the development of the M-1 Garand in World War II."

Howell noticed a couple of Muj leaning against the building. He looked through his ACOG and tried to guess the distance and elevation, figuring it at about 300 yards. It was actually about 600. In the infantry, arbitrary guesses of range and distance to target are called Kentucky Windage. Sometimes Kentucky Windage takes the enemy down. In Howell's case, his zeal to kill overcame his analytical skills. He shot low and missed.

From his vantage point on the roof, Howell could see black smoke rising near the house where 2nd Platoon was making their last stand. The place was crawling with Marines and Muj. It was hard to tell who was who, because the Muj were climbing on the rooftops and outside the windows in the house before being killed. "Those Marines in 2nd were just shooting and killing and shooting and killing," Howell said. "The way they fought was amazing."

As their heads bobbed up and down above the rampart like toys in amusement park games, Howell and Dawson glanced at each other.

"Yo, this isn't good man," Dawson yelled over the gunfire.

"No shit," Howell said. "It's like *Blackhawk Down*."

"Yeah," Dawson agreed. "*Blackhawk Down*." It was code for *we just did eight hours of back-clearing and now we're in the biggest firefight of our lives with no chow, water, or ammo, and if that isn't totally fucked up, I don't know what is.* "Where's the rest of your squad?"

Brian Zmudzinski (left) and Dusty Soudan, enjoying their time off near Seattle, Washington, while stationed at Naval Submarine Base, Bangor. They are on a ferry transiting Puget Sound.
DUSTY SOUDAN

A farewell party at Dusty Soudan's apartment. Cpl Jason Howell is in the center. To his right is Krista Lance, Dusty's longtime girlfriend. Smiling above the crowd in a striped shirt is Cpl Brian Zmudzinski.
DUSTY SOUDAN

Then-Cpl Dusty Soudan patrolling southern Shiite Iraq, summer 2003. The 1st Marine Division did not sustain a single combat fatality after May 1, 2003. When they returned to Iraq in February 2004, young Marines thought they would be bored, handing out candy to children and seeing little action. They were wrong. DUSTY SOUDAN

Grunts from Lima 3/7 work on an informal off-duty assignment: reading the novel *Gates of Fire*. Marines of all ranks consider this tale of epic heroism at the battle of Thermopylae to be required education in the fundamentals of the warrior spirit.

DOMINIQUE NEAL

Cpl Brian Zmudzinski and Cpl Dan Amaya. They first met at Bangor and then were assigned to the same platoon, serving under the command of Lieutenant Stokes. They were partners, both on and off the battlefield.

BRIAN ZMUDZINSKI

MajGen James N. "Mad Dog" Mattis addressing a battalion of Marines to give them their final marching orders. Although this picture was taken in early 2003, the scene was replicated hundreds of times during Mattis's command of the 1st Marine Division. "A general has a responsibility to have a close relationship with his troops," said Mattis. ANDREW PETRUCCI

Cpl Craig Atkins and Cpl Dustin Schrage on liberty. This picture was originally taken in Las Vegas, with rowdy neon colors in the background. Dustin Schrage's mom, Nina, superimposed the Marines on a picture of a sunset near her home in Indian Harbour Beach, Florida. NINA SCHRAGE

Market Street in Husaybah, Iraq. This photograph was taken in March 2004, as the Marines left the base for one of their first patrols. DUSTY SOUDAN

Although this picture was taken in Karbala in the summer of 2004, it accurately depicts the streets on a typical afternoon in an urban area of Iraq. The unpredictable traffic patterns, as well as infinite numbers of potential car bombs, were constant navigational hazards for Marines. DUSTY SOUDAN

Cpl Jarod "Shady" Stevens taking a smoke break. After leaving the Corps in the late 1990s to follow the tech boom, Stevens reenlisted after September 11. He was assigned to a headquarters unit, where he installed Internet networks, drove humvees on convoys, and conducted other kinds of covert operations. JAROD STEVENS

Fallujah, Iraq. The charred corpses of four American security contractors were hung on March 31, 2004, from what became known as Blackwater Bridge. FRANCIS SLEIGHER

Cpl Jason Howell, 1st Platoon, Bravo 1/5, after sharing candy with an Iraqi girl in a village near Fallujah. Hailing from southern California, Howell joined the Marines as a stepping-stone to another passion—the L.A. County Sheriffs. One crazy night of liberty almost derailed his dream. JASON HOWELL

A view of a fishing village near Haditha Dam, where Kilo 3/4 was stationed before fighting in Fallujah. When they arrived in March, there was little enemy activity, and the operations tempo in Haditha was slow. Times would change. BRIAN ZMUDZINSKI

April 12, 2004, near Fallujah. After two straight days of urban combat operations, exhaustion sets in for 3rd Platoon, Kilo 3/4. The Marines slept like dead men, huddling in their uniforms for warmth. BRIAN ZMUDZINSKI

Lance Cpl "Dirty Steve" Nunnery, fire team leader with Bravo 1/5. His squad leader, Cpl Jason Howell, called him "the bravest sonofabitch I've ever met." MARK PERKINS

The "brain trust" of 3rd Platoon, Kilo 3/4: (left to right) Lieutenant Stokes, Cpl Brian Zmudzinski, Cpl "Ozzy" Osborne, and Cpl Dan Amaya.

BRIAN ZMUDZINSKI

The corporals of 3rd Platoon, Kilo 3/4, before the first Battle of Fallujah: (left to right) Garcia, Zmudzinski, Osbourne, and Amaya. Garcia, who is holding an M-16 with an M-203 grenade launcher attached, took over for Amaya on April 11.

BRIAN ZMUDZINSKI

Cpl Jason Howell displays the fin of the mortar that wounded Pfc Matthew Brennan on a rooftop in Fallujah.

JASON HOWELL

Cpl Bob Dawson, Bravo 1/5, manning a vehicle checkpoint in spring 2004. Because of their vulnerability to enemy car bombs while on watch, Marines referred to this as "the suicide post." MARK PERKINS

A Marine from 1st Platoon, Bravo 1/5, expresses enthusiasm for Hotel Fallujah and the sandbagged fighting position he has just rebuilt. To keep the men occupied for several days, the platoon leadership ordered the sandbagged bunkers torn down and reconstructed. JASON HOWELL

Then-Capt Richard J. Gannon II, company commander, Lima 3/7. This picture was taken at the funeral service of another fallen Marine. Gannon's leadership, commitment, and character earned him respect and esteem throughout his unit. DOMINIQUE NEAL

After the April 17 battle for Husaybah, two Iraqi girls stand near their concrete home, which was located near the Marine camp. They continued with life amidst chaos. DUSTY SOUDAN

A mosque located near Bravo 1/5's "Hotel Fallujah." Calls to prayer and other Arabic chants from the mosque frayed the edges of the men's sanity. JASON HOWELL

A few days after May 2, 2004, a Marine from Fox 2/4 reflects on the banks of the Euphrates River. In the background is the island that the Marines from Cpl Dustin Schrage's 3rd Squad planned to raid. NINA SCHRAGE

These outhouses, which Marines called burn shitters, were a poor man's Port-a-John. For units stationed in remote regions where waste transport tankers were unavailable, burn shitters were the privies of choice. This photo illustrates waste disposal. MARK PERKINS

3rd Squad, 1st Platoon, Fox 2/4, took this picture at the bank of the river as a gift to the Schrage family. Along with the photos, they sent sand from the riverbank. Behind them was the raid site for Operation Treasure Island. CRAIG ATKINS

Cpl Justin Green and Corporal Atkins, 1st Platoon, Fox 2/4, strike a pose in a Snake Pit barracks room.
CRAIG ATKINS

Ted Nugent and Toby Keith, Camp Fallujah, Iraq, brought down the house during a midnight concert over Memorial Day weekend, 2004. JAROD STEVENS

Left to right: Corporals Richardson, Alarid, and Atkins, 1st Platoon, Fox 2/4. The trio remained squad leaders for the rest of the company's 2004 deployment to Ramadi. CRAIG ATKINS

The Cigarette Girl, Fox 2/4's diminutive contraband runner, and Cpl Craig Atkins. Behind her is one of the dozens of Marines who might have been responsible for her free English lessons. CRAIG ATKINS

Cpl Jason Howell relaxes after a patrol with Bravo 1/5 translators (terps) Ahmed and H-Money. The Marines depended on these Iraqis for information, and the terps expected privileges for risking their lives by declaring loyalty to the Americans. As they spent time together, their camaraderie grew. JASON HOWELL

Doc Mark Perkins, who went from corpsman to security guard during the June 8 combat in Karmah, holds a fin from a rocket-propelled grenade. MARK PERKINS

Howell and an Iraqi policeman, near the time of the June 8 Battle for Karmah. Before and after June 8, Bravo 1/5 was responsible for training the Iraqi Civil Defense Corps, which evolved into the Iraqi Security Forces. JASON HOWELL

Capt Jason Smith, Bravo 1/5 company commander, stands with H-Money. The picture was taken a few days prior to Bravo's departure from Iraq.
JASON SMITH

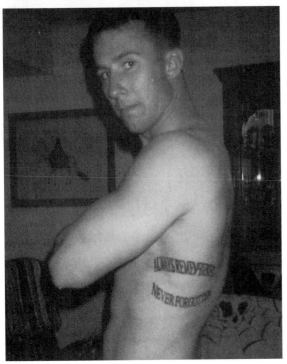

Sgt Jason Howell, USMC, inactive ready reserves, will never forget. He continues his service to country in law enforcement, as a member of the Los Angeles County Sheriffs. JASON HOWELL

September 2004. With the running trails of Camp Pendleton in the background, the Magnificent Bastards celebrate their return home. Left to right: Deb Edwards, Cpl Craig Atkins, mother Bev, and youngest brother Mitch. BEV ATKINS

Cpl Brian Zmudzinski after returning home from Iraq. His comrade-in-arms is his father, John, a Marine veteran who served with a motor transport unit in Vietnam. BRIAN ZMUDZINSKI

After two enlistments and three promotions to his rank, Cpl Jarod "Shady" Stevens poses with his bride, Andrea, at their reception. Displayed in front of their cake is the NCO sword. JAROD STEVENS

Marines from 3rd Squad, 1st Platoon, Fox 2/4. Standing are LCpl Justin Oliver, Cpl Craig Atkins, Cpl Dustin Schrage, Cpl Jeff Green, and LCpl Russ Bullock. Kneeling is Cpl Justin Richardson, who accepted the responsibility of passing on Schrage's dog tags to his family. Nina Schrage commissioned the portrait after Schrage and Green died; they were drawn without their combat gear. The others remain armed in memory of their fallen brothers. ASHLEY VERKAMP

Howell had been trying to answer that same question. When they had been split up, most of the squad had wound up following Dirty Steve into the other house. Howell had been calling Lewis over the radio, looking for Dirty Steve. Gunfire kept breaking up their transmissions.

"Howell, we're in the house right next to you," Lieutenant Lewis said. Howell looked up. *Crack, crack.* Howell got down. At least ten houses were right next to him. Bullets and RPGs were flying out of most of them.

Suddenly, ignoring the frenzy of enemy action, Dirty Steve—ugly glasses and all—stood up on the rooftop of another building and waved his hands. "We're over here!"

Amazed that Dirty Steve had gestured so obviously in the middle of the gunfight, Howell, Dawson, and the rest of the men moved over to the house, meeting up with the platoon.

As Howell and Dawson were making their way towards the building, Dirty Steve looked down and realized there was another problem he needed to fix. While Dirty Steve had been fighting, his SAW gunner, LCpl Jeff Elkin, had been crouching down where he was protected against the wall. Elkin was not engaging the enemy.

Caught up in the fight, Dirty Steve needed to find a way to get his SAW gunner snapped back into it. Pausing briefly from laying bullets and grenade rounds into Mujahideen, Dirty Steve looked over to his Marine. "Hey Elkin! Get over here! Be a man and light me a cigarette!"

Elkin got up, ran over to Dirty Steve, and did exactly that. Dirty Steve's command had shook Elkin out of his combat stress. Cigarette dangling from his mouth, Dirty Steve and his SAW gunner laughed and, together, turned their attention back to the Muj.

Back in the courtyard, just when they thought they might be overrun, Sagredo's men from 2nd Platoon brightened. "Tanks! I hear tanks!" they yelled to each other.

And tanks it was. With six humvees and three military ambulances in tow, four M1A1 Abrams tanks from the 1/5 QRF clanged down the street, blasting away at the enemy. Running back and forth throughout the column was Capt Jason Smith, who was carrying a rifle and firing at the Muj. He had been seated in the last humvee when, soon after departing friendly lines, the convoy had ground to a stop at an intersection. They were taking enemy fire. Smith had dismounted, exposing himself, in order to direct fire into the enemy position. Since it was easier for him to run back and forth on foot through the narrow streets, Smith remained outside of the vehicle, scouting, encouraging, and leading until the convoy made it to Bravo Company's Marines.

Arriving at the 2nd Platoon Alamo, Smith ran into the house and found Staff Sergeant Sagredo's rifle pointing back at him. Of the twelve Marines in 2nd Squad, eight had been wounded. The Marines loaded them onto the ambulances and used a tank to tow the amtrack back to safety. Ordinarily, Marines would have simply used an incendiary grenade to permanently disable the downed amtrack. However, Corporal Kolm's body was inside and could not be retrieved. Smith was determined to bring every Marine off the battlefield.

By now the Muj assault had been repulsed and the Marines were ready to finish their fighting withdrawal. The battalion had coordinated an air strike. Smith ordered all of his Marines to pull back. Fast.

The radio buzzed with the word: ALL UNITS PULL BACK EAST TO ORIGINAL POSITIONS. AIR INBOUND.

Back at the blocking position to the north, Dawson heard the transmission over the radio. He looked at Howell and Lieutenant Lewis. "Yo, sir, we gotta get out of here now!! It's Slingshot!!"

Howell had no idea what Slingshot was, but Dawson kept repeating the word like it was the most important thing in the world. He later learned that Dawson's unit had used Slingshot as a code word for an immediate airstrike during OIF I. To Dawson, the term had come to mean anything requiring a prompt withdrawal.

"Slingshot! Slingshot!" Dawson reiterated to the men, who were staring blankly at him. "Sir, we gotta go *right now!*"

Howell looked out at the area where they were planning to run. It was a wide, muddy field—probably some type of farm— with one house standing in the middle. Behind the field was another row of houses. From there, they would link up with the rest of Bravo and move back to the warehouse. But first they had to deal with the open field.

Howell, and presumably Lewis as well, did not want to run through the field. They were looking around for another route with better cover they could use to withdraw.

In garrison, Marines are taught the Fighter-Leader Concept. The idea is that the chaos of combat creates so much fear, adrenaline, and confusion that Marines forget what the common-sense thing to do is until they see someone doing it. Then they follow along. Captain Smith had applied the Fighter-Leader Concept when guiding in the tanks.

Dawson, who wasn't in the mood to deliberate, decided to apply the Fighter-Leader Concept himself. "I'm going, sir!!!" He ran out of the house and into the field.

Well, Howell thought, *Bob Dawson isn't running across that field alone.*

Howell ran out of the house and into the field, trailing Dawson. "I'm with ya, Bob!" Howell affirmed. "I'm with ya, Bob!"

Dawson and Howell had not said a single word to their squads before they started running across the field. Not even a "follow me." After they had ran about fifty meters, they looked back. The entire platoon was following them.

As the Marines sprinted across the field, the F-15s roared above them, dropping bombs that turned the Mujahideen havens into infernos. Lungs heaving for air, the men ran for their lives toward the row of houses. The snaps and whizzes of both enemy and friendly firepower—machine guns and tank rounds were also pounding away at enemy positions—surrounded them. Howell was staring at Dawson's boots, trying, literally, to follow his footsteps so he could avoid tripping over the muddy ruts.

1st Platoon made it across the field and seized an empty house. The Marines dispersed throughout the house to maintain security and reflect on the first time in several hours that they weren't being shot at. They were tired, strung out, and wanting to know what was happening. Up to that point, it was the most intense fight any of them had experienced. They said the words to each other over and over like a mantra—"What the fuck was that?"—as though they couldn't believe they had actually lived through the last three hours.

With the rescue completed and all Marines and gear accounted for, Lieutenant Lewis told Dawson and Howell to run their squads back to the warehouse. Howell dispersed his squad in a column with Dirty Steve in front. The Marines ran for their lives. As they sprinted, they ignored the potshots they received from the remnants of Muj still holding out in the gutted, smoldering structures.

Then something happened that made Howell lose it.

Marines started walking.

Howell could appreciate that the men were exhausted, dehydrated, and frayed to the point of sanity. But he could not accept his guys quitting on him. "What the *fuck* are you doing?" Howell screamed at one recalcitrant Marine. "Don't you see that *this is life and death!* You have a better chance of living behind the gates at that warehouse. You slow down, we're all at risk that much longer." Of course, Howell planned to be the last one through the gate. "Now *fucking move!*"

The Marines moved. Over the next ten minutes, Howell repeated the lecture half a dozen times to his squad before they dragged themselves into the warehouse. As they ran, Howell saw several humvees speeding towards the area where they had just been fighting. Perhaps they were heading out to mop up the remaining Muj. Howell was too tired to care. The vehicles had reminded him from another scene in *Blackhawk Down* near the movie's end where the exhausted Rangers walk back instead of taking the United Nations troop carriers.

There were no cups of ice water or UN relief workers waiting for Howell and his squad at the warehouse the platoon called home. They flopped down on the concrete floor and lay still, using their flak jackets as pillows. No one said a word. Their hamstrings, calves, shoulders, and forearms took turns cramping up. Ravenous for electrolytes, they took the salt and sugar packets from their MREs and dumped them straight into their mouths.

And they reached for the Lamasil.

CHAPTER 8

All Quiet On the Western Front

War is an ugly thing, but not the ugliest of things.
The person who has nothing for which he is willing to fight,
nothing which is more important to him than his own
personal safety, is a miserable creature and has no chance
of being free unless made and kept so by the exertions
of better men than himself.

—*John Stuart Mill*

At Camp Husaybah on the Syrian border on April 16, 2004, Sgt Dusty Soudan was lying on his cot and flipping through the stack of mail he had received a few days before. Krista had sent letters, along with a picture. He held the letters to his face, savoring their scent.

Krista had gone back to Girard when Dusty left Bangor for Iraq in 2003. She had worried constantly during OIF I. Television reports blared with news of the war. When the statue fell and Dusty went to southern Iraq, she rejoiced. They had thrown an enormous party for 3/7 when they had returned to Twentynine Palms the previous September.

One month later, Dusty had to tell her he was going back to Iraq. When he had come back from OIF I, she had been so excited. You made it! You're home! You're alive! A month later, she cried as he broke the news. Like a mother birthing her second child, this time she knew exactly how painful the uncertainty and separation would be. And nobody in Girard understood.

Dusty would always sugarcoat the truth whenever he called. "No honey, it's really not that bad." *Boom!* "Oh, that noise . . . it's nothing . . . just a truck backfiring." In three weeks, a lifetime of events had happened that he couldn't talk to her about until he got back . . . if he got back. There was April 8, with Wasser, Benatz, and the IEDs. Two days ago, on April 14, the Muj had executed a series of ambushes. One of them involved a grenade attack that critically wounded one of his buddies, Cpl Jason Dunham. Witnesses at the ambush said that Dunham had jumped on the grenade to protect his squadmates.[*]

As Sgt Dusty Soudan drifted off to sleep in Husaybah, Major General Mattis was facing a challenge. Over the years, Mattis had trained himself to think that way: *It's not a problem; it's a challenge.* Mattis was strict with any lexicon that could weaken the morale, mental flexibility, or fortitude of either him or his men.

Blue Diamond's challenge was to figure out a way to maintain the offensive on the insurgents even though high-ranking American politicians had decided to halt the attack. Mattis knew his enemy would exploit the Marine siege of Fallujah. They would claim victory over the Americans and be emboldened. Also, he knew many of the Muj in Fallujah—as well as local Iraqis who had recently chosen the path of *jihad*—had already left the city and scattered into the outlying countryside. No political authority

_____

[*] *The Gift of Valor* by Michael M. Phillips takes a detailed look at the death of Cpl Jason Dunham. For sacrificing his life, Dunham's chain of command, including the Commandant of the Marine Corps, Gen Michael Hagee, recommended him for the Medal of Honor.

restrained him from sweeping his Marines through the area to look for bad guys.

Which was exactly what he did. Mattis called the commander of the 7th Marine Regiment and told him to take the majority of his forces—including tanks, light armored infantry vehicles, and an entire battalion of grunts—and sweep from west to east toward the Fallujah outskirts. Like kicking the hornet's nest in Karmah, the mission was part show of force, part search-and-destroy. Remaining behind was 3/7, with the majority of their strength at Al Qaim. Captain Gannon and his company-sized detachment remained at Camp Husaybah. When the regiment left for the sweep on April 16, 3/7 was the only battalion left in western Iraq.

Somehow, the Muj noticed this.

Counterinsurgency experts and historians will debate about the level of organization in the Iraqi insurgency for decades to come. Many insist that they (always the ubiquitous "they") are fragmented, uncooperative, and lacking in political cohesion. All of these things might be true. Nonetheless, "they" sensed something. Perhaps some of these men had fought Russians in Afghanistan or Chechnya. Or Israelis in Palestine. Or Indians in Kashmir. Or maybe Americans in Afghanistan.

Wherever "they" came from, over 300 of them united the night of April 16 in Husaybah, ready to martyr themselves for God or each other. The Mujahideen forces infiltrated hundreds of well-trained fighters—martyrs like Muhammad from Fallujah—ready to die for *jihad*. With the Marines bogged down in Fallujah, the Muj thought they could exploit the American weakness and seize the undersized Marine base.

On April 17, Sgt Dusty Soudan woke up at 6 A.M. to the sound of twenty-six mortar impacts. Twenty-six *booms*. The Marines put their gear on and waited behind Hesco barriers and sandbagged bunkers. They weren't even scared. By now, they were dulled to the sound of mortars.

Wearing his gear over a green T-shirt, Soudan walked over to the company CP to give his accountability report to the first sergeant; everyone was okay. Second Lieutenant Benatz had returned a couple of days before from the field hospital in Al Qaim, but things hadn't been the same since he got back. Soudan had been running the platoon, and the Marines were growing accustomed to his leadership. Benatz would have to try and fit in again. If he could.

Soudan gave his report and brewed himself a cup of coffee in the company CP while waiting for Captain Gannon to give the "all clear." Piled in the concrete bunker were stacks of junk food, baby wipes, and other toiletries sent from care packages. The company bulletin board prominently displayed miscellaneous paperwork, including a motivational letter to all hands that Mattis had penned to his division before taking them back to Iraq.

While the coffee brewed, Soudan's platoon was getting ready for their next patrol, which was in two hours. Weapons Platoon, which was called 4th Platoon in Lima Company, was still out on patrol. Also out was a five-man team from the Recon Marines. Gannon wanted the Marines to maintain a constant presence in Husaybah. "Patient, persistent presence," Mad Dog Mattis would often say, "is the key to winning over innocent civilians terrorized by our enemy."

Not long after the mortar barrage, Soudan began hearing gunfire. The radio bleeped and crackled as the Recon unit squawked in a report:

"Lima CP, this is Recon. We found group of Muj setting up an IED ambush. We engaged them and killed four. We're in a heavy firefight and need backup. Can you get CAAT out here?"

With their armored vehicles and mounted heavy weapons, Marines from the combined anti-armor team (CAAT) rolled out of their cots, threw on their gear, and flew out of the base in two minutes. Most of the men were shirtless, wearing flaks and helmets over naked torsos with desert boots and pants. Sergeant Soudan sent word back to his platoon: something's going down. Be ready to roll.

Led by Lieutenant Moore, CAAT drove out of the base toward the site of Recon's ambush. Two minutes after they left the base, the CAAT convoy drove past a building covered with several windows. Like a stack of fallen dominoes rising in reverse, Mujahideen armed with RPGs popped up and fired a series of rockets at the Marines. On the other side of the street, Muj shot at them with AK-47s. Using a dated ethnic slur, Marines referred to this double-sided attack as a Polish ambush; the enemy could easily kill one another with stray rounds.

Soudan could hear the .50-caliber gunfire and Mark-19 grenades exploding from the base. He cheered. He loved the sound of Marine weapons. It gave him a warm, comforted feeling. For Soudan, it wasn't the thrill of the kill; it was because hearing those weapons meant his Marines were less likely to die. Gunfire meant victory, and a greater chance of going home physically intact.

The CAAT-Muj firefight continued for about five minutes while the Recon-Muj firefight waned. CAAT took two casualties—one shot in the leg, one with shrapnel wounds throughout the body—and called for assistance. They also lost two vehicles: a humvee and a 7-ton. The reinforcements called Lima CP. They needed more reinforcements.

As Soudan had anticipated, Captain Gannon called 3rd Platoon into action. Soudan told his squad leaders to make sure the Marines were fully loaded with a day's supply of water, ammo, and MRE remnants stuffed into their cargo pockets. At first, their mission was only to secure the northern LZ to evacuate CAAT's wounded, but Soudan thought things might get a little crazy. He had no idea.

North of Husaybah, Soudan and 3rd Platoon secured the northern LZ. After the MEDEVAC, 3rd Platoon went back to the CAAT ambush site, linking up with Lieutenant Moore and the remainder of CAAT. Captain Gannon told Gunny Vegh, the company gunnery sergeant and Soudan's erstwhile mentor, to handle the MEDEVAC for the CAAT casualties while he went to check on 4th Platoon.

Commanded by Lieutenant Carroll, 4th Platoon was heavily engaged at the southeast end of Husaybah. LCpl Gary VanLeuven of Klamath Falls, Oregon, lay dead in the back of a humvee, killed by a sniper's bullet. Exactly one month before, VanLeuven had received his first Purple Heart from a mortar explosion. His second was posthumous.

Also dead were Cpl Chris Gibson, LCpl Ruben Valdez, and LCpl Michael Smith. Gibson had been shot in the leg, and Smith and Valdez were dragging him to safety. The pair of Marines pulled their comrade into the courtyard of a house, through a door in the concrete wall. Concealed behind the wall was the Muj machine gun that killed them. At least five well-armed Muj were crawling around inside the house.

Like their brethren from Kilo 3/4 in Fallujah, the Marines now faced the challenge of invading a fortress. The Muj had the entrances covered by machine-gun fire, and the concrete was thick enough to protect them from rockets, which the Marines were volleying into the building. The Marines could see their fallen comrades in the courtyard, their blood staining the sand red. They couldn't get to them.

By this time, Captain Gannon had arrived. He was on another side of the house, close to Lance Corporal Palmerton's fire team. Gannon and Palmerton did not yet know that Gibson, Valdez, and Smith had been killed.

"Stay here. I'm going around the corner to check on the other team," Captain Gannon said.

"Roger that, sir." Palmerton replied.

A company commander's job is to go to the point of friction—on his own, if necessary—make decisions, and give quick orders. So when Gannon said he was going to check on his guys, no one would have thought to stop him. He wasn't trying to be a hero. He was just trying to do his job.

What did Gannon see when he ran around the corner? Were Gibson, Valdez, and Palmer still alive, gasping for breath? Did Lima Six try to find another way into the house? Did he run toward his Marines, seized by the passion of the Highest Good?

It was about 10 A.M., and Husaybah had exploded. Patrolling the southwestern corner of the town, 2nd Platoon was engaged in a firefight and taking casualties. Camp Husaybah itself, guarded by 1st Platoon, was also under attack. Every Marine in Husaybah was patrolling, shooting, guarding, or being MEDEVACed.

At the CAAT-Muj ambush site, Soudan, Gunny Vegh, and Lieutenant Moore cleared several houses while taking sporadic fire. One Marine was hit by a sniper's bullet on his flak jacket. The Kevlar insert stopped the round. The Marine just kept fighting.

While they were clearing out buildings, several other Marines towed the destroyed vehicles back to Camp Husaybah. With the ambush site cleared, 3rd Platoon swept east towards the former Ba'ath Party headquarters building. They captured several hundred rounds of 7.62 ammunition as well as dozens of AK-47s,

RPGs, and machine guns. "Lima Six, this is Lima Seven," Gunny Vegh called Captain Gannon.* He received no answer.

With 2nd Platoon in a firefight to the southwest and 1st Platoon repelling an attack on Camp Husaybah, 3rd Platoon, Recon, and CAAT moved to the southeastern fortress 4th Platoon was attacking. The Muj had fortified the house with ceramic tiles, concrete, and other stacks of debris they had turned into bunkers and fighting positions. Inside the concrete wall, the multi-story house was abutted against another wall that had no windows and was not guarded. Against this wall was a stack of tires that led up to the roof. Like many houses in Iraq, the roof was surrounded by another four-foot wall. The Muj had not secured the stack of tires leading up to the roof of the house.

At this time, Lieutenant Carroll, 4th Platoon commander, was the senior Marine at the house. When 3rd Platoon arrived, Gunny Vegh wanted to know where Lima Six was. "He went back to base" or "He's with 2nd Platoon" were the answers Vegh received. This would have made sense; with the entire town in chaos, Gannon would have gone back to call the battalion commander and report what was happening.

Marines from 4th Platoon were on top of the roof and surrounding the building. A staircase ran down from the roof. Below the staircase, the Muj controlled the courtyard and the interior levels. Whenever a Muj exposed himself, Marines would unload a few machine gun bursts in his general direction to keep his head down.

3rd Platoon had brought a stack of shoulder-fired rockets and grenades. Lieutenant Carroll went up to the roof and

---

* Every Marine rifle company has standard numeric call signs. One through Four are platoon commanders. Five is the company executive officer. Six is the company commander. Seven is the company gunny. Eight is the first sergeant.

directed 3rd Platoon's Marines into position, advising them on the best angles of fire. While Carroll and several other Marines were standing on the rooftop, Soudan and another Marine volley-fired a pair of rockets into the building. A dust cloud erupted with the explosion, obscuring their vision.

The dust drifted past.

The building remained intact.

Carroll conferred with Lieutenant Moore, the CAAT platoon commander. They had decided to smoke out the Muj. A Marine grabbed a grenade and a five-gallon fuel can. Military fuel cans are made of hard plastic with a pair of tops that unscrew, one wide and the other narrow. The Marine unscrewed the wide top, pulled the pin on the grenade, tossed it in the fuel can, put the top back on, and threw it down the staircase. About a minute after the explosion, smoke billowed from the building. The Muj ran out shooting and were mowed down by hundreds of Marine bullets. Hundreds was not an exaggeration.

Positioned in front with Corporal Link's 1st Squad, Soudan saw one last Muj run out towards them. The Marines killed him. He had been shooting at them with an American 9mm. At this point, four to six dead Iraqis were lying in the courtyard, along with three dead Marines.

Carroll called the Recon team and asked if they could clear the building. He "asked" instead of ordered because Recon technically fell under a different chain of command. However, Carroll was the senior Marine present, and the Lima Company Marines were almost out of ammunition. It made sense to send Recon in. Understanding the need for unity of command, the Recon Marines voiced no objection.

As Recon went to clear the house, Soudan and his men carried Gibson, Valdez, and Smith out of the courtyard. Everything was silent, which was a sound distinct in and of itself after the deafening noise of the past day. By now it was early afternoon. The Marines had been fighting for six hours.

The Recon Marines began yelling to get out. Flames from the grenade/fuel can were burning near a propane tank. They ran out of the house. Oblivious to the activity, a pair of Recon Marines remained in the house; they hadn't heard the warnings being shouted behind them.

Suddenly, the Marines heard gunfire and shouting in the house. Double-taps of gunfire. More shouting. The two men from Recon emerged from the house carrying a third Marine who was already dead.

Now everyone was confused. Who was this Marine? The leaders of Lima's platoons had accounted for all their men. The Recon Marines looked around their unit, trying to figure out who else was missing.

Sergeant Soudan, Corporal Link, and Lieutenant Carroll were standing in the back of a humvee. After triaging the wounded from the dead, they had placed the bodies of Gibson, Valdez, and Smith in the humvee with VanLeuven. The Recon Marines ran up, muscling the body of the other dead Marine into the vehicle.

Soudan, Link, and Carroll looked at their fallen comrade. Their faces went white.

Captain Gannon.

Lima Six was dead.

They killed our company commander. Pain switched to fury and an immediate demand for vengeance. *These fuckers killed Captain Gannon.*

To say Lima Company liked and trusted Gannon would be an understatement. Gannon's presence, authority, and compassion radiated to all his men. His actions and convictions had bolstered the morale of every Marine at Husaybah. Standing there, seeing his corpse, every Marine was struck with guilt and anger. To this day, they anguish at not having been present when he died. Nobody will ever know exactly how it happened, only that it did.

In triage, a dead Marine was a routine casualty, not an urgent one.[*] When 4th Platoon reported Lima Six as a routine casualty, 1stLt Dominique Neal, the executive officer, was back at the CP. In an instant, he knew what had happened. He came on the radio and said, "Lima Five is now Lima Six." One of Neal's seniors told him that an executive officer had not replaced a company commander who was killed during combat since the Vietnam War.

Unbeknownst to Soudan and 4th Platoon, 3/7's battalion commander had already begun organizing for a big fight. After hearing of the heavy action in Husaybah, LtCol Matt Lopez had driven down from Al Qaim to fortify the town and to repel the enemy attack. News of Gannon's death steeled him, and Lopez resolved to cleanse Husaybah of the Muj that day. Lopez called the remaining companies in the battalion and ordered them to leave Al Qaim and join the fight in Husaybah.

The platoons on the east end of Husaybah did not know the battalion commander had arrived, but they knew they had a lot of work ahead. By now it was well into the afternoon. The mixture of adrenaline, fear, and fight-or-flight instinct created a distorted sense of time. Events that Marines later swore took hours to happen actually occurred in minutes. They were thinking in terms of mission: *What's my next task? Where's the enemy? Who's my new team leader?* They were struggling to deal with the death of leaders and close friends. They were deafened from the ringing

---

[*] Combat casualties are sorted into three categories: urgent, priority, and routine.

in their ears. Their eyes were alert for any sign of activity. They wolfed down whatever food they had and speed-loaded their magazines with urgency.*

3rd Platoon's next mission was to visit the Iraqi Police station. The Marines in Husaybah hated the police. They knew most of them were corrupt, which was a relative term in Iraq. Most, if not all, members of Iraq's security forces were crooked by American standards. Payoffs and bribes—*baksheesh*—were normal business. A typical transaction in Iraq required a 15 percent skimming fee for every layer of bureaucracy involved. This was expected as well for law enforcement officials.

The Iraqi police in Husaybah were wolves in sheep's clothing. They not only tolerated and supported the Muj, but often constituted them as well. Several weeks later, a search of the police station turned up a stockpile of weapons, ammunition, and duffel bags filled with Muj-style black jump suits. Circumstantial evidence suggested that the policemen would change clothes at work and go hunt Marines, using the same weapons and gear provided to them by the American Coalition.

Sergeant Soudan and his Marines were not paying a friendly visit to fellow law enforcement officials. While Husaybah had been exploding the entire morning, the police had stayed in the station—or perhaps they were changing clothes. Regardless, they had done nothing to assist Marines with securing the town and safeguarding the people.

The Marines arrived. They grabbed the policemen and threw them against the wall, frisking them down and releasing pent-up aggression. Marines and hajjis stared at each other with mutual

---

* A speed-loader is a metal clip shaped like the bottom of an hourglass. The wide bottom fits onto a magazine, which allows Marines to jam ten-round clips onto the narrow top. They can then load all ten rounds into the magazine at once instead of loading each round separately.

hate. The policemen glowered, faces canted sideways with cheeks pressed onto the concrete.

As they were searching, 3rd Platoon got new orders over the radio: leave the police station and link up with Lieutenant Colonel Lopez on the east side of Husaybah. Without any tangible evidence, the Marines could take no further action against the police. To signal their disapproval, the Marines took the police cars and drove them to the linkup point with Lopez. This action had a two-fold purpose: it deprived the police/Muj of transportation, and it allowed the Muj to observe the police cars near Marines. The Muj might think the police had split their loyalties.

3rd Platoon linked up with their mates from Lima on the deserted outskirts of the town's eastern edge. A stream of humvees and 7-tons poured in from Al Qaim carrying hundreds of angry Marines yearning to demonstrate why their battalion motto was The Cutting Edge. Elements from the entire battalion rallied, rehearsed, and maintained security, waiting for the word while their commanders huddled with Lopez.* Marines from H & S went to Camp Husaybah and relieved Lima's 1st Platoon from security duties so they could move into the attack.

As Soudan later explained, Lopez wanted at least a squad on each street, moving methodically to search each house. 3/7 would sweep through the town from east to west and consolidate at Camp Husaybah, which would soon be renamed Camp Gannon. Any Iraqi man carrying a weapon in the streets was considered hostile. From Soudan's perspective, Husaybah had just become a free-fire zone.

---

* Like weapons platoons, an infantry battalion also has a separate weapons company. Sized like a regular infantry company, the weapons company contains the CAAT platoon and 81mm mortar platoon. Some battalions also place their snipers in weapons company.

As Lopez was giving his brief, snipers and other intelligence agents saw several dozen Muj carrying weapons while running to a pair of mosques on the northwest portion of the city to coordinate their own attack. Wearing facemasks, *kheffiyahs*, or even baseball caps, the Muj had turned the mosques into forts. Gunfire emanated from the building as they prepared defensive positions near the minarets, stockpiling caches inside hidden rooms where Americans would not search.

Geneva Protocol I states: "Acts of hostility toward places of worship in international conflicts are prohibited." However, the Protocol also says, "Places of worship may not be used in support of a military effort." Seeing masked men with guns fleeing into the mosque gave Lopez the distinct impression that the mosque was no longer simply a place of worship. Soudan stood next to his battalion commander as he requested a laser-guided bomb for each mosque.

With the political currents of the Battle of Fallujah swirling, approving an air strike on a mosque was a challenging task. Still, a pair of AV-8B Harriers flew into the town to acquire the target. Their passes roared less than 100 feet from the ground, and the reverberations were so strong they detonated several IEDs that had not been discovered. After that, Soudan and other sergeants wryly requested Harrier fly-bys before they went into town on patrol.

With Sergeant Soudan standing next to him, Lopez soon received the word from Col Craig Tucker, the regimental commander. Disapproved. Whether the decision was made because of politics, cultural sensitivities, or not wanting to endanger troops on the ground, air wasn't an option. Soudan watched, maintaining security for his battalion commander as Lopez reconsidered the best way to attack the city.

The Muj had picked a good time to stage their Husaybah uprising—all of the tanks and light armor that might have been available to the battalion were in Fallujah. Lopez called a pair of AH-1 Cobra helicopters and asked them to make a pass over the city. Two blocks into the town, the Cobras took heavy fire. With engines, props, and fuel tanks pierced by bullets, the Cobras hobbled back to the base.

When Marines attack an enemy position, they like to use armor, air, and other assets to quickly destroy their foe while minimizing their own casualties. They call this the combined-arms effect. Lopez was short on combined-arms options. Every house and street would have to be personally cleared by his Marines. They would be on foot the entire time. Lopez looked up and down the lines into several hundred stony faces. His men were ready.

Soudan and his buddies looked at each other. They had been through more action in one month than they had seen during the entire war in 2003. Having spent the better part of the morning outside of an Iraqi house and having lost five Marines, they knew what the price of clearing the town would be. "Hey, hope to see you back at the base," they said. A few embraced. Soudan and Link walked around, voicing encouragement, distributing ammunition, and backslapping.

At 5 P.M., Lopez ordered 3/7 into the attack.

When Marines were killed in Iraq, company and battalion commanders—by order of Major General Mattis—organized memorial services as quickly as they could. The services enabled

Marines to grieve for their fallen brothers, remember their unique contributions, and reestablish their commitment and trust both to their leadership and to each other. Kilo 3/4's memorial service for Cpl Daniel Amaya happened in late April, after the first attack on Karmah, around the time the men from Lima 3/7 began planning their own memorial service for their fallen commander and Marines.

In *Odysseus in America: Combat Trauma and the Trials of Homecoming*, psychiatrist Jonathan Shay describes the importance of communal grief in preventing psychological injury from developing into severe cases of post-traumatic stress disorder. Shay illustrates how a fraternity of warriors—characterized by unique, asexual devotion and love (the Highest Good)—fights and survives more effectively when they can grieve together as a unit.

Held at the Camp Fallujah chapel, the memorial was simple and heartrending. A pair of empty desert boots was placed on the ground. Between the boots was a rifle, muzzle pointed down. A helmet was set on top of the butt stock of the weapon. Amaya's dog tags were suspended from the rifle.

Ever the jokester, Cpl Matt O'Brien stood up and reminded the Marines about Amaya's favorite nickname, Kung Fu. GySgt Paul Courville talked about Amaya's strengths as a squad leader. Captain Savage said a few words. Thundering Third's chaplain prayed.

The company first sergeant called off the roll as each Marine affirmed their presence. Captain Savage. "Here." Lieutenant Stokes. "Here." Corporal Zmudzinski. "Here." He called each name in Kilo Company, well over one hundred and fifty.

"Corporal Daniel Amaya," the first sergeant intoned. Silence.

"Corporal Daniel Amaya," he said again.

"Corporal Daniel Amaya." Three times to commemorate an irreplaceable loss.

All was quiet in the Camp Fallujah chapel, except for the soft sounds of brave men weeping.

Retired Marine brigadier general Thomas V. Draude, a Vietnam and Desert Storm veteran who served with 3/7, once told a story about an intense firefight in Quang Ngai Province when he ordered his Marines to fix bayonets. In April 1966, then-Captain Draude had been ordered to take Mike Company and seize an enemy objective. "As the metal clicked in place, a solemn—almost peaceful—silence rolled through the steamy Asian jungle," Draude said. "Individuals looked at that rifle with renewed respect: in a few minutes someone was about to die—on one end or the other." Although Lima 3/7 did not have their bayonets mounted, the same quiet intensity and resolve filled the hearts of The Cutting Edge.

The moment 3/7 stepped off to clear out Husaybah, they heard gunfire up and down the line. The cracks of AK-47s mingled with the rhythmic *thunk-thunk-thunk* of M-240G and .50-caliber medium and heavy machine guns. Even for Marines like Soudan that had been fighting all day, the noise level had ratcheted up.

Lieutenant Colonel Lopez wanted to clear the town in a battalion line, blanketing Husaybah in a fierce wave of green. This meant that every time a unit took casualties, the other Marines would halt. India Company had the far south, or left, flank. Lima had the right. The battalion was attacking east to west.

It took almost an hour to move six blocks. The battalion was held up twice for casualty evacuation. Enemy dead were left in the streets; no one moved to pick them up. As the attack progressed, word filtered down that, at the time, Soudan attributed to Lopez: "Anyone on the streets is considered hostile." Marines were thrilled. For the most part, women and children had stayed in the houses, but even women had been running in the streets. Some were carrying guns and shooting at Marines. They were now targets. One woman ran towards a trio of officers screaming, carrying a basket as if it was a bomb. She was killed.

Almost three hours after they started, the sun had set, and the Marines were halfway through the town. Soudan had seen about fifteen dead Muj on his street alone (Husaybah had about two dozen streets). Nobody was really counting, there were so many dead littered about. By this point, Marines were working in tandem with adjacent units, flushing people toward the north or south by fire, and then yelling across to the other Marines: "You've got one headed your way!" *Crack, crack*. One more dead body.

Soudan had also lost count of the friendly casualties. One Marine was shot in the face. Others took shrapnel and bullets in arms, legs, and hands. At one point in the attack, a bullet ripped through Soudan's desert cammies half an inch from his left knee. Unharmed, Soudan killed the man shooting at him. Amazingly, the Mujahideen had not killed any other Marines since The Cutting Edge started their sweep.

Night fell, but the Marines methodically continued the assault. Five blocks before they arrived at the base, Soudan saw a man without a weapon walking behind a five-year-old child. He saw Marines instinctively lower their weapons, as if they had all collectively decided to save what little remained of this child's innocence. Sergeant Soudan later regretted not shooting the man in the head; he thought the Iraqi was most likely a combatant using the child for cover.

At 11 P.M., 3/7 consolidated at Camp Husaybah. They renamed the base Camp Gannon. Covered in sweat, dirt, and blood, the men gulped down water (most of them had forgotten to drink during the fighting) and collapsed on their cots. Many didn't even bother to eat. They had taken six hours to clear the town. Normally, they patrolled the length of Husaybah in thirty minutes.

With the exception of a 107mm rocket hitting Camp Gannon (causing no injuries), the next day was like the morning after a hurricane. The women of the town—and any remaining men—had piled the bodies along Market Street so families could claim and bury their dead. Between 200 and 300 people had been killed. Over 100 bodies were unclaimed; these dead were foreigners, and nobody knew who they were. Husaybah also had noticeably fewer policemen.

That day, the Marines swept the town again. They did not attack, but instead performed a detailed search of each house and street. They found weapons caches, surface-to-air missiles, and over fifty IEDs strewn along the road. The Muj had intended to detonate them, but the Marine attack the day before hadn't given them time to do so. The Marines took sporadic fire and killed a few more Muj, but the sweep back through the town was not as intense as the one the day before had been.

On April 19, Major General Mattis and the division chaplain, Father Bill Devine, arrived in Husaybah. Captain Gannon's death hit Devine especially hard. Gannon was Catholic, and Devine had baptized him. He knew Gannon's family well. Although Devine felt the loss, he still bolstered the Marine's spirits. If anything, the loss of Gannon made both the priest and his flock feel more devoted—to their mission and to each other.

The men of Lima Company formed up behind 1stLt Dominique Neal, the executive officer who, two days earlier, had become their company commander. Neal was a slender, bald, young African American with high cheekbones and a demeanor of quiet strength. Originally a member of the U.S. Naval Academy's class of 1998, Neal graduated in December 1999. At the time, Neal was the only midshipman in Naval Academy history who—with academic waivers—took five and a half years to complete a four-year program.

Neal's status as an academic underachiever belied his skill as an officer and commander. His performance during OIF I had earned the respect of the company and his Marines. Just as Capt Morgan Savage of Kilo 3/4 had been replaced by a battalion staff officer during the Battle of Fallujah, the men in Lima had expected higher headquarters to send down another captain as Gannon's replacement. Instead, Major General Mattis frocked Neal to captain and put him in charge of Lima.*

The battle for Husaybah became the defining event for 3/7 during their 2004 deployment to Iraq. It was the yardstick by which the Marines measured each other's performance. Sgt Dusty Soudan had hardly seen Lieutenant Benatz on April 17. The Marines said that Benatz had spent a lot of time in a house or on the radio. Whether it was true or not, Soudan believed that Benatz had intentionally avoided the heaviest fighting.

Benatz's struggle to win the respect of his platoon sergeant represented one type of perception problem: that of small assumptions, or inactions, having a compounding negative effect. Like the mistaken—and widespread—belief among the junior Marines who thought they would not find much of a fight when they relieved the "screwed up" 82nd Airborne in February 2004, Benatz, for whatever reason, was unable to address the lack of confidence Soudan had in his abilities. Fortunately, despite

---

* A frocking is a special promotion where rank and privileges are awarded, but increased pay is not. A Marine is frocked to a rank at a commander's discretion if he has already been selected for promotion, but his official promotion date has not arrived.

their initial faulty impressions that they would have no mission more intense than handing out candy to kids, the men of Lima 3/7 were ready when they had to adjust. 2nd Lieutenant Benatz would have to find a way to bring Soudan on board and keep his platoon off the skyline.

But sometimes, as Cpl Craig Atkins and the men of Fox 2/4 in Ramadi's Snake Pit would soon learn, too much confidence is not always a healthy thing.

Sometimes overconfidence can bring dire consequences.

CHAPTER 9

The River

Complacency kills.

—*Motto posted on American*
bases throughout Iraq

In Iraq, a Marine's status was measured by where he went to take a shit.

Like everything in the military hierarchy, toilets have their own form of a pecking order. At the top are the head (restroom) trailers. Found most often at pogue hangouts like Camp Fallujah, Camp Taqaddum, and Al Asad, the prefabricated, air-conditioned, mobile-home-style head trailers turn defecating into its own type of morale boost. They require constant pumping from sewage tanks, and the logistical capacity to make it happen. Head trailers mean headquarters.

Next are the Port-a-Johns. Proliferating at transient camps like Al Qaim, Baharia, and the Snake Pit, Port-a-Johns are the basic no-frills means of making a daily deposit. The hotter the weather becomes, the more uncomfortable they are for a Marine to use.

The stench increases with the heat, making the entire experience claustrophobic and nauseating.

Burn shitters are a poor Marine's Port-a-John. A burn shitter is a standing outhouse built with plywood. Marines sit on benches with holes. Underneath the holes are open oil drums cut in half. When they have filled up, boots, outcasts, and other unlucky souls remove the drums, add diesel fuel, and burn them, stirring the mixture with a rotted two by four until it's consumed. Burn shitters are popular in remote areas like Husaybah. In one case, the infantry company that guarded Camp Fallujah—India 3/24—maintained their own burn shitters. They were motivated by both solidarity to their grunt brethren and the practicality of having local facilities; the head trailers were on the other side of the base.

Of course, the grunts in Fallujah wound up with the worst of all available options. They could either dig a hole in the ground and squat—a difficult chore in the concrete jungle of urban warfare—or they could use the hajji toilet. There was no lesser of these two evils.

Ensconced in an Iraqi house that 1st Platoon, Bravo 1/5 had started referring to as Hotel Fallujah, Cpl Jason Howell was sick of the stench that radiated like a weapon of mass destruction from the hajji toilet. The commode was installed into the floor of the house like a sink with a wide hole stuck into the ground. The Marines had placed a hollowed-out chair over the commode so they could sit instead of being forced to squat. They flushed the hajji toilet by pouring a bucket of water down the drain and scraping the pipes with a sawed-off broomstick. After two weeks, the privy—which was being used by the entire platoon—had started overflowing. The feces attracted flies, making the climate of sweat and filth feel even nastier than it already was.

Human offal was not the only type of shit overflowing in abundance. After dozens of rumors, the false information floating through Hotel Fallujah on the Lance Corporal Network grated on Howell like a bad reality TV show. Every day for the past two weeks, a new rumor had flown through. We're leaving Fallujah! We're going back to the MEK! We're attacking to the Euphrates tomorrow! Pack up! Stand down! Fill more sandbags! Do rehearsals! The general is visiting—get this area cleaned up!

After the insanity of April 13, a relative calm had settled over 1st Platoon. Like the rest of Bravo 1/5, they were quartered in a house in the middle of the city. Because of constant Muj attacks, the Marines in Fallujah had not immediately observed the mandate of halting offensive action. In keeping with the standing rules of engagement—which seemed easy to understand but actually depended on the prevailing political winds—Marines had responded to Muj hostilities with their own.

By the end of the month, city leaders in Fallujah had curbed the violence to scattered mortar and rocket attacks. They sat down to negotiate a compromise to the siege. The Fallujan interlocutors included the infamous Sheikh Abdullah al-Janabi—a notorious jihadist who later worked hand-in-glove with Abu Musab al-Zarqawi—and the Fallujah city mayor, Ibrahim al Juraissey, who garnered little respect from either Iraqis or Marines. It was common knowledge among the American negotiators that the mayor of Fallujah was politically inchoate. It was also common knowledge that he was gay.

During the last two weeks of April, the negotiations dragged on fruitlessly. Although the Fallujans claimed to represent the local civilian community, the debates did not focus on humanitarian issues or economic redevelopment. Instead, Janabi repeatedly insisted that Marines move the tanks from their checkpoints and stop flying reconnaissance airplanes. "After that is complete," Janabi said, "we expect full claims to be paid for damages." It became clear that Marines were negotiating with the enemy, not neutral civilians.

The last week of April 2004, a pair of Saddam Hussein's former generals stepped forward. "Give us control of the city," they said. "We will form the Fallujah Brigade. They will patrol the city on their own, restoring order and trust between the Fallujans and Americans."

Mattis did not like the idea from the start. Instinctively, he distrusted the Fallujan rhetoric. To him, it looked like a double-cross. Nonetheless, the idea generated momentum within I MEF as a solution to the stalemate. Using clandestine go-betweens from American and Iraqi (Mujahideen?) intelligence agents, the idea of the Fallujah Brigade began taking shape.

At that time, Howell knew nothing of the Fallujah Brigade. For two weeks, he had filled more sandbags than he ever knew existed. Like other small units in the area, 1st Platoon, Bravo 1/5, was building a defensive fortress to keep up the siege. Large enough to house both a Marine platoon and an Iraqi family, the three-story building was surrounded by a quadruple layer of sandbags stacked five feet. *Somewhere back home,* Howell thought, *a sandbag company is making a fortune on this war.*

After almost two weeks of nonstop action, Hotel Fallujah had been a nice break. Located on a major intersection directly across from a mosque, 1st Platoon was responsible for maintaining security and defending the perimeter. After the first few days of resting their bodies, Staff Sergeant Campbell, the platoon sergeant, and Lieutenant Lewis saw the Marines getting lazy and lacking in motivation.

The obvious solution to this problem was work. Eventually, a routine settled in: if they weren't on watch, the men were filling sandbags. Once all the sandbags were filled, they built up the fighting positions, adding concrete blocks and heavy wooden doors. If the fighting positions were finished, they dismantled them and put up new ones. Busywork kept the men from griping, bullshitting, and thinking.

When they weren't filling sandbags or assembling fighting positions, they were cleaning. Of course, the Marines constantly cleaned their weapons, but they also swept the floor, stacked and re-stacked Iraqi carpets and rugs, and wiped down the furniture in the occupied house. When the Marines eventually left, the Iraqi family they had evicted returned, undoubtedly confused by the mixture of pristine carpets, bullet holes, swept floors, and tactical fortifications.

While Bravo Company stayed at Hotel Fallujah, Captain Smith allowed the squads to go back to the MEK once a week for a day off.* Marines maintain a Spartan tradition of reversing luxury in hard times: food is always served in ascending order of rank, from private to general. Officers eat last, or go without if rations are sparse.

Howell applied that attitude toward showering privileges. After over two weeks of living in filth, the simple act of smearing soap and running water over their bodies was like a royal Jacuzzi bath. As the squad leader, Howell took the last shower. Because of water rationing, they turned the water on to rinse their bodies, then off as they lathered up, then back on again to remove the soap. The water looked like tar as it drained.

If they got mail, they read it. If they got care packages, they distributed them among their mates. If they got a ride to the MEK/Camp Fallujah PX, they purchased dip, junk food, and a

---

* 1/5 was actually bivouacked at a camp adjacent to the MEK. However, the Marines were able to enjoy the Camp Fallujah amenities when off the lines, including hot showers, hot food, and the PX.

copy of *Maxim*, which they took with them into a head trailer or Port-a-John for their long-awaited sexual fantasy and release. Ten minutes undisturbed in a Port-a-John accompanied by the cover girl of the month boosted a young Marine's morale more than all the care packages in the world.

But then it was back to the grind of filling sandbags and waiting, watching and guarding empty, desolate streets. One day, the higher-ups removed part of the cordon and let some of the Iraqis back into the city. The mosque was flooded with activity. They began receiving occasional gunfire—scattered potshots, not dangerous sniper fire. Nobody was hit.

The worst thing about Hotel Fallujah from Howell's perspective was the singsong Arabic chants that echoed from the loudspeakers on the *muezzin* towers in the Muj-controlled portion of the city. They sounded like nursery rhymes and mind-fucked Howell and his Marines. *A Sa . . . A Sa Laam . . . A Sa Laam Uleikum.* The noise and endlessness grated on their spirits, a different form of psychological warfare.

While the Fallujah Brigade negotiations continued to their east, Sgt Dusty Soudan and the Marines in Husaybah had enjoyed two weeks of something approaching bliss. Women and children were smiling and waving. His Marines hadn't been attacked. Birds chirped when the sun rose in the morning. When the Marines patrolled, locals stopped them in the streets. Life was as picturesque and bucolic as it could possibly be in the Root of All.

When the Marines patrolled, hajjis were stopping them on the street. "*Shukran! Shukran!*" Profuse gestures of gratitude dripped from their mouths. They told stories about how evil men from other countries had come into the town. The poor, unfortunate souls of Husaybah insisted again and again that they had absolutely nothing to do with the violence. "May they never return and may we have peace, *inshallah*," they said.

One day during the last week of April, an Iraqi policeman came to Camp Gannon. "The foreigners are coming back," the policeman said. "They are hiding out at this house in town. You must go and get them, or they will bring misery and war back to the people."

As word spread about a raid that was being planned for May 1, Soudan and his Marines were skeptical. They didn't trust the information. They smelled a trap. Still, what if the man was telling the truth? The civilian population would want to know why the Marines hadn't done anything. The policeman claimed they were not strong enough to act on their own; without the Marines, they would be defeated. Or so they said.

Much to Soudan's frustration, Lieutenant Benatz seemed particularly enthusiastic about the intelligence, which might have affected Captain Neal's decision to order the raid. All of 3rd Platoon loaded up in their 7-tons and headed out. They had an entourage with them, including combat engineers and a pair of Marine photographers. After weaving through the town, about fifty Marines arrived and dismounted. They were not running, but they were "moving with a purpose" toward their assigned sectors.

The locals were nowhere around.

BOOM!

Soudan never figured out why the Muj didn't detonate the IED when the whole platoon was collected in front of it. Perhaps they weren't ready yet, or maybe they hadn't seen the crowd show up. For whatever reason, the enemy held off until a stack of eight Marines had lined up against the wall, waiting for the word to take down the building.

Seven of the eight Marines were lying on the ground. Only Soudan, who had been the last man in the stack, was unscathed.

Oh shit, Soudan thought. *They got all seven.*

All the men got up, except for the combat engineer—shrapnel had torn through his leg. Once again, they called for a MEDEVAC, describing the injuries over the radio using brevity codes and short explanations: "Gates is hit in the eye. Metal shards are in Spadafore's face. Palmer has shrapnel, too."

Ashen-faced, the photographer was trembling. He held up his M-16. The explosion had snapped it in half.

Before the IED detonated, 3rd Platoon had cordoned off the building in preparation for the raid. About ten minutes later, with the cordon still intact, they started taking sporadic fire. The shots were not well aimed—just a couple of Muj off in the distance—but the fire was steady enough for concern. Two squads maintained the cordon while the rest of 3rd Platoon took cover under a bridge, calling CAAT for backup.

Lt Isaac Moore, Sergeant Soudan's old platoon commander, rolled out with CAAT. The armored vehicles pinned down the attackers in another building several blocks from the raid site. CAAT set up a cordon. The Muj were inside.

Moore called Benatz. "Lima Three, can you clear the objective?" CAAT only had enough Marines to maintain the cordon. To clear the building and kill the bad guys, they would need some help.

Before Moore had even called, Soudan had read his mind. Moore and Soudan had worked well together during OIF I; Soudan knew what his old boss was thinking. Instinctively, both believed the current threat was not the raid house (which had already been a trap), but the house CAAT had attacked. In that house were Muj who were actually shooting at them, not some bullshit raid location that had been the product of duplicitous intelligence.

Benatz told Soudan to halt. "Negative. Lima Three is maintaining the cordon."

Moore was furious. "Lima Three, *we need you over here now!*"

Perhaps Benatz and Moore had their own clashes. Maybe Benatz sensed that his Marines were prone to follow the orders of other officers they respected more quickly than his own. Maybe he was jealous. Or maybe he really thought the raid was the most important thing.

For whatever reason, 2nd Lieutenant Benatz refused to budge. Instead, Moore had to call another platoon from Camp Gannon for support. Without vehicles, the reinforcements pushed two miles across Husaybah on foot. By the time they arrived to clear the building, it was empty.

3rd Platoon performed the raid, and that building was empty too. Shaken and angry, the grunts returned to their base. The peace of two weeks was no more.

If a Marine bled from his eardrums, was he wounded? Technically, yes, but many young grunts said no. 3rd Platoon, like young Marines in general, had its own litmus test of what did or did not constitute a wound and, consequently, a Purple Heart. For some of the men in 3rd, a blown eardrum was not recognized as serious enough to rate the medal.

Thus, when Lieutenant Benatz was awarded his second Purple Heart for blown eardrums from the May 1 IED, further rumblings against him stirred. Gannon—who was posthumously promoted to major—had seen many Marines hiding minor wounds. His blanket policy for Lima was that, if a Marine was treated for injuries sustained in combat, then he rated a Purple Heart. Period. In keeping with Major Gannon's policies, Captain Neal signed off on Benatz's recommended award.

Even though Benatz had nothing to do with the decision, receiving a second Purple Heart for a minor wound only fueled the distrust his platoon sergeant harbored for him. Marines like to think they always have all the relevant facts in a decision, but just as often, they act on perception, assumption, and instinct.

Sometimes they are dreadfully wrong.

In Ramadi, the Magnificent Bastards had found a hell of a fight. During the first two months of 2/4's operations around places like the Snake Pit, 19 Marines were killed, and another 138 were wounded. A number of those injuries were caused by mortar and rocket fire. On April 4, 2004, the 2/4 operations section issued a warning order to Capt Mark Carlton and Fox Company for an event they were calling Operation Treasure Island. 2/4's higher headquarters, the Army's First Brigade Combat Team (also known as The Big Red One, or 1-BCT) had named the operation.* The mission of Operation Treasure Island would be to conduct ambushes on the major islands and banks of the Euphrates River. They would be looking for enemy weapons caches or other signs of activity.

---

* Major General Mattis refused to permit Marines to name individual operations. To prevent confusion of effort, he wanted everything classified as part of their main Operational mission: Iraqi Freedom. Although 1-BCT fell under the operational command of Marines, they named their operations. This happened because 1-BCT had been in Iraq prior to the Marines' arrival and had already established a pattern of naming their major missions. Consequently, Mattis let them keep their existing policy.

On April 6, while Bev Atkins was chatting online and jumping at doorbells, Echo Company was attacked and devastated. The Marines stepped up their patrolling throughout Ramadi. Battles ensued. Fallujah happened. All of Iraq went ballistic. Everyone forgot about Operation Treasure Island for a couple of weeks. Eventually, during the last week of April, somebody remembered the operation and planning began again.

Infantry battalions stationed on ships become part of a Marine Expeditionary Unit, Special Operations Capable. To earn their "SOC" qualification, companies are trained for waterborne, heliborne, or mechanized operations. Fox Company was the waterborne unit, or Boat Company. During their eleven months on Okinawa in 2003, they had trained extensively for beach landings, surf passage, and water operations in black rubber rafts called zodiacs. Additionally, sixteen Marines from 1st Platoon had attended a three-week scout swimmer course in 2002 in Coronado, California. Cpl Dustin Schrage and Cpl Craig Atkins were two of them.

The course was grueling and intense. Coronado was the same beach where Navy SEALs trained, and the scout swimmers had lengthy classes on ocean swimming, beach landings, and boat raids. The course included lessons on proper fin techniques; only a handful of the Marines had used fins before. By the end of the course, the Marines were proficient at assessing ocean currents and scouting terrain for beach landing sites.

The scout swimmer course did not cover river crossings, but 2/4 had trained for that as well at the Mountain Warfare Training Center in Bridgeport, California. At Bridgeport, Schrage and Atkins had learned how to cross a swift-moving shallow river. They had also learned how to build a one-rope bridge to secure Marines and gear, keeping them from being separated by the current. The preferred technique for testing current was to toss a stick in the river.

The Euphrates River was neither an ocean nor a swift, shallow creek. When it is spoken of in the Bible, the Euphrates is simply called the River, which is the same name—*Al Furaat*—that Iraqis commonly use today. Descending from the Armenian mountains and winding through southwest Asia for over 1700 miles, the Euphrates normally flows at less than one knot through a deep, narrow gorge out onto the broad Mesopotamian plains. For millennia, the River has flooded during the annual mountain snowmelt in the springtime, which causes currents to reach as high as five knots from the middle of March to the end of May. In the summer heat, the runoff evaporates and the River decelerates to a tranquil speed and level.

According to river diving expert Larry Taylor, only master divers should operate in any current greater than two knots. The reason for this, Taylor says on his diving website, is because deep rivers are unpredictable. "In intense current, one feels like one is in the middle of an underwater thunderstorm." Flood stages increase current speeds and risks. The presence of obstacles, such as dams, or the varying depth can create microclimates of turbulence. Taylor calls these vortexes "drowning machines" because they cycle like a vertical tornado instead of a spiraling horizontal whirlpool.

When the Fox Company scout swimmers heard about the mission, they were thrilled. A real-world operation for Boat Company! Hoping for a mission on the Euphrates, the company had packed a crate filled with swim gear—goggles, booties, wetsuits, and life vests—as well as a zodiac. Only one thing was missing.

When they unpacked the gear, the Marines discovered the fins were gone. This might have raised a red flag, except the island they were supposed to raid was so damn close! The target location for the Treasure Island sweep was only fifty meters from the shoreline. Fifty meters! "If the wind was right, we could have pissed onto the damn island," Cpl Craig Atkins said, with his southern Indiana twang.

A group of Marines from 2/4 had established an observation post on a tall building. They noted, "We've been here for a week and haven't seen anyone coming or going. The Marines don't really need to swim across. We don't think anything is there."

Apparently someone thought that estimate was wildly off the mark. Someone in the chain of command insisted that the insurgents were using the island as a possible stockpile or weapons cache. Besides, the men thought, it will be an easy swim and a good raid. It will be good for the Marines to do a real-world boat mission.

Treasure Island was a go.

The operation called for the scout swimmers to cross the river and establish security on the island. They would carry a rope with them that was attached to the zodiac, which would be loaded with a dozen Marines and their gear. They would guide the zodiac across, just like they were taught at Bridgeport. The zodiac would ferry back and forth until all the Marines were on the island.

Fox Company had five scout swimmers for the mission. Since swim teams always travel in buddy pairs, GySgt Dirk Lens, the company gunny, volunteered to replace another swimmer who had injured his ankle. Schrage and Atkins were the first pair of swim buddies. Cpl Jeffery Green and LCpl Brandon Winneshiek came next. A corporal named Pretrick who had been raised in Micronesia was partnered with Gunny Lens. All the Marines considered themselves expert swimmers.

Even though Gunny Lens was the senior Marine swimming, he planned to sit back and let the corporals run the show. The senior scout swimmer was Cpl Dustin Schrage, and Lens wanted to let him make the calls. Senior enlisted Marines encourage their young Spartans-in-training to "step up and take charge" at every opportunity.

On the day of the mission, May 2, while the Marines who would come across in the zodiac were practicing their techniques, Corporal Schrage reviewed the plan with the swimmers. They were wearing life vests, trousers, and swimming booties. They were carrying weapons and ammunition. They did not have fins.

"What about a waterproof pack to use as a shooting platform?" Gunny Lens asked.

Schrage thought about it. "That would slow us down. We weren't trained that way at the course in Coronado. Besides," he added, "the swim is only fifty meters. We need to get over there quickly to get the zodiac onto the island."

Although Schrage did not want every swimmer bobbing across the Euphrates with a waterproofed pack for floatation or stability—speed was essential—he agreed with Lens that one man with a pack was a smart idea "just in case something happened."

That evening in the chow hall at Hurricane Point, 2/4's senior enlisted Marine, SgtMaj James Booker, was talking with the Marines about the mission. "You guys had better watch out for the current," the sergeant major said.

The night of May 2, the designated Marines from Fox Company loaded up in 7-tons and drove to their insertion point on the bank of the River. They removed the zodiac and set up security on the riverbank. Sergeant Navarro—who had been running the QRF when LCpl Andrew Dang had been killed weeks before—was standing on the riverbank when he noticed areas where the water was moving in both directions. He thought the current looked extremely fast. Navarro wanted to find the swimmers and warn them.

They had already dropped into the water.

"You all right, Green?" Winneshiek said.

"Yeah," Green said. They both whispered. All the Marines used the sidestroke as they swam. Green was easily recognizable; he looked like a cross between Muhammad Ali and Will Smith.

Corporal Green and Winneshiek were having a smooth swim. They had started downstream of the other two pairs, but by swimming into the current at an angle, they found themselves upriver of both Pretrick and Gunny Lens and Schrage and Atkins.

Behind Green and Winneshiek, the other four swimmers were almost in a column. Pretrick swam in front of Gunny Lens, who was slowed down by his pack. Because Gunny Lens was on the pack, Corporal Schrage had asked him to carry the rope across that was attached to the zodiac back on the beach.

Pretrick was also pulling upriver and swimming into the current. Although he noticed the current was strongest in the middle, he had spent his childhood swimming in Micronesia. Pretrick had a genetic edge. Behind Lens, Schrage, and Atkins were having the hardest swim. They had been pulled downriver by the current.

Halfway to the island, Schrage and Atkins were both sucked into what Larry Taylor had called a drowning machine. Swept further downstream—only meters but just enough to pull them into the vortex—the last pair of swimmers was fighting a monster.

"I'm not sure I can make this one," Atkins heard Schrage say.

Craig grunted. He couldn't answer. He could hardly breathe.

The current was separating them. They were both bobbing up and down.

"Atkins . . . Atkins . . ." Schrage said.

Thirty meters upstream, Winneshiek was almost at the island. Reeds were right in front of him, about ten feet away. "I'm trying to touch the bottom," he said.

"Okay," Corporal Green, his partner said.

Winneshiek couldn't touch the bottom. He kicked a couple more times. Winneshiek grabbed the reeds. "Green, I got it."

"Green?"

He was gone.

"Green! Green!"

Just then Pretrick swam ashore. "Green?" Winneshiek asked. "No, it's Pretrick."

Winneshiek and Pretrick started looking around, calling Green's name. They looked back across the riverbank and yelled, "We're missing Green!" breaking the tactical silence that had been in place for the past ten minutes.

Pretrick was looking around for Gunny Lens. He had also been right behind him. Where did he go?

Atkins was thrashing against the vortex . . . pulling . . . pulling . . . pulling. He had already tried pulling the lanyard to activate the life vest, but it hadn't worked; something was wrong and he didn't know what or why. He tried to manually inflate his life vest, but he couldn't get a breath. The vortex was winning. Atkins was under the water.

From beneath the surface, Atkins felt something.

A rope.

He snatched it and pulled.

The rope was attached to the zodiac on the beach. Gunny Lens held the other end.

From under the water, Atkins yanked on the rope. A few seconds later, Atkins felt something solid and grabbed it.

His head was finally above water. Panicked, Atkins sucked in air.

Gunny Lens had been moving at a good clip toward the island when suddenly he was yanked back. Somebody had grabbed his leg and pulled him under the water.

"Mother fucker!" the Gunny sputtered. Atkins had dunked him. "Take the fuckin' pack, goddammit." Lens gave the pack to Atkins, who grabbed it, wrapping his arms around the straps, kicking and holding on for his life.

By now, Captain Carlton and the Marines on the riverbank knew something was wrong. Carlton told Lt Matt Brooks and SSgt Kevin Shelton—Atkins's platoon commander and platoon sergeant—to throw tactics out the window. No more raid or ambush or whatever. They launched the zodiac, desperate to find their missing men.

Gunny Lens arrived on the island, next to Pretrick and Winneshiek. "Green?"

"Goddammit, I fuckin' got dunked by Green." Gunny meant to say Atkins. "I gave him my pack. He's still out there."

Floating with the pack, Atkins had made his way to the reeds. He grabbed them. He was exhausted. He looked around and called for Schrage. No answer.

The Marines in the zodiac rowed over to Atkins, pulled him into the boat, rowed to the island beach a few meters away, and dumped him off. Atkins knelt on the beach, retching up the water he had swallowed.

"Where's Schrage?" Winneshiek and Pretrick said. Atkins didn't know. He told them what had happened.

LtCol Paul Kennedy, the battalion commander of the Magnificent Bastards, brought in divers and aircraft. Believing Green and Schrage might have been swept hundreds of meters downriver by the current, they combed the area to their east for two days. Eventually, someone thought of the possibility of a vortex. They started searching closer to the island and found Green facedown in the reeds with a contusion above his left eye. The coroner thought perhaps Green was knocked unconscious.

Schrage was found a day later. He had inflated one side of his life vest, but it still wasn't enough to save him from the vortex. Lieutenant Colonel Kennedy immediately ordered a formal investigation.

But the investigation meant nothing to Atkins. Guilt-ridden and anguished, Cpl Craig Atkins had been forced into a promotion. The good-hearted kid from Dubois County, Indiana, who was the all-American deer hunter with the funny accent had just become 3rd Squad leader. Dustin Schrage—his friend and swim buddy—had drowned right next to him one chaotic night in the River. At that moment, as far as Atkins was concerned, Schrage's death was his fault.

Atkins had always wanted to be a squad leader, to have a dozen men watching him with *that look*, waiting for his orders. But no Marine wants to take over a squad because of a fallen friend. Still, all eyes in Fox 2/4 would be on Corporal Atkins, watching to see if he could handle the pressures and professional responsibilities amidst the tragedies and personal remorse.

CHAPTER 10

Inshallah

It's increasingly becoming a war of
all against all, with no rules.

—*Toby Dodge, author of* Inventing Iraq

Cpl Shady Stevens sat inside the humvee, eyes peeled as he waited for Captain Anderson to finish talking to the hajjis. They were in a village on a ridgeline north of Fallujah. Millions of years ago, that ridgeline had been the edge of the River, which now ran through the southwest corner of the city. Shady was with two lance corporals: radio operator "Kid" Montcalm and his wingman "Sky" Hawthorne. They were watching Captain Anderson as he chatted with a few soldiers from Iraq's latest militia: the Fallujah Brigade.

On May 10, 2004, four days after the bodies of Jeffrey Green and Dustin Schrage were discovered in the Euphrates, Major General Mattis took a convoy with several vehicles from the Thundering Third of 3/4 into the governmental headquarters of Fallujah. Their mission was to drive into Fallujah, meet with city leaders—including General Latif (the new Fallujah Brigade commander), the Gay Mayor, and several town shiekhs—and return the city to their control. They had agreed to form the Fallujah Brigade and police the area. Theoretically, the Iraqi government, in partnership with American forces, would control the Fallujah Brigade. It was like accepting a pledge of chastity from a buxom blonde at the Mustang Ranch brothel.

Before the May 10 convoy, Mad Dog Mattis had visited Kilo 3/4 and Cpl Brian Zmudzinski, who were dug in south of the city as part of the siege/cordon. Major General Mattis was easy to recognize because he was the only Marine wearing a desert-camouflage cap (a "soft cover," in Marine parlance) instead of a helmet. He walked over to a group of his Marines. Zmudzinski was among them.

"Sir, how much longer do you think we'll be here?" a Marine asked Mattis. The tone was informal but respectful.

"Men, I'll tell you the truth," Mattis said. "I have no idea. It could be days. Could be months. Could be years. I really don't have a clue." The general clapped the Marine's shoulder and looked him in the eye. "But the best thing we can to is keep our spirits up and take things one day at a time. The folks back home understand that we've got a tough job to do. They'll support us."

Mattis turned to go. "Keep up the good work, my fine young warriors. You have honored your families, the Corps, and the American people. I am very proud of you."

"Oooh-rah, sir!!"

Mattis could have told his Marines to invade Syria, trudge mindlessly through the desert, or swim the Euphrates carrying a pack of lead weights. They would have done anything for him. As it turned out, Mattis was compelled to order his fine young men to do the one thing none of them wanted to do: give Fallujah back to their enemy.

After the Mattis convoy left the city on May 10, all of Fallujah exploded in a victory celebration. Next to the contemptible Sheikh Janabi, General Latif mingled with jubilant crowds who were chanting and shooting AK-47s into the air. The rumor in Fallujah—sort of a Muj version of the Lance Corporal Network—was "the Marines have surrendered!" The Muj said that Mattis had taken the convoy into the city so he could sign the final documents of American capitulation.

On the outskirts of the city—and not knowing the enemy thought his general had just surrendered—Corporal Zmudzinski had other observations. "I just kept seeing assholes riding around in trucks cheering and firing into the air," Zmudzinski said. "I had no idea what was going on, except that I couldn't do anything about it."

A few weeks after the formation of the Fallujah Brigade, Captain Anderson's convoy traveled to a train station on the northern edge of the city. Although the Fallujah Brigade was independently owned and operated by the Muj, funding for the enterprise, per the CPA/Marine/Iraqi agreement, came directly from the American taxpayer. Vehicles, radios, rifles, and other gear had been issued to the Fallujah Brigade so the Iraqis could "bring law and order" to Fallujah.

The mission of this small convoy that had brought Shady to this village was to pay the soldiers' salaries. The convoy had several stops to make—the train station, a Fallujah Brigade "camp," and a headquarters unit. Each time they went near the Fallujah Brigade, the Marines got the same icy reception.

"Hawthorne, go stand next to the captain and make sure those assholes don't touch him," Shady said. The crowd was mostly teenage punks. They were wearing older Saddam-era uniforms and smoking cigarettes. They sat like schoolgirls, giggling and laughing. One boy had wrapped his arms and legs around his male friend, like a collegiate with his first main squeeze.

Anderson offered his right hand in friendship. They stared back. *La, la.* They waved their hands and shook their heads, smiling, laughing, and pointing to indicate they had no interest in shaking his hand.

As Shady remained perched in the driver's seat of the humvee, Hawthorne had walked over and stood next to Anderson, who was glaring back while offering a false smile. "*Min Fallujah?*" Anderson asked. His pidgin Arabic was improving. *You from Fallujah?*

Hearing Anderson speaking Arabic made some of the teenagers shift to a more respectful posture. The deferential ones replied, "*na'am,*" saying "yes" with a formal word. The cockier kids stared back. "*Eee, eee.*" *Yeah, yeah.*

What's it to you, American dog? The hate in their thoughts could be seen in their eyes.

Shady looked over to Kid. Captain Anderson was in a parking lot a few dozen meters away. The Fallujans were all carrying AK-47s. They didn't have magazines inserted, but Shady didn't know that. They were being extremely casual with the muzzles of their weapons.

"If those fuckers flag the captain again, I'm shooting them," Shady said. Flagging meant pointing a weapon at someone, either accidentally or intentionally.

Shady and Kid aimed their M-16s at the Fallujans, who had turned their back to them. Ever since Anderson had been wounded, Shady had felt protective of him. Anderson was the captain, but he had a way of finding trouble. He was used to being surrounded by grunts and had found himself uncomfortable around most of the other staff officers. He cared little for the illicit creature comforts Shady provided for everyone else. Ironically, this made Shady trust him more. They had become something like friends.

Captain Anderson looked over at Shady and waved him off. He turned back to the Fallujans. *"Inti jundi?"* Are you a private? *"Na'am, na'am."* They had grown deferential. Anderson spoke just enough Arabic to make them think he knew more than he did. It caught them off-guard. They were smiling and gesturing more in conversation, a sign of fear as much as happiness.

Anderson and the convoy moved on. It took about two hours to pay each unit. In the late afternoon, one Fallujah Brigade officer motioned to the Marines. "You had better go," he muttered. A few elements within the Brigade had been whispering about an ambush. Annoyed by the entire charade, the Marines left without paying the last battalion—if there was such a thing as a battalion.

Anderson and Shady agreed that there were many things worth dying and sacrificing for. The Fallujah Brigade did not appear to be one of them.

Throughout the Fallujah attack and siege in April, the MEK had sustained a barrage of mortar and rocket fire. Because of this, May 2004 in Fallujah seemed almost serene. As the pressure remained steady on Ramadi and areas south of Baghdad, the May 10 convoy and the "victory" of the Fallujah Brigade brought the American bases around Fallujah a reprieve from mortar and rocket attacks. Like in Husaybah, the lull did not last for long. Instead of bands and parades, sporadic shelling kicked off Memorial Day weekend at Camp Fallujah.

As the sand and summer heat ruined more computer circuits, Shady spent more of his time on base and less on the road. Less action and more boredom raised the demand for libations. His contraband business was now thriving: more of the good stuff was coming in from the Green Zone, and he still had a steady supply of the cheap hajji whiskey.

Holidays in a war zone like Iraq often meant little private celebrations, like the splitting of MRE pound cake instead of fireworks and barbecues. For many grunts, holidays were nothing special—just another day away from home. Memorial Day 2004 was different: the first USO show to be held at Camp Fallujah was coming to town. The performers had specifically asked to play for the Marines.

Weeks before the attack on Pearl Harbor in 1941, President Franklin D. Roosevelt formed the United Services Organization (USO) to handle the needs of soldiers, sailors, and Marines on leave. Throughout World War II, the USO became the hub of activity for community participation in the war effort. Although technically a private organization, every American president has served as honorary chairman since its inception. Volunteers typically outnumber paid staff twenty to one.

Since the MEF Headquarters Group was responsible for Camp Fallujah logistics, both Shady and Anderson were involved in USO show preparations. In April 2004, Shady had gone from being a computer repairman to provisional combat leader. For the USO show, Shady became a provisional concert sound manager. His job was to convert the base chapel into an auditorium. Captain Anderson was one of several Marines escorting the celebrity entourage. The main guests were Ted Nugent and Toby Keith.

Anderson told Shady that he wasn't particularly impressed by the idea of a has-been 1970s rock star and a country musician grooving into a war zone. The captain shrugged off the rumor that Nugent—known simply as The Nuge—and Keith had specifically asked to do a show for Marines as a demonstration of honor and respect. A natural cynic, he thought the whole thing was a gimmick set up to help their careers. He thought of celebrities as prima donnas, craving the spotlight and the glitter of the red carpet without having any substance of character behind their fame.

Flying in helicopters under cover of night, the USO team was supposed to arrive at Camp Fallujah at 10:15 P.M. Sure enough, a pair of helicopters landed at 10:15, but they were the wrong birds. The VIPs had been delayed, and nobody knew when, or if, they were arriving. One earlier show at another base had already been cancelled, and the USO party was supposed to arrive at their overnight site in Baghdad no later than 11:00.

Anderson figured they wouldn't show up. After all, these guys were celebrities. Certainly their handlers would force them to get their beauty sleep.

Around 11:30, the twenty Marines at the LZ heard the distinctive whirring of inbound helicopters. A pair of Army Blackhawks landed. After the sand settled down, a man wearing baggy trousers, a T-shirt, and a scruffy beard jumped out of the Blackhawk and wandered out in the general direction. Anderson thought it was a contractor or reporter—a celebrity wouldn't just stroll off a helo in a war zone.

The figure approached Anderson and pumped his hand. "Hey, man, I'm Toby Keith."

Keith looked over his shoulder and gave a thumbs-up to the rest of the posse. "We're good!" he called back, giving the hand-and-arm signal for the crowd to follow him out. Rather than being handled, Anderson realized Keith was the driving force in the entire operation. Keith was acting more like a squad leader than a country music star. Anderson was surprised.

The entourage of eight people—musicians, military escorts, and USO staff—moved off the bird and over to the escort party. The Blackhawks flew away. Wearing jeans, a camouflage cowboy hat, and a weird triangular goatee, the Nuge was a little farther back in the crowd, but no less animated in his excitement to be with Marines.

Nugent and Keith began walking about, chatting with their admirers, signing autographs, and backslapping. They smiled for pictures taken from the same cheap disposable cameras the Marines had received months before, when a USO volunteer had handed them a brown zippered bag stuffed with items and stamped with the words Operation Care Package as they walked toward the World Airways jet bound for Iraq.

Once things settled down at the LZ, the Marines loaded up for the drive to the chapel. By this point it was past midnight, but two thousand Marines had packed in for the show. Nugent took a seat in a Humvee next to Anderson.

"Whoo boy! It's been *crazy* today!" the guitarist known as the Motor City Madman said. "We woke up this morning in Afghanistan. Went to Camp Anaconda, Balad . . . maybe some-place else. Only reason I know we're in Fallujah is 'cuz we're with Marines." He looked tired, but wired. "Damn good to be with you folks!"

"You had any food?" Anderson asked.

"Not since noon. Uncle Ted don't get too hungry out here on the road," said the Nuge. "We're too busy." The duo was plan-ning to play the night show, fly to Baghdad, sleep for four hours, and then play two more shows the next day.

Knowing they would be at the chapel in moments, Anderson ripped open a couple of MREs and rifled through them. He grabbed the items that could be eaten quickly—peanut butter, crackers, M&Ms, and Tootsie Rolls—and handed them over to Uncle Ted.

The Nuge was impressed. "Yeah man! Improvise, adapt, and overcome, baby!!" He pointed to his belt for emphasis, "If those raghead fuckers try anything tonight, my Glock is loaded, and I'm ready to rock and roll." The Nuge lowered his voice to a conspiratorial whisper. "Just don't tell the USO staff. I ain't supposed to be packin'."

Anderson raised his eyebrows, appraising the situation. Toby: sober squad leader. Ted: goofy lance corporal. He made a mental note to tackle the Nuge if the base took mortar fire—rock star or not, Marines don't react well when weapons are quickly brandished by civilians.

As the humvees turned onto the main road leading towards the chapel/concert hall, Nugent's door kept slipping ajar. The Nuge fumbled in his pocket, whipped out his Gerber multi-tool, and jimmied with the hinge until it was fixed to his satisfaction.

The humvees arrived at the chapel, and Toby and Ted walked onstage, packing six-string acoustic guitars like six-shooters. Shady had rigged a pair of microphones to a speaker system. That was it. High school garage bands have used better equipment.

It didn't matter. Joking that they were "just like Lennon and McCartney, only with guns," Keith and Nugent played a mix of country and classic rock for an hour and a half nonstop. They hadn't showered in three days. There was no manager, no make-up person, and no costume changes. They were tired, hungry, and dirty. But they appeared to be enjoying every minute of it.

Backstage, Shady heard Anderson strike up a conversation with Sarah Farnsworth, the USO chief of staff who accompanied the troupe. "Are they always like this?"

"Yeah," she said, smiling. "Usually we have to tell them when to leave. They always want to stay longer than we can."

At 1:45 A.M., the entourage returned to the LZ. As the Black-hawks landed, Keith and the Nuge offered a final round of hand-shakes amidst the wind, noise, and dust.

"Was it what you expected?" Shady asked his captain.

Anderson smirked. Shady knew of his earlier sarcasm. "Those guys earned my respect," he admitted.*

"Mine, too," Shady said, looking out towards the empty LZ. Respect meant as much as friendship in combat, sometimes more so. Especially from leader to led, and vice versa. Shady knew his captain respected and trusted him, which was why he was careful not to say anything about his business.

Shady's ambition and devotion to his black market enterprise would eventually cost him the things he valued most.

Cpl Craig Atkins pulled his laundry out of the hajji washing machine and walked out to the clothesline. The hajji washing machine was an oversize plastic container with an electric-pow-ered fin attached inside. Marines filled buckets of water, dumped them into the machine, and turned it on. If the Marines wanted a rinse cycle, they had to dump in another bucket of water. Usu-ally the men just took the detergent-filled clothes out to the line

---

* At the time, neither Anderson nor Shady knew that Ted Nugent had avoided the draft during Vietnam. In a July 15, 1990, interview for the *Detroit Free Press*, he claimed that thirty days before his physical, he stopped all forms of personal hygiene, that in the last ten days he ate nothing but junk food, and that a week before he stopped using the bathroom altogether. This left his pants caked with excrement and urine. That spectacle, Nugent said, won him a draft deferment.

and placed them out in the heat to dry, leaving them with soapy stains on their otherwise-clean garments.

Lost in his own reverie, Atkins hung out a pair of desert cammies, a green T-shirt, a brown towel, and a bunch of white socks. The trousers still smelled like the Euphrates. Of course that scent brought everything back. Atkins was more comfortable planning or executing a patrol . . . that was the only time he stopped thinking about it. The guilt never really left.

Sometimes the dreams were good times and memories, he and Schrage laughing about guns or girls. Schrage the City Boy, Atkins the Country Hick. Sometimes he woke up thinking he couldn't breathe. The water was in his mind, but not around him. Sometimes he just woke up scared, flinching involuntarily from imagined or real explosions.

"Need a hand?" LCpl Justin Oliver asked. Oliver, a SAW gunner in the squad, was becoming one of his go-to guys, just like Atkins had been for Schrage.

"Nah, I'm good. Just gettin' a load o' wash clean n' done before we go out tonight." Craig grabbed a pair of clothespins and stuck a white sock next to a green Under-Armour T-shirt.*

The Marines had adjusted quickly to Cpl Craig Atkins. He was different from Dustin Schrage—not better or worse, just different. Even out on patrol, Schrage was usually a jokester. Atkins was intense and serious. He rarely lightened up.

"The Cigarette Girl's here," Oliver said. "You gonna buy anything?" Oliver bought town goods from the Cigarette Girl on occasion. All the Marines liked the *hubbous* flatbread, which they sometimes bought or had given to them on patrol by a local in a generous mood.

---

* Made from a sweat-wicking polypropylene that helped keep Marines cool, Under-Armour T-shirts were extremely popular in Iraq as field replacements for the standard green T-shirt.

"Nah. Don't think so." Atkins was truculent.

Cigarette Girl walked up to the pair. She was ten years old, four feet tall, with black hair, black eyes, and tanned skin. She wore a T-shirt and jeans. Her limited knowledge of English had come from lessons courtesy of Fox 2/4.

"*Shaku maku,*" Oliver said.

"Hey. You want the bullshit?" Cigarette Girl asked. She had a bag with cigarettes, lighters, and generic Arabic cans of diet cola. The Cigarette Girl could get anything the Marines wanted— food, drinks, or even hajji whiskey—out in town. The senior enlisted Marines at the Snake Pit had a soft spot for children and thought it would be a nice gesture to let her on base. Meanwhile, her parents used her as a proxy to run their own contraband operation.

"*La, la. Shukran.*" Oliver said.

"Please?" Cigarette Girl stopped, giving her best little-princess smile. "The bullshit!" She held up her bag of trophies. Cigarette Girl could have sold ice to Eskimos.

"*La, la.* Go see Mister Richardson." Oliver pointed over towards the gym where another corporal was working out.

"Fuck." Cigarette Girl kicked the dirt and turned her back, walking towards the gym. "Richardson?" she said, smiling and pointing.

The Marines nodded.

"Okay. See you later." Cigarette Girl waved goodbye, innocently chirping with profanity.

Not long after the concert, Shady was up late on a sweltering night, finishing up a cigarette in the smoke pit, the hub of Network life. A mile toward the southern end of Camp Fallujah, an acrid pile of white was rising from the trash pit, where the refuse—like the burn shitters—was disposed of in a homemade bonfire twice each day. Nearby, a cacophony of other headquarters Marines were playing an enthusiastic game of "beach" volleyball. A radio blared.

In the moonlight, refracted from the shadows of the burning trash and volleyball game, Shady saw the silhouettes of four girls sitting on the curb smoking cigarettes. Fatima was there, a *hijab-*covered Iraqi beauty of twenty. Along with the other girls, she worked as a translator for Americans in Iraq.

The oldest of three sisters, Fatima oozed an alluring blend of innocence and insouciance. Her father had been a soldier under Saddam during the Iran-Iraq War, and her mother had been a biologist in Basrah before her marriage. Having learned English from watching movie subtitles, she volunteered for a job as a translator after the American occupation began.

In early 2004, Fatima found work at Camp Fallujah with Titan Corporation, a San Diego–based defense contractor the Pentagon hired to provide linguists. Her Sunni father said she was a foolish girl, but her Shiite mother gave full permission. Fatima hoped to use her job with Titan as a springboard to navigate her way to America. She conspired to forge her father's signature if he would not sign the papers. Grudgingly, he agreed.

As they chatted, Shady became intrigued with her questions and answers. Childlike naïveté mixed easily with resigned acceptance of reality.

"I don't fear the guns, the bombs, the missiles, or the terrorists," Fatima said. "I don't even fear my father. Everyone in my family thinks I'm crazy, but I only fear what would happen if I never took a chance at having my dreams come true."

Shady nodded quietly. In many ways, Fatima was twenty going on fourteen. As they smoked and talked, Shady heard *booms* off in the distance. He absent-mindedly wondered if the rounds were incoming or outgoing; they were well outside the compound, and not loud enough for him to care one way or another. The volley-ball game continued. It was a normal night at Camp Fallujah.

"Did they make you join the Marines?" Fatima asked.

"No. I left, then I volunteered to come back in."

This shocked Fatima. "You mean they didn't make you come over here?"

"Well . . . yes and no." Shady told Fatima his story.

Why, she asked, wide-eyed, did you come back in after you had left?

How do I explain this? Shady thought. *How do I explain that I came because I wanted to help . . . I wanted to serve . . . I wanted to defend freedom?* He tried to tell her how he had grown to care very much for other Marines.

"There are good people and bad people in the military, just like everywhere else." Shady explained that, despite his illegal business, he considered himself one of the good guys. He felt like he had a responsibility to do something when his country was at war.

Fatima gave him an odd look that said, "Why did you leave your family to come to Fallujah?" For her, family and tribe were everything. It was only for the hope of a better life that she had left them, and Shady's life in America had obviously been much better than Iraq.

"I'm not much different than you," Shady explained. "The Marines are like family to me. They are my tribe. No matter what I do, wherever I go, I will always be a Marine. And if Marines are in trouble, I will want to be there with them. That's just the way it is."

She asked Shady if he planned to stay in the Marines after his contract was done. He told her he wasn't sure yet. He had just been offered a chance to extend his tour in Iraq. He was thinking about doing it. He made good money with the tax-free salary. Plus . . . he liked it. Being there made him feel like he was actually doing something with his life, contributing to something bigger than himself instead of living the rat race, scrounging for a buck.

Fatima was completely dumbstruck. "Why would you volunteer again for something like this?"

Her interrogation became merciless. "Aren't all these years of wearing the same clothes every day and following the same orders and routine enough for you? You should go back to America! Find a wife! Have a home! Make a family! Why can you not return to your country and help in some other way? Have you not done enough fighting?"

Shady mumbled pithy answers about somebody needing to fight the terrorists, but his mind was elsewhere. *Perhaps hers are the feelings of a girl who has seen too many people die,* Shady thought, trying not to think about the way he had alienated his ex-wife.

Fatima stared back at him, angry that he didn't have enough good sense to return to his beautiful homeland. How could he run away from America and leave such a wonderful place? She was happy that Shady—and the Marine Corps he represented—came and freed her from a dictator's tyranny, but unhappy that he was unable to leave it all and go back to his home.

"You know, I danced and sang when I heard the sound of bombs and planes in March 2003," Fatima said, "but I still want you to go back home. Not for my sake, but for yours. Go back to America. You deserve it."

Shady couldn't help but wonder if she would be disappointed if she ever arrived in Washington, D.C., or Kennedy International Airport. Would she be able to handle her freedom, or would the same material trappings of most Americans enslave her? Would she groan under the pain of absence from family and familiar cultural surroundings? Would her liberty be mortgaged to a low-paying job or an oppressive husband?

The volleyball game had ended, and with it the late summer recreation. Other than goodnight, little remained to be said. Shady walked away, confused by Fatima's support for his nation and simultaneous disapproval for his own willingness to take personal risk. Despite all of her life's struggle and pain, Shady couldn't help thinkng of her as a grown-up little girl.

"I know my rights! This is abuse! I will not go on any more patrols if you keep treating me this way!" H-Money bellowed to Capt Jason Smith, company commander, Bravo 1/5. "You send me on patrol all day while the other Iraqis stay at the MEK and do nothing. This is not acceptable."

"Calm down," Smith said. Lt Stephen Lewis stood behind him, arms folded.

"I want to go back to the MEK," H-Money replied. "No more patrols."

The Iraqi translator, a short, baby-faced Iraqi in his late teens whose Arabic name of Haeder (which means "lion") had been shortened to H-Money by Bravo Company, was in no mood to calm down. As one of Bravo's two Iraqi Arabic translators, H-Money was a scarce and valuable commodity. So valuable that he was averaging two eight-hour patrols a day in the city of Karmah, the town northeast of Fallujah where Cpl Brian Zmudzinski and Kilo 3/4 had destroyed the mosque and killed dozens of fighters/martyrs/angry residents during the battle in April.

After Fallujah was given back to the Mujahideen, Bravo 1/5 withdrew from the city and settled into a more normal routine.

They pitched camp at an Iraqi schoolhouse in Karmah and rotated Marines through patrols in the city. They taped up posters, passed out soccer balls, waved to kids, and painted over anti-American graffiti. Occasionally, if they had good intelligence, they raided homes and arrested potential enemies. They found weapons caches and took down IED manufacturers. H-Money was present for it all. H-Money was getting sick of it.

"This wasn't what I signed up for," H-Money said. "I volunteered to serve the new Iraq, not to be treated like a dog."

Smith had had enough of the tantrum. "Listen, I don't care what kind of deal the folks at Titan offered you. You're with us now. Lieutenant Lewis needs you for this patrol. I need you to do it." Smith paused. "I'll give you a day off tomorrow."

Like a slave who had finally vented his spleen, H-Money, whose young body was scarred with torture marks from Saddam Hussein's reign of terror, moved from sullen to ambivalent. He shrugged. "Okay, captain." It was obvious to Smith that H-Money didn't believe he would actually get a day off.

Lewis and H-Money left and went on patrol. That evening, H-Money came back and talked to Ahmed, the other translator. A Marine knocked on Smith's door. "Sir, H-Money wants to see you."

Smith walked outside. "I apologize for my anger," H-Money said. "I was upset and tired. I do not want to leave Bravo Company."

"No problem," Smith said. It wasn't as if he had never seen a guy get upset. "We really do appreciate what you do for us."

"Than why do we not have the ID cards yet?" H-Money asked. It was a respectful and legitimate question. ID cards carried weight. They meant access through checkpoints and conferred status, both on American bases and out in town. With translators and contracted Iraqis killed at three times the rate of American soldiers and Marines, H-Money and Ahmed knew the risks of aligning with the Americans. It was only fair, H-Money thought, that they should have the privileges they had earned.

Smith nodded. "I'll take care of that," he said. "Go enjoy your day off."

H-Money brightened. Here, for the first time in as long as he could remember, was a man who actually kept his word. Perhaps he could trust the Americans after all.

CHAPTER 11

Social Energy

You cannot exaggerate about the Marines.
They are convinced to the point of arrogance that they
are the most ferocious fighters on earth. And the
amusing thing about it is that they are.

—*Father Kevin Keaney, Chaplain,*
1st Marine Division, Korean War

"C'mon, corporal. Have a smoke," Ahmed said as they walked down the streets of Shahabi, a village east of Fallujah, north of Camp Fallujah and south of Karmah. The mustached Iraqi grinned while offering Howell a pack of British cigarettes.

Howell hesitated. Dirty Steve notwithstanding, cigarettes were typically a no-go on patrol. But Howell knew most Iraqi men smoked, and it would look good to the natives who were watching his reaction. He took a cigarette and lit it, reflecting on the irony of his Iraqi interpreter handing him a British smoke as he stood on a street on Mesopotamia.

Ahmed grinned as they shuffled along, his hand brushing past the forged ID card that sat in his wallet as he pocketed the cigarettes. At Captain Smith's orders, the Marines of Bravo had used digital photography, an English-Arabic computer program, and laminating paper to manufacture a pair of "official" identifications for Ahmed and H-Money. They were as authentic as any other ID cards being made for Iraqis, and the gesture had satisfied the terps.

But in Fallujah, the stalemate was taking a toll on the spirits of the Marines. The Fallujah Brigade openly mocked the authority of American forces by turning the city into a Mujahideen sanctuary. Marines referred to their episodic patrols into Fallujah, which were supposed to act as a "proof of concept" for the Brigade's effectiveness, as a "spoof of concept." The scorching summer heat increased the inverse effect on morale; in addition to the enemy, many grunts battled their own discouragement and psychological malaise.

Since the Fallujah Brigade experiment could not be easily undone—it would take the Second Battle of Fallujah in November 2004 to actually "disband" the unit—the Marines decided to continue the patrolling effort on the outskirts of the city. This included the town of Karmah and the nearby village of Shahabi, where Cpl Jason Howell and Bravo 1/5 continued to maintain their presence at the former UN compound.

While Cpl Shady Stevens was playing sound manager for Ted Nugent and Toby Keith, the grunts of Bravo 1/5 were bouncing back and forth from one job to another. They were on high alert and then off again, which kept them awake at all hours. Tired and disgruntled, Corporal Howell had seen little action since April. His only highlight was that the static routine allowed for more frequent *Maxim*-accompanied visits to the Port-a-John.

Howell finished both the patrol and the cigarette without incident. He had been busy with the new Iraqi Civil Defense Corps—also called the Iraqi National Guard, the New Iraqi Army, and finally the Iraqi Security Forces. Headquarters in Baghdad kept changing the acronyms and, like Depression-era US government programs, the Marines lost track of the alphabet soup of names that uniformed Iraqis were supposed to be called. Despite the myriad of monikers, grunts continued to refer to them as the ICDC, a catchall term that represented individuals whose loyalty to American forces was somewhere between that of the Shahwanis and the Fallujah Brigade.*

In addition to training the ICDC, Bravo began working more closely with 1/5's intelligence assets. Human intelligence Exploitation Teams, or HET, were important for American infantry forces in Iraq. A distilled version of HET's job is to recruit local spies, pump them for information, determine if it is useful, and then pass it on to commanders. In Iraq, the HET groups became the grunt-level counterintelligence operators.

After the battle of Fallujah had ended in stalemate, both infantry battalions and HET had turned their attention from Fallujah to the fence-sitters in the surrounding villages. In late May, after learning that the residents of Karmah were offended by their presence at the schoolhouse, Bravo Company moved to an abandoned UN Oil-for-Food building in the village of Shahabi. Captain Smith suspected—and the HET Marines confirmed—many of their sources were also Mujahideen moles. Additionally, the moles were moonlighting as Iraqi Civil Defense Corps employees.

On June 7, Bravo made their move. They raided several houses near the police station in Karmah, arresting several Iraqis-turned-Muj. The afternoon of June 8, while Howell's squad was standing guard in Shahabi, the Muj coordinated an attack on the police station. Although the prisoners had already been sent back to a different American detention facility, the Muj thought they would be able to rescue their captured comrades.

---

* A few months later, the new catchall term became the Iraqi Security Forces (ISF).

The good news was that the ICDC had, for the time being, sided with the Marines. In contrast to Husaybah, the Marine training in Shahabi appeared to have taken root. Inspired by a mixture of loyalty, nationalism, and fear—not unlike the Marines who had trained them—the Iraqis at the police station were fighting alongside the Americans.

Because 1st Platoon was the quick reaction force for Bravo, they were immediately ordered to the scene when fighting happened at the police station. Along with his platoon sergeant, Staff Sergeant Campbell, Corporal Howell's squad piled into humvees and drove north, heading from Shahabi to Karmah. As they headed out, they heard a steady stream of AK-47 and RPG fire.

Howell's adrenaline rose. Days before, children had been smiling on the streets in the city, running up to him as if he was their hero. He felt protective of this town and angry at whoever was invading it. Even during the chaos of Fallujah, Howell hadn't had the personal experience of looking through his sights and having a confirmed enemy kill in combat. He still wanted it. Fiercely. Howell would soon get his chance.

What Corporal Howell later learned, based on the identities of the men they fought in Karmah, was that the Muj had came from their sanctuary in Fallujah on June 8 when they were attacking the police station to rescue their comrades. At the time, Howell didn't know where they had come from or why they were attacking. And he didn't care. Those abstract details didn't matter to him.

Additionally, Howell was lost. In the rush to deploy and defend the police station, both Howell and his platoon sergeant, Staff Sergeant Campbell, had left their maps sitting next to their gear. The pair kept driving the humvees down and back narrow streets, threading and careening closer to gunfire while trying to find a parallel road to switch back to the police station.

"Turn here at Route Bethsheba! This is the intersection we want! Take a left!" Howell and Campbell yelled and gestured over the noise of humvee engines and gunfire like a pair of fraternity brothers taking a wacky out-of-state road trip.

Making the turn was a good call on Howell's part. One intersection ahead was the police station, where Marines, Iraqis, and Muj were engaging in chaotic building-to-building combat. They had almost driven into the firefight—a bad place to make a wrong turn.

The pair of humvees pulled into an intersection of alleys two blocks southwest of the police station to plan their next move. Staff Sergeant Campbell's front humvee found what they thought was a covered position, but Howell's rear humvee was stuck in the intersection and exposed.

"Pull forward, goddammit!" Howell's vehicle was ramming the humvee ahead of him like a bumper car. Rounds snapped and whizzed around them; they still couldn't tell from where.

Ever the man of action, LCpl Dirty Steve Nunnery came on the radio. "Corporal, I'm taking my fire team, clearing out this building, and finding some high ground." He dismounted the humvees, developed a plan, assembled his men, briefed his boss, and moved into action. This took Dirty Steve six seconds.

Dirty Steve ran over to the house, broke a window—cutting his hand in the process—smashed a hole, and dove through it. His fire team followed him into the house and onto the roof, which they hoped would have the standard four-foot wall. In happier days, this made for a pleasant veranda in the cool hours of the morning and evening. Marines and Muj alike used the roof walls for cover and observation.

Unfortunately, this roof had no perimeter wall. With Campbell outside in the humvee trying to raise Lieutenant Lewis on the radio, Dirty Steve's team ran out of the one house and found another one to clear.

Howell decided the alley was 2nd Squad's key terrain. He wanted to keep control of this narrow road, which intersected several other avenues of approach, and then use them as a foothold to push toward the Muj flank. Howell told one fire team to secure the intersections while Dirty Steve's team started clearing the rest of the houses in the street.

In the second house, Howell found something suspicious. One Iraqi man was standing in a room. He was about thirty years old, with weathered skin, hollow eyes, and a black mustache. Nobody else was in any of the houses. In fact, nobody else appeared to be in the city. Except for this one Iraqi man. It didn't feel right.

They put the man on his knees. Nobody else was there. Campbell was back at his humvee on the radio. Howell was in the courtyard of the house. The prisoner was Howell's to interrogate.

"You're Mujahideen, aren't you, fucker?" Howell said.

"No, mistah," the man replied.

"Don't lie to me, you sonofabitch!" Howell screamed, putting his face within inches of the man, drill instructor–style, "I know who you are, fucking Muj!"

"No, mistah! No, mistah!" The man's eyes widened as his voice trembled.

"STOP LYING TO ME!" Howell's veins bulged as he moved his head back and forth. "YOU THINK I'M STUPID?"

Thud. The man recoiled back. As his body had moved rhythmically with his screaming, Howell had accidentally banged his Kevlar helmet into the man's face. Surprised, Howell paused.

"Whoa! Hey, corporal, chill out!" Doc Perkins piped up. "Stay cool." He grabbed Howell and pulled him back. Quickly, Perkins examined the Iraqi and slapped a Band-Aid over the cut.

In the small room, the men in Howell's squad looked around at each other. Wordlessly, they all came to several conclusions. First, any further interrogation would be ineffective without their translators. Second, Howell, while going too far with his screaming and head butting, had good combat instincts. This man probably knew things they wanted to know. Third, they needed somebody of higher rank to get the information out of him.

Crack. Howell spun around.

Private First Class Oswalt, whom Howell called, "a shitty Marine in general but amazing in combat," had spotted a Muj running through a side street on the other side of the alley. Oswalt had raised his M-16 to his eye and fired one shot, hitting the Muj in the head. The enemy combatant collapsed behind the building he had been running toward for cover, leaving only his foot exposed.

"Got him, Corporal Howell." Oswalt announced.

"Are you sure?" Howell raised his M-16 and looked through his ACOG at the man's foot. It wasn't moving at all. Not even a post-mortem twitch. Just to be certain, Howell fired twice into his foot. Nothing happened.

"Yeah. You got him, Oswalt."

"Hey, Howell," Staff Sergeant Campbell shouted up into the building, "You got a GPS? I'm trying to call in some support."

Why is this guy on the radio bugging me with this kind of crap while I'm busy leading Marines?

Soon, Howell got his answer. The 1/5 quick reaction force—the same cavalry that had showed up for 2nd Platoon on April 13—arrived within minutes. Accompanying them was Lieutenant Lewis and Cpl Bob Dawson's 3rd Squad.

Howell was just happy to see Dawson. After the mess they had gone through in Fallujah, they both felt better whenever their two squads were working together. Just like the battle of Fallujah, 2nd and 3rd Squads from 1st Platoon happened to be simultaneously in the fight. 1st Squad was on post.

Lewis walked up to Howell. "Corporal, what's going on?"

As Howell briefed Lewis and Dawson, he made a small mental note that stuck with him for a long time. The lieutenant came to him first instead of the platoon sergeant for the explanation. It was a little thing, but it showed that Lewis trusted his judgment. That meant something to Howell.

The corporal handed his canteen to Lewis and gestured towards his empty green CamelBak water pouch. "Sir, could you fill me up?"

Without hesitation, the platoon commander took Howell's canteen and dumped the water into his CamelBak.

1st Platoon was starting to develop social energy.

A man once asked Col Clarke Lethin—a wiry, taciturn officer with black and gray hair who served on Major General Mattis's staff in three combat zones—what his biggest personal contribution was to the post–9/11 global war on terror. "I provided the social energy necessary to keep the cogs moving," Lethin replied.

Social energy? What is that? It is something closely akin to spiritual power, the power that, according to Mattis's favorite saying from Gen. George Marshall, is essential to win wars. To the men of Mattis's staff, social energy was the practical employment of spiritual power. "Spiritual power includes the connection to things larger than ourselves, the feeling and bond warriors have for each other, and the strength to handle any reality," Mattis said. "But social energy is the building of trust and confidence that reduces friction in the heat of battle." Social energy, when established, helps to make the difficult easy.

It's been called different names throughout history. Businessmen have called it synergy. The Chinese once referred to it as "gung-ho," a phrase that means "all together." The French phrase was esprit de corps, which literally is "the spirit of the body [the Corps]." Esprit de corps, however, was rarely mentioned in Iraq—French phrases were not en vogue at that time and place in the American military.

"The combination and focused direction of social energy and spiritual power makes a military organization so tight, all the commander has to do is point his unit in the right direction and tell them what they already know," Mattis said. "Social energy is the framework through which spiritual power flows. Social energy is the pipes and hoses. Spiritual power is the fuel."

By this, Mattis does not mean a specific religion, or even an abstraction like "morale." Spiritual power is the unbreakable commitment of a group of warriors, both to each other and to the mission they've been assigned. This phenomenon of spiritual power often happened around Mattis himself, within the small platoon of men he called his Jump CP.

The Jump CP's mission was to provide Mattis with security, communications, and information capabilities while he traveled around Iraq. Commanded by GySgt David Beall, the Jump CP moved quickly—often on extremely short notice—to whatever place Mattis wanted to go. The Jump CP often got into fights with the Muj; of the twenty-nine men who manned the handful of vehicles, seventeen were killed or wounded.

In April, after the first time Mattis's Jump CP was hit, the general called Father Bill Devine and asked him to be present when the men returned to Blue Diamond. "Everywhere Father Devine went, the Marines felt better about both themselves and their mission," Mattis said. "He was a good listener, but not a crutch. He helped the young men find the power inside themselves."

Devine did as ordered, proffering handshakes, hugs, and words of encouragement to the tired and bloodied. As he was talking to the Marines, Father Devine watched Mad Dog Mattis walk back to his office alone. *Who's going to take care of him?* Devine thought. Mattis had charged his chaplain with maintaining the division's spiritual power. Devine wouldn't be doing his job unless he also ensured his boss's spirit was strong.

Later that evening, Devine rapped on Mattis's door and cracked it open. "Busy tonight, general?" Devine asked with his Boston accent.

"Hey, Bill, come on in." Mattis had been reading a book. The general fixed his chaplain with the same quiet stare he offered to his men. "How are the Marines doing?"

"They're doing fine, sir. How are you doing?" Devine pulled up a seat. The pair talked for about half an hour. "I could see strength in his eyes," Devine said, "but also the pain of the loss." He later learned Mattis had personally written award citations that same night for the men who had earned them.

In June, around the time Howell and Bravo 1/5 surged into Shahabi, Mattis's Jump CP was on a road driving west from Fallujah to Ramadi. A convoy of Army MPs was moving in the opposite direction. As the two convoys passed, the Muj detonated a car bomb, killing and wounding men from both convoys. While tending to their own casualties, Mattis's men quickly oriented their focus onto the enemy. The Army MPs followed in trace, and together, two units who had never even seen each other hunted down and killed the Mujahideen who had exploded the bombs.

After the second attack, Mattis gathered his Jump CP. He told them that he understood he placed their lives at greater risk because of his frequent trips throughout western Iraq. He implied that perhaps the enemy had learned what his convoy looked like and was targeting him directly for assassination. He offered them the opportunity to be assigned to another unit. "It won't affect my esteem of you at all. There would be no loss of manhood in my eyes."

Not a single Marine accepted his offer.

In a back alley of Karmah, Corporal Howell was dueling for his life.

Twenty feet away from him, a Muj with an AK-47 kept popping back and forth behind a corner and shooting a burst. He was shooting directly at Howell. And, every time the Muj exposed himself, Howell was firing at him. It was visceral and personal.

As they exchanged volleys, Howell realized that he had been taking cover behind an empty, rusted trashcan. Five feet away was the armored humvee that he had rammed earlier like a bumper car. Howell had gotten so absorbed in the hunt for the kill that he hadn't even noticed it. He moved over to the humvee and opened the door for cover.

Howell felt a jab of pain in his right forearm. He stopped, looked, and found no blood or evidence of a wound. His adrenaline pumping, Howell went back to firing at the Muj, who eventually disengaged and disappeared.

Further down the alley, a white pickup was driving towards Howell. Two men were inside.

"Sir, I've got a white pickup at two hundred meters headed this way," Howell yelled to Lewis.

Where rules of engagement were concerned, white pickups with Iraqi men inside in the middle of a firefight represented a gray area. Technically, they weren't shooting at him. However, in all likelihood, they represented a threat. Again, Howell intuitively sensed that something was off.

Lewis didn't even hesitate. "Light him up!"

Along with two other Marines from his squad, Howell pumped a steady stream of rounds into the truck, killing one man and wounding his partner. Lewis called a cease-fire while another squad of Marines flanked the truck and captured the wounded Muj, speeding him back to the rear for HET to interrogate. The Marines searched the truck and found several RPGs and AK-47s, confirming Howell's instincts.

Lewis looked over at Howell. "There's some traffic on the radio about a lost fire team near this alley."

"You're kidding, right, sir?" Howell had a good idea of where all the Marines were, including those a hundred meters away. He didn't know what unit they were from, but he knew they were Marines. They didn't appear lost.

Lewis thrust the green handset inside his Kevlar to check. "They're stranded somewhere. Go search a couple of blocks with a fire team and come back."

"Aye, aye, sir." Howell had no problem with Commander's Intent. He was happier doing his own thing. Additionally, it was obvious that his squad was having a good day. If he were a basketball player, Howell would have said he was "in the zone."

Howell and three other Marines moved out to a parallel alley in a staggered and dispersed column on opposite sides of the wall. Further down the alley, a man got into another white truck. The vehicle started revving forward Dukes-of-Hazzard style, tires squealing. A mortar system was next to the truck.

This is it.

Howell raised his weapon. He notched the infrared laser chevron that appeared in the center of his ACOG reticle onto the back of the man's head.

Steady.

He took a deep breath. And released it.

"What do we do, corporal?" a Marine with a SAW asked.

Steady.

Howell heard his SAW gunner, LCpl Jeff Elkin, but wasn't paying attention.

Crack.

Howell's first shot hit the mark. Two feet away, Elkin opened up with his SAW, and the other Marines peppered the truck with bullets.

Convinced the man was dead, Howell and the Marines stopped shooting and ran up to the truck. When they ran up to the man, his body was twitching, as if he were receiving an electric shock.

"What the fuck?" Howell shot him eight more times before his body stopped moving.

Concerned about the possibility of a suicide car bomb, the Marines checked for wires running to other parts of the vehicle. Finding no wires, they spotted a white bag with a powdery substance. The man had been strung out on opium, heroin, or cocaine while mortaring the Marines. Howell never found out exactly which drug the men had been using to get high. Throughout Fallujah, the Muj had been found with all of them.

The Marines grabbed the mortar system and ran their hands inside the tube. It was warm, and they could feel the residue of fresh powder. Howell had killed a man who had just been dropping mortars onto other Marines. He was beyond ecstatic.

Howell ran back to Lewis and told him what happened. "Good work." Lewis called a quick meeting with Staff Sergeant Campbell, Corporal Dawson, and Howell. To their frustration, 1st Squad had remained on post. "We're sweeping through Karmah," Lewis said.

Out of breath and still fired up with adrenaline from the kill, Howell didn't hear exactly what Lewis was saying. Something about sweeping through Karmah. Suddenly, Lewis and Campbell took off with Dawson's squad.

Also standing in the house were the HET Marines and their two prisoners—the wounded man from the truck and the thirty-year-old Howell had head-butted. "Can you give us a Marine to help with security?" they asked.

Howell looked around at his squad. Other than Dirty Steve, whom Howell needed, there was only one man he completely trusted to act independently. He turned to Doc Perkins. "I need you to stay and do this," Howell said.

"What?"

"Just make it happen," Howell said as he ran off. Confused and somewhat frustrated, Doc Perkins—battlefield medic—grabbed one of the captured Iraqi AK-47s and posted security for HET as they interrogated the prisoners.

As Howell ran to catch up with the platoon, the battery in his radio ran out. Having lost communications, he looked around for other Marines and found none. He vaguely remembered the general plan was to sweep from east to west. Howell and his squad were on their own.

While chaos unfolded around them, social energy and good training formed a powerful combination in Howell's 2nd Squad.

They cleared out buildings on instinct, reacting as if they were all different parts of the same mind. When women and children peered out of their windows, the Marines lowered their weapons, took off their Wiley-X sunglasses and called out. *"Awghf! Stop!"* They gestured and pointed, ushering them to safety.

At one point, the Marines spotted five Iraqi males standing in a building. Although they appeared to be harmless, Howell's squad flex-cuffed the men and searched the area. After finding nothing, they cut the men loose, shook hands with them Iraqi-style (mild handshake followed by touching of the heart) and let them go. All this happened with no commands. The men just did it.

Running ahead, Howell saw some Marines from another company. A squad from Charlie 1/5, along with their platoon commander, had been training the ICDC for several months. They had gotten caught up in repelling the attack. Howell had never seen them before. One was sitting on a humvee, bleeding. "Watch out for the fuckers on the roof with grenades," he yelled.

"What are your current ROEs?" Howell yelled back, stopping. Rules of engagement, or ROEs, always seemed to be changing. When attacks were rare, they were restrictive. When the shooting was heavy, some of the Marines tossed the ROEs out the window.

"If it's an Iraqi male, he dies," the Marine from Charlie Company said.

Howell could see the man was exhausted and pissed off. Still, he was proud that his squad had not lost their bearing and humanity. With Spartan discipline, they had killed all the right people and, in their best judgment, not killed any innocents. Howell had taught his men to be discriminating when they pulled the trigger. As much as he had thrilled for his own kill, he knew that the shot was fully justified. Howell had killed an enemy combatant out of devotion to duty, not a random hajji out of vengeance or bloodlust.

Howell and the squad continued running west through Karmah. Just then, Lance Corporal Henderson, a Marine in Corporal Dawson's squad who happened to be driving an Iraqi car, came careening down the street in an Opel sedan he had commandeered. Also in the car were two Iraqi men, a Navy corpsman and a wounded child. The corpsman was treating the child.

Howell and the squad reached the end of the city and found the rest of the platoon scattered near a checkpoint. He posted his squad and ran over to Cpl Bob Dawson, who was relaxing and drinking an ice-cold Iraqi 7-Up that he had just bought from a hajji soda merchant.

"Gimme some, fucker," Howell greeted his best friend in the platoon.

"Anytime," Dawson smiled. Howell gulped the soda.

As the corporals swapped stories, Lewis called a leader's meeting. Everyone was accounted for. The police station had been defended. A large number of Muj had been killed or captured. As the conference ended, several helicopters flew low into the town.

Immediately, scenes from another movie flashed into Howell's head. *Apocalypse Now.* "Walking away from that meeting and seeing the door gunners standing there . . . the propellers thumping . . . hearing the roar of the engines . . . the whole thing was like being in a Vietnam movie," Howell said. "I felt like I controlled the world. I can definitely see how people get addicted to combat. I'll never forget that feeling of power and invincibility."

As soon as air support arrived, the Muj hunkered down. With the town quiet, 1st Platoon patrolled back through the streets they had just sprinted through. Lewis had wanted them to collect all the dead bodies and check them for intelligence. Half of the bodies were already gone. A combination of Islamic tradition—which required burial of the deceased before sunset—and Mujahideen tactics prevented them from collecting most of the dead. "We would walk by and see a fresh bloodstain where a body had been two hours before," Howell said.

Additionally, children were playing in the streets. "It was surreal," Howell said. "An hour before, we were running through, ready to shoot anything. Now kids were waving. Little boys and girls were smiling, giving us the thumbs-up, begging for water or food. They were acting as if nothing had happened.

"We all almost lost it," Howell said. "It was like we had tripped into some alternate reality."

After the psychological jarring from combat to eight-year-old girls giving them the thumbs-up, Howell's squad went back to the house where Doc Perkins, with his AK-47, was waiting for them. They found two dead Mujahideen—including Oswalt's kill on the street—and took their bodies so they could check their fingerprints against other known records. They found numerous weapons stockpiles and took them all.

"We felt like we did something that day," Howell said. "We killed some people and took some weapons off the street and the townspeople thanked us. I couldn't have been any prouder of those men in my squad. They did everything exactly as they had been trained."

Howell went back to the 1/5 headquarters. Several officers interviewed him, asking him to explain why he had shot the men he did. They filled out some paperwork. After that happened, Howell reloaded his magazines. Then he and his squad went back to the warehouse and stood a four-hour shift of guard duty.

One week later, Howell accidentally scraped his right forearm against a wall. He felt something inside it, like a sliver or a scab. He squeezed at the scrape. A sore Howell had not noticed before popped open. Pus, blood, and a small chunk of metal spurted out. The metal was a bullet fragment. Howell had picked it up during his firefight by the empty trashcan. The heat of the shrapnel had cauterized the wound when the fragment entered Howell's arm.

Cpl Jason Howell never said anything to his chain of command about his wound. He didn't want his guys to think he was trying to scam a Purple Heart. Even though he was entitled to the award, he thought his reputation mattered more to his squad's combat effectiveness than his receipt of the medal.

A greedy squad leader on a medal hunt would destroy social energy.

CHAPTER 12

Sophomoric Behavior

A soldier's time is passed in distress and danger,
or in idleness and corruption.

—*Dr. Samuel Johnson*

By the middle of June 2004, the heat of the Iraqi summer was in full effect. Temperatures pushed 120 degrees during the day, falling to a somewhat pleasant 80 or 90 at night. Stinging winds that were only interrupted by more furious sandstorms compounded the misery. Carrying fifty pounds in weapons, ammunition, and gear each day on patrol, the Marines felt like human clams, broiling inside their camouflaged shells.

As the Coalition Provisional Authority prepared for the Transfer of Sovereignty ceremony late in the month, attacks unexpectedly slowed. They happened, but not at the high rate that most observers thought they would occur. Many suspected the lull meant the Muj were planning something big.

Because the Muj had "won" the first Battle for Fallujah, Major General Mattis believed that they were after Ramadi as their next big prize. Like a swing state in an American presidential election, the allegiance of Ramadi's Sunni population could tip the balance of opinion decisively in favor of the Muj. They had already established one sanctuary in Fallujah. They would be after Ramadi next.

Mattis knew the men of Blue Diamond had varying political opinions. But he also believed that his men should be reminded as often as possible that their moral purpose for fighting was superior to that of their adversary. If they didn't believe that, why would they care if Ramadi held? In June, Mattis published a short message, which he directed each Marine in the division to read:

WHY WE ARE HERE

All officers and NCOs/petty officers must understand and be able to articulate to their troops why we are in Iraq. In counterinsurgency operations, keeping our troops informed of their roles, coaching them daily, and explaining the wider situation is critical to their sense of purpose.

This area has been slowly poisoning itself over the past decades, and has recently begun poisoning the rest of the world. It is not the U.S. who used chemical weapons against its own people. It is not the U.S. who has vast oil reserves, but huge numbers of hopelessly impoverished citizens, where the rich say "*inshallah*" and accept the plight of the poor. It is not the U.S. that preaches *jihad*. It is not the U.S. that abuses young people by turning them into suicide bombers, kills innocent people, or demands second-class status for women.

Remind your commands that the U.S. military remains the best hope for peace in Iraq and in the world, the best hope to stabilize a very unstable part of the world, that we will stay here in danger and discomfort as long as we choose to, that we will kill the enemy until he relents, and that we will take every step to minimize our own and innocent Iraqi casualties.

—MAJOR GENERAL JAMES N. MATTIS

Mattis had no way of knowing which units needed to receive this message, but at least one platoon in Iraq needed some type of boost. After a shaky start, Corporal Howell and 1st Platoon, Bravo 1/5, had begun to peak as a team. The tragedy at the River was a blow to Corporal Atkins and 1st Platoon, Fox 2/4, but they would bounce back. And even with Corporal Amaya's loss, Lieutenant Stokes had built 3rd Platoon, Kilo 3/4, into a crew of all stars.

In contrast, by late June 2004, 3rd Platoon, Lima 3/7, had lost their social energy. It wasn't the enemy's fault. After May 1, no other Marines in the platoon had been wounded. They had done it to themselves.

As a result, they were on the skyline. Lima's company commander, frocked Capt Dominique Neal, knew something was festering even before Gunny Vegh came to him. Lieutenant Benatz needs to be relieved, Vegh said. Why, Neal asked. He's not fit for the job, Vegh replied.

The pair talked. Although the company first sergeant was technically the most senior enlisted man in the company, Vegh was the combat leader the young grunts looked to. Within the 150 men of Lima Company, the staff NCOs and officers were the key players who made things happen. Among this small group of alpha males, only Captain Neal—who possessed both rank and moral authority—could trump Vegh.

Moral authority was the commodity that Lieutenant Benatz lacked. Specifically, Benatz stood at odds with two enlisted men whose opinions mattered in Lima: Gunny Vegh and Sgt Dusty Soudan. Soon after 3/7 arrived in Husaybah, Soudan's predecessor, a fiery, enthusiastic staff sergeant, had punched a Marine who was not responding quickly to an order. This staff sergeant, who was relieved by then-Captain Gannon, had had a contentious relationship with Lieutenant Benatz as well. He would frequently hide information from Benatz, which made the second lieutenant look bad to Gannon and other members of the company staff.

Benatz, for his part, knew the power of information. Smooth, urbane, and polished, he had worked for several months at CNN on Bernard Shaw's staff prior to becoming a Marine. Even as his platoon sergeant undermined his authority, Benatz worked to develop close relationships with his squad leaders, especially his senior corporal, Peter "Link" Milinkovic.

When Sergeant Soudan, Link's close friend, came into the platoon in March, he had been a squad leader for several months. Because squad leaders often talked to other platoon sergeants in the company, Soudan was aware of the platoon's dynamics. Soudan had seen Lieutenant Benatz's former platoon sergeant undermine him. He had resolved not to do the same.

Then, three things happened. Soudan observed Benatz keeping information from him; he would pass the word directly to the squad leaders and handle accountability issues—in other words, doing the platoon sergeant's job. On April 17, during the attack through town, Benatz was on the radio in a well-covered house while Soudan and Gunny Vegh were leading an attack to flush out a sniper. And on May 1, even more than the Purple Heart he later received, Benatz had contradicted Lieutenant Moore—Soudan's much-revered former platoon commander from OIF I—in the heat of battle.

As Benatz's 1st Squad leader, Corporal Link saw a different side of the lieutenant. On May 1, after the platoon returned to Camp Gannon, Benatz pulled Link aside. During the skirmish, Benatz had also argued with Link. "I was wrong," Benatz said to Link. According to Soudan, the lieutenant never admitted as much to either him or Gunny Vegh.

After April 17, Lieutenant Benatz and Gunny Vegh rarely spoke. When they did, according to Link, it was usually contentious. Vegh, a passionate Christian, thought little of the Iraqi Security Forces in general and Islam in particular. At one point in a firefight, Vegh exhorted his Marines by standing up, striding the lines, and yelling, "What's the matter, Marines? Are you afraid to meet Jesus?" According to Link, hate might not have been too strong a word to describe Vegh's feelings about Islam.

Benatz didn't hate Islam, and he didn't hate the Iraqis. In fact, although Captain Neal questioned his leadership skills, he thought Lieutenant Benatz's gregarious personality was well suited for dealing with the internecine problems and rivalries that Marines often became embroiled in. When Lima 3/7 was assigned the mission to guard the Syrian border checkpoint, Lieutenant Colonel Lopez told Captain Neal to think carefully about the man he picked to run the job. Neal selected Benatz.

Although Benatz excelled at dealing diplomatically with strangers in a strange land, it was Marines like Link that kept the international incidents out of the CNN cameras. At one of the border checkpoints was a bomb-sniffing dog. Several hundred yards past the checkpoint, a group of Syrians was tossing mortar rounds over the squalid fence that notionally separated the two countries. Smelling the explosive material, the dog charged, escaping his handler. The men fled. The dog chased them into Syria. The Iraqis, Syrians, and Marines at the border all looked at each other. Not waiting to ask for permission, Link ran over into

Syria, chased down the dog, came back into Iraq, and then took his squad to secure the mortar rounds.

For his part, Gunny Vegh made life difficult for Benatz at the border. Benatz wanted to provide supplies to several Iraqis who worked alongside them at the checkpoint. Vegh, who commanded both company logistics and Sergeant Soudan's loyalty, refused. Like the characters in the Oliver Stone movie of the same name, the Marines in the platoon started picking sides.

The counter-mortar operation brought everything to a climax. As the summer plodded on, Camp Gannon started receiving mortar and rocket attacks three times a day. Although no one was killed, the attacks had wounded several Marines, including Corporal Link, who caught shrapnel in his buttocks while walking away from a visit to the burn shitter. Captain Neal called a Lima Company meeting. His Intent was clear: make the mortars stop.

Sergeant Soudan wanted to do another April 17–style sweep through town—the last sweep had terminated attacks for over two weeks—but that idea was nixed. Instead, the platoons began sending patrols into town to observe several fields and orchards that, based on their range, were the likely launch sites of the mortars.

While 3rd Platoon was on patrol and occupying a house facing a field, the Marines heard mortar rounds impacting at Camp Gannon. Based on his instinct and the knowledge of local sights and sounds he had gained from patrolling, Sergeant Soudan was certain that the mortars were being launched from the field.

"Lima Three, were being mortared," squawked a voice over the radio. "We think it's from the field. Can you counterattack?"

The radio call validated Soudan's instincts. He had not seen the actual launch, but that didn't matter. Marines were getting attacked. He could do something about it. He told his Marines to open fire.

"Cease fire!" 2nd Lieutenant Benatz abruptly yelled from across the house. "You can't see what you're shooting at! You don't have a target."

"Sir, the target's in the field behind cover," Soudan said as he kept shooting.

"Hold your fire!" Benatz screamed.

Soudan looked over at his 3rd Squad leader, Corporal Mejia. "Fire a 203 into the tree line past the field," Soudan muttered. Mejia did so.

As Benatz ran back and forth shouting orders, the Marines kept their eyes on Soudan. If he was shooting, so could they. With the unit fractured, it was each Marine for himself. Some of them fired. Some stopped.

After he determined the platoon wasn't receiving any return fire, Soudan stopped shooting. At that point, everyone else did, too.

After they returned, Captain Neal heard about what happened through Gunny Vegh, who urged Neal to relieve Benatz for incompetence. Although he trusted Soudan's combat instincts, Neal sensed the issue was much bigger. As he deliberated, he called Soudan into his office. "There's a problem in your platoon, sergeant, and you need to fix it."

Soudan protested. "Sir, I've tried talking to him before. He just looks at me as nothing more than a sergeant. He doesn't care about my experience. He won't listen to me."

"I'm letting you make the call, Soudan," Neal said. "If you come back to me again with a problem, I'll relieve him. Either way, I expect you to go talk to him. This has got to stop. It's tearing your platoon apart."

Neal treated Soudan not as a sergeant, but as an infantry platoon sergeant, a full-fledged Lima Company key player. But Soudan never told the lieutenant he was on the verge of being relieved. Feeling somewhat threatened by Benatz's intelligence and position, Soudan did not believe that, as a sergeant, he could have a counseling session with his platoon commander. He wanted to, but he didn't know how. So he just didn't.

A few days later, Neal pulled Benatz into his office. "Did Soudan talk to you?" Neal asked.

"No, sir," Benatz replied. Three months ago, then-Lieutenant Neal and Benatz had been on a first-name basis. When Neal assumed command of the company, he immediately became a "sir" to Benatz.

Neal told him what had happened. An angry Benatz stormed over to Sergeant Soudan and Corporals Link, Lightfoot, and Mejia.

"How could you let me be blindsided like this? What the hell is so wrong with me? What is your problem?" Benatz yelled.

At first, no one said anything. Then, Soudan finally found his voice. "Well, look how you're reacting, sir. You're yelling and freaking out. What do you expect us to think?"

So they talked. They talked about April 17, when the lieutenant explained he was on the radio in a building. They talked about Soudan as a sergeant, and what had happened with the previous platoon sergeant. They talked about trust. They talked about responsibilities.

And in the end, things settled as much as they could. But they all stewed, especially Soudan, who thought Neal and Vegh leaned too heavily on him in dealing with 2nd Lieutenant Benatz. Traditionally, the platoon sergeant acts as an advisor and quasi-mentor to the platoon commander, but the officer is supposed to arrive at the unit tactically sound. Although recognized as a stellar Marine, Soudan did not believe he was ready to provide young officers whose judgment he found questionable with their combat learning experience. He just wanted to get his Marines back home.

Officers like to say that these kinds of politics are part of the 10 percent of unsavory issues that take up 90 percent of their time. Mad Dog Mattis had a favorite catch phrase to describe behavior such as this type of bickering and backstabbing that, once started, grew like gangrene within a military unit.

He called it "sophomoric bullshit."

Husaybah wasn't the only place in Iraq where the summer heat had gotten to the Marines and spawned sophomoric activity. Back at Camp Fallujah, Cpl Shady Stevens had run out of luck. In an hour, Shady would be standing in front of his commanding officer, Col Joseph Bruder. The charge? Gross violations of General Order 1-A.

Col Joseph A. Bruder IV—unmarried, thin-haired, and bookish—wore wide wire-rimmed glasses and comported himself with a Pentagon-wise political manner. Bruder had been the MHG commanding officer for only a month, but in that short time, Shady had sensed the difference in his presence. Although Bruder made few major changes at Camp Fallujah during the first weeks of his tenure, he did remove a number of construction hammers from the area, including a foot-long mallet that had been tied to the front grill of an MHG humvee.

Before Bruder even arrived to MHG in June—in the Marine Corps, most units change commanders during the summertime—Shady had started out with the wrong assumptions. When he learned a new commander was arriving, Shady asked several officers that he sold alcohol to about the new boss. Like Major General Mattis, Colonel Bruder was single. The officers told Shady that Bruder was a crazy, hip cat. "He loves to party!" they said.

The intelligence reports weren't accurate. In other circumstances—perhaps years ago—Bruder might have been a boozehound. Not anymore. Bruder was a colonel nearing fifty, comfortable with his rank and committed to the same type of sobriety in a warfighting environment that Mad Dog Mattis espoused. Basing his judgment on what he had been told, Shady approached Bruder casually during their first meeting. As he talked with his new boss, Shady tried to find a low-key way to let Bruder know that he had the stuff the colonel might be looking for. Bruder eyeballed him, wondering what this corporal was trying to say. Shady realized his estimate of the situation was wrong, and he shut up before he dug his hole any deeper.

Shady had followed a number of self-imposed guidelines while running contraband to keep others from learning of his affairs. He rarely sold below the rank of staff sergeant; his logic was that staff NCOs and officers were less likely to put their careers on the line just to rat him out. When he got the goods, he sold them quickly, not holding onto a bottle or flask for more than twelve hours. And, personally, he rarely drank. Like any bar owner, Shady knew it wasn't a good idea to gulp away profit.

Romantically, Shady had drifted after his wife left him. During May and June, as the activity had slowed down, he had started thinking about his ex again. Although he had formed a few quasi-serious attachments, he hadn't really loved anyone since her. And he wasn't really in the mood to love anyone. What he did want was companionship.

In May, after the Battle of Fallujah, a joint Army-Marine Corps firefighting unit of nine to twelve was assigned to Camp Fallujah. Although trained in aviation crash, fire, and rescue, the firefighters were used like an urban emergency medical service. Their mission was to extinguish fires caused by mortars, IEDs and car bombs in the Camp Fallujah vicinity. Half of the firefighters were from a Marine squadron. The others were from the Michigan National Guard. Three of them were female.

One of the firefighters, a thin, athletic, pixie-faced brunette, had caught Shady's eye. She was a Marine. She was a lance corporal. She was nineteen. She was hot.

One night in late June, Shady received a care package. It had the goods. Without the slightest ulterior motive, Shady thought it might be courteous to share some alcohol with his new female friend. Alone, if possible.

They never got alone. She called up a couple of firefighters and told them to come to her room. Following her lead, Shady called up some of his friends and did the same. They turned up the music, mixed up the whiskey, and started guzzling the night away.

The thin brunette didn't weigh much at all. Also, she had been raised in a conservative home where alcohol was forbidden. Finally free to taste the fruit, she didn't know her own limits. She treated the mixture of soda and liquor like it was a slurpee. An hour after they started drinking, she had passed out.

The firefighter's friends guided her, reeking and stumbling, into the medical unit for an IV to get her sobered up. Questions started being asked. Shady's name was revealed. Rooms were searched. His small stash was discovered. Cpl Shady Stevens was going down.

After he learned that he had been caught, Shady went to Captain Anderson, asking him to walk out to the smoke pit outside the concrete bunker where they worked. Important conversations often happened at the smoke pit. Shady told him about the firefighter. He told him about the business, the care package, the roster he kept. He told him everything.

Captain Anderson listened dispassionately. Although he could be vocal when the time called for it, Bill Anderson wasn't a screamer by nature. The constant barrage of mortars and rockets had made him even less so. Throughout his years as an officer, he had told his Marines that the entire Uniform Code of Military Justice could be streamlined into two basic creeds: don't be stupid and don't be a coward. Shady had obviously broken the first rule. At least he wasn't breaking the second.

"You know you'll be punished," Anderson said.

"I know," Shady agreed.

Anderson wasn't going to let him off that easy. "I'm really disappointed in you, Stevens." That got him. "I expected more from you. I always thought you were involved in something, but I never imagined you would get one of our firefighters smashed."

"But I didn't know she couldn't handle it!" Shady protested, trying to rationalize his bad judgment to save face.

Anderson cut him off, slipping into parental lecture mode. "It doesn't matter. What if a car bomb had gone off at our front gate? What if a mortar or rocket attack had tagged a building? Yeah, it's all fun and games and getting a piece of ass until someone's life is on the line and the rescue personnel are too drunk to do their job."

"What do you think is going to happen?" Shady asked. He meant: how bad will my punishment be?

In the MHG command structure, all disciplinary problems were sent directly to the colonel. Bruder had several options. He could string Shady up with a special court martial, which might result in a bad conduct discharge and time in the brig. He could serve him with non-judicial punishment, which would reduce him to lance corporal and cost him several weeks of pay. Or he could do nothing, which, in this case, wasn't really an option at all.

Although he didn't tell Shady, Anderson was also disappointed in himself. Decades ago, LtGen John A. Lejeune had advised Marine officers to instruct and guide their subordinates like fathers to sons. As Shady confessed his sins, Anderson found himself thinking: *What did I do wrong?* He liked and trusted Shady. Skilled, resourceful, and technically competent, Anderson had spoken highly of him to others outside the command. An officer's reputation rests on his own actions and decisions, but also on the performance of his Marines.

Having spent time discussing leadership with Shady—his gift of *Gates of Fire* being one attempt at mentorship—Anderson could have taken the corporal's stupidity personally. He didn't. Shady might have been a knucklehead, but he was *his* knucklehead. Anderson knew he deserved to be punished, but not dishonored. He told Shady that he thought he would remain a Marine, but not a corporal.

Anderson got up and started to walk away from the smoke pit. Shady called him back. "Sir, just one question. If you were the colonel, how would you punish me?"

The captain didn't hesitate. "I would reduce you in rank and fine you," he said. "Shady, I like you. And I'd still take you into combat with me. But what you did was wrong. Being a non-commissioned officer might not matter so much in other services, but in the Marine Corps it's a big deal. All of those young guys will look to you and watch your example. The Marines are built on corporals and sergeants leading and teaching younger troops.

When you wear the blood stripes, you've got a responsibility. From now on, you'd better live up to it."

As helpful as they were in dealing with their fellow Iraqis, the Shahwanis had a habit of treating hygiene with a sophomoric attitude that celebrated their newfound individual freedom with tremendous irresponsibility. When unwilling or forbidden to use the head trailers for showering, the Iraqi men would remove the tops of large military potable water tanks and bathe inside them. Furious American logisticians lost thousands of gallons of fresh water to the whims of these Iraqi men.

Some of the Shahwanis would also defecate wherever it suited their fancy—concrete barriers, sandbagged bunkers, or even tents often doubled as informal Port-a-Johns. In Husaybah, Corporal Link and a few others caught two Shahwanis showering together in a compromising position. The Marines didn't ask, didn't tell, and didn't pursue. But their relationship with the Shahwanis was never quite the same.

Back at the UN Oil-for-Food Compound in Shahabi, the only sophomoric behavior that Cpl Jason Howell and Bravo 1/5 had time for involved sharing *Maxim* and a few XXX-rated skin magazines with their curious Shahwani and ICDC counterparts. Another battalion, 3/1—known, like 3/4, as the Thundering Third—was trickling in to relieve 1/5. Their advance party was already on deck, which meant everyone was busy either accounting for gear or, in some cases, falsifying excuses about why it was missing ("combat loss" was the catchall justification). Advance parties are a skeleton crew sent forward a few weeks ahead of the main body to prepare for their arrival. When 3/1's main body showed up, Howell would go back home.

The job of those on advance party is to mirror up with their corresponding billet holder and learn how they have been doing business. At the end of June, as Shady was getting his drink on, Howell was escorting a couple of Marines from 3/1's advance party on one of his patrols.

They had been out of the four-story compound in Shahabi for ten minutes when, suddenly . . .

BOOM!

Not ten feet ahead of the squad, an IED went off. The explosion had blown forward instead of outboard. No one was hit.

One of the Marines stood up. He started shaking. H-Money, wearing a helmet and flimsy flak jacket, ran over and grabbed him. "Hey, it's cool! You're okay! You're okay!"

"Wires!" Lance Corporal Draime yelled out. H-Money and Draime looked at the side of the road. A coil of red and white wires was leading out of a hole in the ground, away from the road.

The Marine and the translator ran, following the wires. They led behind a building. Standing there, surprised, was an Iraqi man. On the ground was an explosive detonator.

The Iraqi tried to escape, but they seized him. Triumphant, Draime grabbed a pair of plastic flex-cuffs and zip-tied his hands behind his back. They searched the house the man was standing next to and found weapons, ammunition, and other IED materiel. H-Money and Draime dragged him up to Corporal Howell, who started in on him.

"You Muj motherfucker!" Howell said, moving closer.

H-Money stopped him. "Be cool, corporal. I'll do this." Then H-Money stepped into the man's face and began a long harangue in Arabic, repeatedly pointing his finger and punctuating his comments with the word *haara*, which means "shit."

The man started crying.

H-Money switched to English for effect, "Why are you crying? You did this. You shouldn't cry. You should be proud of what you did. You should be proud that you are a disgrace to your family. You should be proud that you are killing children. You should be proud that you ran away like a coward. You should be proud that you are now crying like a woman."

Smiling, the Marines stood back. H-Money finished with a flourish.

"And you should be proud that you are now on your way to Abu Ghraib."

CHAPTER 13

Season of Harvest

Courage is endurance for one moment more.
—Attributed to an unknown Marine
second lieutenant in Vietnam

As the Marines counted down the days until they would board their airplane home, most Iraqi families were counting the days until the date harvest. Date palms defined the primordial fertility of the Root of All. Each harvest season, the clusters of succulent fruit that began budding in June and blossomed in August and September served as a reminder of the earth's gifts that, *inshallah,* God graciously provided. The date—*tamur*—was a fixture of Iraqi culture, the manna of Iraq.

Dates began turning granny-apple green at the beginning of summer before ripening in early fall, turning brown before dropping off the tree. The sweet inner pulp was meaty, fleshy ambrosia. Although Iraqi date-sommeliers insisted there were over three hundred variations, most Iraqis agreed on at least eight basic forms. Iraqis said that regular consumption of dates was essential for overall health and vitality.*

For grunts, however, there was only one date that mattered—the date they would step onto the Freedom Bird. The closer they got to that date, the more paranoid they became. In Ramadi, Cpl Craig Atkins and the rest of 1st Platoon, Fox Company, 2/4, thought about all the close calls that had brought them to this point. They had survived IEDs, ambushes and mortars. They had survived March 21, April 6–7, and May 3. They had survived car bombs, RPGs and rocket attacks. They had survived three coordinated Mujahideen assaults in July, where the enemy massed, fought, and died by the dozens. How much longer could their luck hold out?

Mattis had been right: having "taken" Fallujah, the Muj were after Ramadi as their next big prize. Throughout the summer of 2004, 2/4 and other units in Ramadi encountered the heaviest fighting in all of western Iraq. A major setback occurred on July 28, when the Muj kidnapped the three teenage sons of the Al Anbar Province governor, Abdul-Karim Burgis. They burned his house to the ground when they departed. The Muj told him to repent of his involvement with the Americans and resign from office, or his sons would die. Ten days later, on August 6, Burgis stood under the infamous black flag of Abu Musab al-Zarqawi and said, "I announce my resignation at this moment. All governors and employees who work with infidel Americans should quit." His capitulation was a disappointment for the Marines.

The governor's resignation fueled the determination of both Muj and Marines to gain and maintain control of Ramadi. On August 13, Marines learned that a group of Muj had massed in

---

* Dates were also known as an aphrodisiac, which gave the English expression for a scheduled romantic encounter a clever dual meaning from an Iraqi's perspective.

central Ramadi to plan another major attack. Five days earlier, a Muj sniper had killed LCpl Jonathon Collins of Fox Company. After hearing that the Muj were massing again, Fox 2/4, led by Lt Jon Mattison, was going to fan out, patrol, and find the enemy.*

Cpl Craig Atkins, 3rd Squad leader, had no idea exactly where he was going, but with Collins's recent death on their mind, the Marines were ready for payback. What he knew was that 1st Platoon, led by Lt Matt Brooks and SSgt Kevin Shelton, had been ordered to take two squads out to an area where they had never been (Golf Company normally monitored this region, but they had been heavily engaged for two days) and search for the enemy. Atkins's squad was looking for a fight.

Sweltering in their body armor in the searing midmorning heat, Corporal Atkins and the rest of 3rd Squad jumped onto the back of their battered 7-ton and sat down on green benches, twisting their bodies to face outside of the vehicle just the way they had when they convoyed up from Kuwait. Corporal Alarid's 2nd Squad was in front of them, along with Lieutenant Brooks. Staff Sergeant Shelton was with 3rd Squad.

The 7-tons dropped them off, and the Marines headed out on foot. Atkins and his squad got on a roof, maintaining watch as Alarid's 2nd Squad patrolled. They waited an hour. Nothing happened. 2nd and 3rd Squads switched places.

1st Platoon sergeant, Staff Sergeant Shelton, was patrolling with 3rd Squad. "Staff Sergeant Shelton and Lieutenant Brooks

---

* Because Fox's platoons and squads rarely did company-level operations, this narrative has not done justice to Capt Mark Carlton, Fox Company commander. "Everyone loved Captain Carlton," Atkins said. "We thought we had gotten the best company commander in the Marine Corps." Weeks before, Carlton was wounded by an RPG; he lived because of his body armor. His executive officer took over the company.

were very well respected. They trusted the Marines to do their jobs and took care of them as well," LCpl Justin Oliver said.

Casualties had reduced 3rd Squad to just two fire teams, which were led by Cpl Justin "Babe" Richardson and LCpl Glenn Bullock. When Atkins had taken over the squad, he had planned to make Oliver the 2nd Team leader. Oliver had a natural instinct for when to separate himself from the rest of the group; to him, maintaining respect was more important than being liked. In the lance corporal pecking order, however, Bullock was senior to Oliver—he had been a lance corporal a few months longer. Lieutenant Brooks wanted Bullock in charge of the second team.

Like a corporate executive grooming his up-and-coming vice president, Atkins put Oliver in the third-senior billet: 1st Fire Team SAW gunner. Oliver liked carrying the SAW. He cleaned it constantly, and the weapon never jammed once—an impressive feat in the desert with a machine gun that had a reputation for frequent stoppages.

Like all squad leaders throughout the Marine Corps, Atkins had established a SOP that addressed which Marines walked where on patrolling. They rehearsed this over and over again so they knew, instinctively, which man was to the left and right, behind and in front of them.

Patrolling with the team was Staff Sergeant Shelton. Even though he was the platoon sergeant, Shelton was participating as another member of the team, feeding information back to the team leader, who would tell the squad leader and then the platoon commander. At the front of 3rd Squad, Staff Sergeant Shelton, LCpl Aaron Brown, and the team leader, Corporal Richardson, prepared to round a corner into a wide dirt road that had buildings on both sides. Oliver, carrying the SAW, was behind Richardson.

Suddenly, Shelton had a funny feeling. "Oliver, switch with Richardson."

"Staff sergeant, that's not how we usually do it," Oliver said. He was used to patrolling directly behind the team leader. That was the squad SOP. Both the platoon sergeant and platoon commander had told the Marines not to do anything special just because they were around.

Shelton calmly looked back at Oliver. "Switch. Because I said so."

Without another word, Oliver and Richardson switched places.

Just after they had rounded the corner and started walking down the path, bullets started hitting the wall all around them. Standing in the open, Shelton fired while Brown took cover. Acting on instinct, Oliver crouched down, firing his machine gun. Then he looked up and realized what had just happened.

Oliver had taken cover behind his staff sergeant, and the suppressive fire from the SAW had momentarily silenced the Muj.

On the other side of the corner, they heard a scream. "Bullock's hit!" Lance Corporal Bullock had been shot in the right buttocks, shattering his femur. While Doc Jared White—who Oliver had said was more of a Marine than a corpsman—went to work on Bullock, Oliver stood up from behind Staff Sergeant Shelton and poured fire into the buildings. After emptying his magazines, Shelton ran over to a concrete wall, took cover, and reloaded his ammunition.

Suddenly, everything was quiet again. Shelton called a ceasefire and ran back towards Atkins to check on Bullock.

As Corporal Atkins called in the MEDEVAC, Lieutenant Brooks and Corporal Alarid's squad came down from the roof and sprinted towards the Marines. When Oliver looked over he saw Brooks running in front of the exhausted Marines. In the Iraqi heat, it had been a long run. It appeared not to affect Brooks, except that he was so focused on the MEDEVAC that his Marines had to yell "Sir! Take cover!" three times before he responded.

As Doc White stabilized Bullock, Corporal Atkins examined him and offered some words of encouragement. "Well, Bullock, I guess it's a good thing you've got such a fat ass, or else your dick might have been shot off." The MEDEVAC vehicle arrived from Hurricane Point, picking up Bullock as he began his journey to Bethesda Naval Hospital, via Landstuhl Regional Medical Center in Germany, where care was provided for all wounded personnel evacuated from the area.

Atkins called Oliver on the squad radio. "You've got Bullock's team."

With Bullock gone, Oliver's new fire team set a cordon around the house. Atkins took Cpl "Babe" Richardson's team and searched the house. It was empty. 2nd Squad was also cordoning and searching. Nobody could find anything. The Muj, it seemed, had vanished. It was like a cat and mouse game where the roles kept reversing.

The platoon was moving down the road toward railroad tracks where they planned to consolidate with the rest of the company. At one point, they took AK-47 fire from a second-story window. Oliver was walking below the window. Not noticing Oliver, the Marines on the opposite side spun and returned fire. Blue-on-blue. Oliver dove on the ground, and his buddies stopped shooting. The Muj inside the house stopped shooting as well.

Looking up, Corporal Atkins saw muzzle flashes inside of a window sixty meters away. Behind them was a human silhouette. Atkins fired twice, and a red mist sprayed the air, confirming the kill. "It really felt like a beautiful thing," he said. Atkins had no time to mull the human tragedy of war. He was busy just trying to survive it.

It was quiet as the squad walked past an alleyway, where a truck was blocking most of the route. Suddenly they began taking heavy fire from the far end of the lane. Oliver and Doc White, who was carrying an M-16, happened to be right next to the truck.

Oliver looked at White. "Let's shoot back."

They counted to three, stood up, and fired. In the process, they shot out the windows of the truck.

Suddenly, Babe Richardson ran up with an AT-4, which was among the same type of shoulder-fired rockets that Lance Corporal Nelson of Kilo 3/4 had used in Fallujah. Since July 28, when the fight for the governor's mansion raged and the Fox Company Marines could do nothing but watch, Babe had been actively searching for a chance to put a rocket into the Muj.

"Can I take a shot?" Babe asked Atkins.

"Hell yeah!" Atkins said. "Shoot that motherfucker!"

Lieutenant Brooks ran up. "Wait! Can you see a target?" Atkins thought he was concerned about collateral damage and didn't want do destroy property unless it was absolutely necessary. "First do no harm" was still part of Blue Diamond's motto.

"Yes, sir. We've been taking heavy fire from that alley," Atkins said. Corporal Atkins, at this point, was not the least bit worried about collateral damage. He wanted Babe to shoot the AT-4. "No worse enemy" was also part of the division motto.

"Is there anything down there?" Brooks asked Atkins.*

"You're goddamn right there is!"

---

* Lieutenant Brooks later explained that he had actually been concerned about the number of AT-4s in the platoon, not damaging the buildings. There were only one or two other rockets available, and Brooks didn't want to shoot them unless absolutely necessary. "I probably shouldn't have said anything because I trusted Atkins to make those kind of decisions," Brooks said. "Fortunately, it had no effect on the outcome."

Babe shot the AT-4, which exploded at the end of the alley, damaging several buildings. One by one, they squeezed past a space on the side of the truck and searched the alley. They found nothing, but no more fire came from that direction.

Corporal Alarid of 2nd Squad ran up. "You guys okay?" He thought the AT-4 shot had been a Muj RPG.

The platoon reorganized and continued toward the railroad tracks. By this time, they had been out for three to four hours. Low on ammunition and water, the Marines were beginning to lose focus.

In the midst of all the Disorder, civilian life continued. Women shrouded in black strolled by with carts. Shepherds herded flocks. Children rode past on bicycles. One Iraqi vendor was selling ice-cold sodas. Lieutenant Brooks ran over to the soda vendor and gave him twenty dollars. "Give all these men a cold drink," Brooks said, smiling and *shukran*-ing, thanking the man as he shook his hand and then placed it on his heart. Happy with his windfall, the Iraqi began distributing sodas to the Marines.

Oliver was towards the end of the column when he walked past the vendor. "Soda for you!" the Iraqi announced, offering him a pirated Arabic version of Diet Coke.

Oliver didn't drink hajji soda. Besides, he was thirsty for water. "*Mai, minfadlek.*" *Water, please.*

Smiling, the vendor pulled out a bottle of brackish liquid that looked as old as Ramadi itself. Not knowing that Brooks had bought drinks for everyone, Oliver paid the Iraqi, who quietly pocketed the additional dollar, thanking God for the day's good fortune.

Eventually, they made it to the railroad tracks, linking up with the other elements of Fox Company. Lieutenant Mattison, the company commander, called for vehicles to come pick them up. The platoons dispersed, fanning out into a perimeter.

"Oliver, I'm going around the corner to check things out," Lance Corporal Boston, a member of 3rd Squad, said.

Just as he rounded the corner, an RPG impacted.

"Oh shit!" Oliver was sure Boston was dead. Instead, Boston walked back around the corner, thanking God for his own good fortune.

Another firefight started. The Marine vehicles arrived to pick them up. Mounted on the vehicles were Mark-19 grenade launchers and .50-caliber machine guns. The Marines dumped Mark-19 and .50-caliber fire into the general area, which temporarily silenced the Muj.

Oliver had been sipping on the water he bought from the vendor when he began seeing spots. Feeling nauseated, Oliver told Doc White that he might pass out. He sat down next to a building across from the railroad tracks and, perpendicular to a wide two-lane road, took several deep breaths and collected himself.

Oliver looked around. Lance Corporal Ocasio from 2nd Squad was on the other side of the wide road.

"Hey, Oliver, you want some water?" Ocasio called out, displaying a half-empty plastic liter bottle. For their daily dose of hydration, soldiers and Marines imported huge quantities of bottled water from Kuwait. In Iraq, Marines either poured bottles of water into their canteens or CamelBaks, or drank straight from the plastic bottle. On patrol, they often had a bottle stuffed into a large pocket on the front of their trousers.

"Hell yeah!"

Down the street, shots rang out.

"Well, come get it."

Oliver considered his priorities. He decided he needed cover more than he needed water. "I'm not running over there!"

"Well, I'm not running over there either!" Ocasio announced. The two Marines reflected on the impasse, staring at each other from opposite sides of the road like Mel Gibson and Danny Glover from *Lethal Weapon.*

"Catch?" Ocasio gestured. Oliver nodded. He later said that one hundred and thirty degree water had never tasted so good.

The mixture of humvees and 7-tons had arrived to extract the Marines, but the roads were too narrow for them to turn around. Each driver of each vehicle began making his own decision about what to do. Some of the humvees started making three-point turns. Some of the 7-tons started driving forward, looking for another road to use to backtrack. Marines were jumping onto the 7-tons, then back off of them. The Muj sporadically fired the entire time. "It was a complete cluster fuck," Oliver summarized.[*]

Before he joined the Marine Corps, Craig Atkins used to have nightmares about being in a firefight and having his weapon jam. As he took cover behind a 7-ton and shot towards the Muj, his nightmare became reality. For the second time in the Root of All, Atkins thought he was about to die. Enemy bullets snapped and whizzed near his helmet. Atkins cursed. He tapped the magazine with the palm of his left hand, racked back the charging handle, and, frantically, began banging out all the rounds he had left.

Finally, the Marine convoy rolled out. Oliver could think of only one thing: *We're gonna get hit with an IED.*

They didn't get hit with an IED, but Fox Company did take AK-47 and RPG fire all the way back to the Snake Pit. When they

---

[*] In the middle of this "cluster fuck," a Muj sniper shot Cpl Brad Collier. The bullet shattered his rib and collapsed his lung. In response, the Marines unleashed a hail of lead and explosives into the general area the sniper had fired from. This began a new firefight, which continued until the Marines drove away. Four days later, on August 17, a sniper—believed to have been the same man—shot and killed LCpl Caleb Powers from Fox 2/4.

returned, the platoon gathered for a debrief. When Brooks and Shelton finished, they dismissed the men to their squads.

After Schrage and Green had drowned, Corporal Atkins had become a stern disciplinarian. He was strict with the squad, especially the boots. With only a few weeks left, he didn't want them to lose their combat mindset. But this was the first firefight he had led them through, and he was proud of their performance. Atkins wasn't much for putting his feelings into words, but he felt like his men had earned a compliment.

"Y'all used to be a bunch of girls," Atkins said. "But now, you're women."

Cpl Jason Howell and the Marines of Bravo 1/5 had turned in their gear and were basking in the luxury of Camp Fallujah. The PX. The pool. The girls. And, especially, the head trailers. They had started their week of decompression time before departing for California.

Endorsed by Mattis, the decompression time was designed to give Marines a few days to process their combat experience before going back home. They had several classes on what their return to a civilian environment and reunion with their loved ones would be like. They sat down as platoons and squads and talked about their experiences and reactions to them.

During the decompression time, when one of the chaplains told Howell that he would probably miss his squad and platoon mates after the first weekend he was away from them, he laughed. "There's no way I'll miss these assholes," Howell said. "We've been together for *too long*. We need some *space!*"

While the rest of Bravo 1/5 relaxed at Camp Fallujah, Capt Jason Smith remained behind at the UN compound in Shahabi to finish the turnover with 3/1. As the commander, Smith only thought it right for him to be the last Marine from his company to leave the area.

The last day he was there, Smith walked around. Names and faces cascaded through his mind's eye. Lieutenant Palmer. Staff Sergeant Harrell. The wounded and dead, both in his company and in others. The enemy they killed. The enemy that remained alive. His family who waited for him at home.

He thought about the details a company commander scrutinizes; tried to explain the hotspots, friendly regions, and badlands. He knew that within a few weeks, they would have it figured out. And then they would teach it to another Marine battalion that would rotate into the fight.

How long would they be here? It didn't matter. Those were other people's decisions. Would it be worth it? Smith sure hoped so. If nothing else, they had showed the world that United States Marines would fight and die for each other. They had shown courage and, at times, compassion. They had, as the creed from the Marines' Hymn mandated, fought for right and freedom and kept their honor clean. That alone had to be worth something.

As Smith was lost in reverie, H-Money knocked on the wall to get his attention.

"You are leaving for America now?" H-Money asked. "You are going back home?"

"Yes, I'm returning to my family," Smith smiled wanly at the Iraqi youth.

"I will miss you, Captain Smith. You and your Marines are good men. I was proud to fight with you. We are like brothers now."

Smith looked at H-Money, who was holding a knife in his hand. Their eyes met, and wordlessly, they both nodded. The ceremony transcended the cultural divide. It needed no translation.

After they cut themselves, locked arms, and let their blood mingle, Smith gathered his pack and walked out to the humvee that would take him to Camp Fallujah. H-Money walked him to the vehicle. They embraced farewell—a warrior's embrace: part handshake and part bear hug.

"You must come and visit me after the war is over!" H-Money said, overflowing with the hospitality Arab culture has always been famous for. "You will stay in my home. I will introduce you to my whole family! There will be much to see in the new Iraq . . . *inshallah.*"

As Smith waved farewell, glancing at the newly formed scar on his arm, he wondered what would happen to H-Money. Would the new battalion appreciate his sacrifice? Would they treat him fairly? Would he, like the men he had captured, become a double agent for the Muj?

Smith forced the thoughts out of his head. Today, that became 3/1's problem. He still had Bravo Company to run.

And *inshallah,* Bravo Company was heading home.

Cpl Brian Zmudzinski and 3rd Platoon, Kilo 3/4, had assembled in the chapel at Al Asad Air Base, which was about an hour's drive from Haditha. They waited and chattered. Father Bill Devine would arrive soon to kick off their decompression classes.

In May, after returning to Haditha from Fallujah, 3rd Platoon—because of their fine performance and Lieutenant Stokes's solid reputation—had been designated the raid force for the entire battalion. Considered one of the best assignments, the raid force was not sent out on IED sweeps, mundane patrolling efforts, or other tedious missions. They trained with an Army Special Forces team known as Triple Nickel, which meant they were operating independently for most of the summer.

Like SWAT house takedowns, the raids required detailed planning. Most of the time things went smoothly, but not always. On one raid, a group of young Iraqi women wearing white *hijabs* surprised the Marines by screaming and beating at them with their fists. The Marines tried to calm them down, but the women continued swinging and screaming. So they detained them. "A couple of them were really cute," Zmudzinski ruefully admitted. On another raid, a pair of Muj opened up on Triple Nickel as they tried to escape. They were killed.

But the Marines of 3rd didn't take any casualties after Fallujah—no Marines were killed or wounded doing the raids. They were a glorified SWAT team; explosive breeches with fast, violent entrances into a (hopefully) surprised enemy's home whom they snatched up. Targets were not chosen randomly. They were studied for weeks, even months, and then prosecuted in disciplined fashion.

And Haditha itself was nice. The base got hit with an occasional mortar or rocket, but nothing beyond that. They had good food. They had the breezes from the dam in the summer heat. They had meaningful work. It was almost better than Twentynine Palms.

But it wasn't. The men were amazed at how much they were looking forward to seeing their other desert home again. When they had arrived at Twentynine Palms, they had condemned local bars like Club 29 as hangouts for skanks and sluts, low-lifes and losers. There was some truth to this. Just the same, they couldn't wait to drive past those familiar nasty hangouts again. The idea of cruising down Adobe Road and Highway 62 had never seemed so beautiful.

Father Bill Devine arrived to begin the presentation. They ooh-rahed, enjoying the familiarity of his thick Boston accent. Before he was appointed the division chaplain, Father Devine had served with 7th Marine Regiment during OIF I. Since both 3/4 and 7th Marines were based in Twentynine Palms, most Marines in 3/4 had known Devine for several years. Seeing him up onstage was like visiting an old friend.

"What you are going to do today is very important," Devine said. "Listen to this stuff. All of you have seen and done things that most people in America will never see or do. Each of you has changed. Each of you will react differently. However, there are at least some feelings almost everyone experiences. For example, you will probably feel guilty about having survived in combat when others did not.

"You might feel empty. The fantasy life you thought would be waiting for you in southern California could be quite different. Perhaps people you love have changed in your absence. Perhaps you will feel like you cannot trust anyone except for other Marines from your unit.

"And you might find yourself angry with people. Angry with those who haven't been where you have been. Who haven't seen war or fought it. These are things inside yourself that you have to confront. Don't forget," Devine concluded, "the enemy within you can be just as powerful and dangerous as the enemy on the battlefield."

As Devine spoke, Cpl Brian Zmudzinski and the men in 3rd Platoon nodded. They knew exactly what he meant as far as the guilt and emptiness. They had felt that every day since Easter.

And they thought they knew what the chaplain meant about anger, but they wouldn't really understand until they returned.

It was more than the infantry battalions that were heading home. James "Mad Dog" Mattis had finished his two-year tour commanding the Blue Diamond. He had been nominated for a third star and would be in Quantico, Virginia, for his next assignment. As a lieutenant general, he would be running the Marine Corps Combat Development Command, which would give him a strong voice in framing the next generation of warriors. "Over the years, I had often thought about leaving the Corps, but I stayed in because of the people," Mattis said. "There was no abiding calling—I just loved being around Marines. There's no finer team in the world to be a part of."*

Not far from the Al Asad chapel where Cpl Brian Zmudzinski received his decompression brief, the general turned over his command at a ceremony in an empty airplane hangar. In his short speech, Mattis deflected attention from his own accomplishments, which would be for others to chronicle. In particular, the final portion of his farewell address put the spotlight on those who deserved it most—the young Marines.

"Today, I haven't the words to capture what is in my heart as I look out at these beautiful grunts who represent thousands of cocky, selfless, macho young troops of our infantry division.

---

* When Mattis was asked if he made a conscious choice to remain unmarried as a Marine officer in the fashion of a warrior monk, devoted to the Spartan Way and nothing else, he shook his head. "Not at all. I've had a lovely life with the ladies. I almost got married once," he said, smiling winsomely, "but I didn't." His voice trailed off without finishing the sentence or revealing the personal story behind it.

Infantry—infant soldiers, young soldiers, young soldiers of the sea—who have given so much, and who have taught me courage as they smiled, heading out to risk their lives again, to destroy the enemy.

"So lacking the words, I will close with a warrior's prayer from a man who understands:

> Give me God, what you still have. Give me what no one else asks for. I do not ask for wealth, success, or even health. People ask you so often, God, for all these things that you cannot have any left.
>
> Give me what people refuse to accept from you. I want insecurity and disquietude. I want turmoil and brawl. And if you should give them to me, my God, once and for all, let me be sure to have them always.
>
> For I will not always have the courage to ask for them."

A few hours after the ceremony, Mad Dog Mattis flew to Kuwait, boarded an airplane and, for the eighth time in his military career, returned to the United States from the Middle East.

CHAPTER 14

Hail the Conquering Hero

*I have neither the time nor the inclination to explain myself
to a man who rises and sleeps under the blanket of the very
freedom that I provide, and then questions the manner in
which I provide it. I would rather you just said thank you
and went on your way. Otherwise, I'd suggest you pick up a
weapon and stand a post. Either way, I don't give a
damn what you think you are entitled to.*

—Col. Nathan R. Jessep,
as played by Jack Nicholson in A Few Good Men

No one ever forgot the plane ride home.

The Marines streamed into Kuwait from up north. Some of
them went on one last convoy south through Scania, Navistar,
and Camp Victory; others boarded C-130s at Al Asad Air Base
and Camp TQ, where a shuttle bus ferried them from terminal
to terminal. They stayed at makeshift camps, sleeping on their
packs, reveling in the absence of mortars but also flinching involuntarily every time they heard a loud noise.

They went through customs, where dogs sniffed their packs
and inspectors looked for explosives, AK-47s, or any other prohibited souvenirs they had tried to smuggle (in some cases, even

dirt was confiscated). Finally, they walked onto an air-conditioned Al-Hamadah Logistics International bus in Kuwait with plush red velour seats. Chatty Arabic drivers from Jordan, Palestine, or Egypt operated the buses. Rich from oil money, few Kuwaiti citizens actually worked; those who did wouldn't dare become bus drivers. The Al-Hamadah bus drove them to the tarmac, where they walked onto a chartered 747.

The interior of the plane was festooned with patriotic ribbons, balloons, and bunting. The officers and staff NCOs sat in first class, corporals and sergeants in business class, and the non-rates had the cheap seats. It didn't matter where they were sitting. They would have jumped in the cargo hold. They were going home.

Cpl Jason Howell relaxed and reclined in his business class easy chair. Howell had never sat anywhere on an airplane besides the cheap seats. The grunts were still filthy and sandy, smelling with man-funk desert stench. Many of them had not showered since their decompression time, which had been almost a week before.

Even then, the flight attendants swooned over them. "You know, these were the guys that fought in Fallujah . . ." one admiring stewardess whispered to another, using a tone of voice that others have reserved for encounters with Brad Pitt or Britney Spears. Howell overheard the remark. He felt like a rock star.

After departing from Kuwait, the plane landed somewhere in Europe to change crews and refuel. The airport terminals had alcohol, and the Marines lined up to buy bottles of German beer, Irish stout, or Czech whiskey. USO volunteers from Europe—old ladies who spoke German-accented English, perhaps remembering their own GI many years ago—proffered cell phones for five-minute calls home to loved ones.

When the moment arrived, the pilot announced that the airplane had flown back into American airspace. "You're back in the United States!" he said. Passed out from their first drinking binge in months (pogues and contraband smugglers notwithstanding), they woke up and cheered. The plane landed somewhere on the east coast for another refueling. No matter the hour, USO volunteers lined the airports in Maine or North Carolina or wherever the plane landed to welcome them home. Several raspy veterans from Guadalcanal and the Chosin Reservoir corralled the bleary-eyed Marines to sing a rousing rendition of their Hymn.

The plane changed crews again, excitement building up and ebbing. On some flights, the attendants read poems their friends and children had written to honor the warriors. They distributed pastel-colored construction paper cutouts with cheery messages from schoolchildren: *Welcome back from Iraq. We love you, Marines. Thank you for fighting for us.*

As they descended over California, they looked out the window. Trees! Grass! Mountains! After months in the desert, the scattered shrubbery seemed tropical and lush. Sometimes when the planes landed at March Air Force Base, fire trucks were shooting water from their hoses in phallic salute, which, of course, was exactly what the Marines had on their minds.

Rumors flew on the Bravo 1/5 Lance Corporal Network about the actual day they would arrive, and Howell decided to start a betting pool within the platoon to guess which of twenty days they would return. Each Marine could pay $5 for one of forty twelve-hour blocks. The pool quickly swelled to $200. As they prepared to land, Howell handed the money over to the winner: Dirty Steve Nunnery.

Doc Perkins, who was making a home movie, filmed the award ceremony.

"What are you gonna do now, Dirty?" Perkins asked, expecting the clichéd banter about Disney World.

Dirty Steve wanted to take a trip to a different fantasyland. "I'm buying beer and getting strippers!"

On September 25—which happened to be his twenty-second birthday—Cpl Craig Atkins, LCpl Justin Oliver, and the Magnificent Bastards of 2/4 had their gear searched again before boarding the white rickety USMC buses that would take them back to San Mateo at Camp Pendleton.

The wives, parents, and girlfriends were stacked, celebrating and waiting for the reunions on the large asphalt parking lot that Marines call a parade deck. Bev Atkins and Mitch, the youngest of the Atkins boys, were tailgating with Deb Edwards and several families they had met from the 2/4 chat room. Bev's husband, Gordon, was working at the sawmill, and their middle son, Garrett, was starting his freshman year at the University of Southern Indiana.

Atkins had been engaged with the Muj on and off until the day he left. A week after August 13, he was on a patrol with a squad of Shahwanis when they took AK-47 and RPG fire from a nearby building. Without hesitation, the Shahwanis ran forward to attack the assailant. The Muj escaped. But when the Shahwanis emerged, one of them was cradling a child who had been injured. "I loved them bastards," Corporal Atkins said.

The day before he left for decompression week, Atkins had been at the Snake Pit relaxing and packing his gear. He walked over to use the piss tubes—PVC pipes stuck into the ground at an angle for public urination. He had unbuttoned his fly and was positioned to begin when, without warning, the Snake Pit came under attack. Bullets flew past him. *I ain't getting shot with my dick hangin' out,* Atkins thought as he tucked it in and ran back inside to grab the rest of his gear. The attack was repulsed, but that was the first time the Snake Pit had been assaulted beyond the near-daily mortars and rockets. For Craig Atkins, it was his third brush with death.

The fantasy vision of *that moment,* the glorious warrior's cele-bration with their family, friends, and resplendent sexy sundress-wearing ladies, couldn't come fast enough. The Marine Corps, of course, kept frustrating it. After they departed the plane at March Air Force Base, they were rushed onto buses that took another two hours to arrive at their destination: either Camp Pendleton or Twentynine Palms.

Loved ones placed posters on telephone poles and fences at corners, turns, and junctions on the road into their respective base. Marines opened the windows, craning and waving at onlookers. They drove into their gate . . . saw the crowd . . . and . . . just as the moment had built to a climax . . .

. . . the bus dropped them off at the armory, where civilians were forbidden.

The line formed quickly. Marines working at the armory snatched back rifles and pistols; the weapons had been their con-stant companions in Iraq for the past seven months. In return, they were given their brown credit-card-style weapons-custody receipt. They felt somewhat naked and vulnerable without their weapons. Their defense mechanisms were deserting them. They were going into unfamiliar terrain.

Instead of waiting to form up and march over to the parade deck, some of the Marines just ran from the armory to their lover and departed, determined not to let the Corps take any more from them than it already had. They received icy stares from the rest of the well-wishers. *What makes you so special that you can be an individual?* Those who had assembled had learned of the Spartan Way from their Marines, even if not all chose to practice it. Individualism at such a moment was not acceptable. Their journey had started together; it should be finished with the same unity. Down to the final march.

And the march finally happened. The Magnificent Bastards left the armory, calling a bold cadence for two blocks, passing the supply building and barracks on their way to the parade deck. As they strode onto the pavement, the crowd cheered and roared like they had all just scored the winning touchdown. The electricity was palpable.

As the Marines stood in one final accountability formation before being released, Deb Edwards craned her neck, peering through the mass of waving arms, looking for a glimpse of Craig Atkins.

Finally, their eyes met. They smiled. Atkins walked closer, with a sandy pack thrown over his shoulder. The couple embraced and kissed, as though it had been an odyssey of twenty years. Bev and Mitch took their turns as well.

After they hugged, Mitch quickly handed his older brother a can of beer. Bev had kept her word to let her youngest son imbibe at will, but not until the exact moment his big brother returned. As hundreds of other mini-celebrations—screaming, laughing, hugging, crying, cheering—happened around them, Craig and Mitch Atkins smiled, cracked open their beers, and chugged them down in unison.

The sprawling suburb of Palmdale, California, where Jason Howell was raised, is about three hours north of Camp Pendleton, depending on the traffic. The drive didn't matter to over a dozen of Howell's childhood friends. They skipped school or work and made the trip to the Marine base to welcome him home.

Instead of marching, Bravo 1/5 had been bussed from the armory to their parade deck. After getting off the bus, the Marines got into formation. All Howell could see was a sea of people. He noticed one woman in particular was waving and screaming.

"Get back, ma'am," Bravo 1/5's company gunny ordered.

Howell looked again. The woman was his mother.

Finally, they were dismissed. The moment arrived. Howell ran over and embraced his mom. Then he hugged his dad, who was trembling. Then a couple of his buddies. And then he hugged his mother again.

That was when the dam broke.

The last time Jason Howell had remembered crying was in 2001, after he finished the Crucible in boot camp. The Crucible—the culminating event of Marine recruit training—is a fifty-four-hour marathon of squad obstacles, food/sleep deprivation, and standard Marine misery. At the end, recruits are formed into their platoons. The emblem of the Marine Corps, an Eagle, Globe and Anchor, is pressed into their hands.

When his drill instructor walked up to him, shook his hand, and pressed the cold metal into his palm, Recruit Jason Howell had just become Pvt Jason Howell. He had been baptized into the Spartan Way. He had earned it. He hadn't been able to stop the tears.

And he couldn't stop them now. They had made it. They had survived.

They were home.
But they weren't.

After they left Husaybah, relations within 3rd Platoon, Lima 3/7, improved noticeably. By the time they returned, few outside the platoon would have known that Lieutenant Benatz and Sgt Dusty Soudan had been so angry at each other. Since July, Benatz had addressed the platoon on issues of leadership and, presumably, had reflected on things himself. What was done was done, but his Marines thought he had matured. The experience seemed to change him for the better.

Other than LCpl Chris Wasser, Sgt Dusty Soudan had brought all of his Marines back home, which was the only measure of tangible accomplishment he could explain or identify. The whole thing had, in some ways, been like a bizarre adventure theme park, a carnival of explosions and gunfire where he had been both participant and spectator in a life-and-death drama. Survival, it seemed, was more like a game of Russian roulette than a tactical plan of outfoxing the enemy.

As Krista Lance embraced Dusty Soudan, welcoming him home to Twentynine Palms, she—like most girlfriends and wives of returning Marines—thought she knew what his life had been like. After all, she was a veteran girlfriend, not a boot! She had already done one civilian combat tour! Her Marine had already fought the war! The peacekeeping stuff was the easy part. That was what Soudan had said when he left.

And so, after the cheering and hoopla and flag-waving had finished, a feeling of anticlimax and melancholy set in. The dull chatter receded as Marines like Soudan took their packs, gear, and lovers to the local Motel Six for their release, which—lacking any real intimacy—proved as carnally satisfying as ever but was good only for a moment.

The stories came slowly, but over the next few days, Krista would learn about Husaybah. And she would understand and even accept why he had kept so much of it from her. She had known her Marine long enough to know that, like Al Pacino's character in the movie *Heat*, Soudan was the type who had to "hold onto his angst . . . to keep him sharp . . . out on the edge . . . where he had to be." Sergeant Soudan didn't want to risk losing the ability to do his job under stress. But Krista knew him. And it was okay, because now he was back.

But for every couple like Krista Lance and Dusty Soudan, there was another couple, a couple who hadn't done so well, who had argued, or stopped talking, or maybe *started* talking to somebody else in the other person's absence. They would each confront the chasm of tragedy in their own way. Some argued for days, weeks, or months. Some divorced and moved on with their separate lives. Some maintained their marriage or relationship as a comfortable façade. Some worked it out and actually grew closer as a result of the hardship.

As Marines like Soudan tried to explain to their lovers what had happened to them in Iraq, they realized there were things that had made perfect sense to say or do in Husaybah that didn't make sense anymore. Some feelings no longer seemed real. They had walked on the edge of death for seven months with their combat mindset as the guardian of their sanity and psyche. And they had lived to tell about it! But when they tried to explain their feelings, all they received in return were blank stares.

They wanted to be back with their fellow Marines. Their fellow Spartans.

Maybe they would understand.

After an hour, the Fox Company celebrants began dwindling away. Craig Atkins and Deb Edwards left the 2/4 parade deck to have, as Bev delicately put it, "a bit of alone time." Bev wanted to stay with Kim and Jeff Hunt, parents of a Marine from Golf 2/4, and wait with them for their son, Pfc Andrew Marenger. Mitch wanted to stay, drink beer, and hang out with Marines.

Mitch Atkins did not appear drunk in the least, which was disconcerting to Bev after she had watched the amount of alcohol Mitch had consumed. It appeared that Mitch, now in his sophomore year, had built up a tolerance to alcohol at some point without her knowledge. Savoring the moment, Mitch saved the beer tabs in his front pants pocket; he didn't want to lose count of how many cans he had polished off with his mom's full permission. When Marenger and Golf Company finally arrived, Mitch pulled them out to check. He had thirteen.

Mitch felt a need to hang out with the Marines who had no family or lover to welcome them home. He became a surrogate kid brother for all the men who had left formation and who, without their comrades, were planning a lonely walk back to the barracks. Plied with beer, the Marines told their tales. "You'll run the Crucible there during boot camp," they said, pointing at a hill called the Grim Reaper.

Mitch Atkins was drinking and surrounded by cool guys telling cool stories. The Spartan Way sounded pretty good to him.

After the reunion, Jason Howell stayed in his desert cammies, not bothering to change into civilian attire as his family and friends took him into nearby San Clemente for pizza and brew.

Howell's dad, a detective for the City of Burbank, was worried about him. From his perspective, his son didn't appear to be all there. "You okay?" he kept asking him.

"Dad, I'm fine," Howell reassured him several times. But already a small ache of loneliness had set in. He would try to tell the stories, and then realize his friends and family couldn't appreciate them. He would remember Fallujah and Bob Dawson and June 8 and H-Money and Captain Smith, but when he tried to explain it, it never quite came out right. He had barely left his squad and already he missed them—just like they had said he would during decompression week.

The entourage went to Howell's house. He tried to unwind, but his mind was on his squad. He laughed and joked and heard about all the local gossip that had taken place in seven months. He learned who was dating and who had broken up. What music was cool and what TV shows and movies everyone was watching. Howell soaked it all in, hoping they didn't notice him flinching every time a door slammed.

Eventually, Jason Howell cleaned up and went to bed. The next day happened to be Friday, which meant all of his friends were ready to party. They took him out to the local bar. "Jason just came back from Iraq!" they yelled to the patrons. He didn't buy a single drink.

Howell had a beer in his hand when he started feeling a bit claustrophobic. He wanted to step outside and get some fresh air. Someone tapped him on the shoulder. He turned around.

"Hey buddy. You can't take that beer outside with you," the steroid-ripped bouncer twice Howell's size muttered with a husky voice.

Corporal Howell stopped, assessing the situation. It had only been seven months since he had followed an order from anyone other than a senior ranking Marine, but it seemed like years. He had never liked bouncers anyway; they always walked around like they were so big and tough. *Where was this guy when I was getting shot at?* Howell thought. *Probably sticking himself in the ass with a bunch of needles while I was leading Marines.*

Glaring, Jason Howell walked back inside. The tough bouncer nodded his approval.

One of Howell's buddies walked up. "Dude, it's cool. Our boy Jason here just got back from the war!"

The bouncer looked at him. "You were over there?" he asked, with a gravelly 'roid-enhanced monotone.

"Yeah." Howell didn't feel like talking to him. Or to anyone else in the bar.

"So how was it?" Suddenly the bouncer became chatty, even voyeuristic. "Did you kill anyone?"

"Yeah."

"Wow. That's cool," the tough bouncer said.

Howell didn't say anything.

"Did any of your friends get killed?" he asked.

Howell nodded, clenching his jaw.

"Yeah," the bouncer said, as though he and Howell had been lifelong drinking pals, "we sure have lost a lot of good guys over there."

What the fuck? Howell set his beer on the bar as he felt his face turn red. *That's it.* The bouncer had just violated something sacred. Here was this buffoon, this *fucking civilian*, pretending to understand killing and sacrifice and the Spartans and the Highest Good and Order and Disorder when he had never done a fucking thing in his life besides throw around lead and play tough and shoot himself full of drugs while SSgt William Harrell and Lt Josh Palmer had given their lives. *His idea of sacrifice was to throw a block for his quarterback. What does this asshole know about losing guys?*

"Who the *fuck* are you to say that?" Howell started in on the bouncer, drill-instructor style, just like he had with the Iraqi months before in Karmah.

The bouncer stared back, wondering what he said to make this dude freak out.

"You heard me!" Howell shouted, "WHO THE *FUCK* ARE YOU TO SAY THAT?" People were turning to watch them. "YOU WANNA TALK ABOUT LOSING SOME GOOD GUYS? WHO DO YOU THINK YOU ARE? WHAT DO YOU KNOW ABOUT LOSING SOME GOOD GUYS? YOU DON'T KNOW SHIT ABOUT LOSING GOOD GUYS, DO YOU MOTHERFUCKER? *DO YOU?*"

"Whoa, Jason! Chill out, man!" Howell's friends grabbed him and pulled him out of the bar as the bouncer stared back, dumbfounded.

Jason Howell stood on the street corner, trembling, tears in his eyes. His hometown friends put their arms around his shoulders and led him down the sidewalk. In a way, he felt guilty. The bouncer had meant no harm. But the anger never seemed to go away. Neither did the loneliness.

Weeks before, Corporal Howell had been counting the days until he came home. Now all he could think about was there were only three more days until he would be back with his squad . . . and Bob Dawson . . . and Dirty Steve Nunnery . . . and Doc Perkins . . . and even Lieutenant Lewis.

He wasn't in Iraq, but war had made Jason Howell a stranger in his own hometown.

Returning veterans felt lost in other places besides their hometown. The Marines even felt strange around other Marines, especially the ones who hadn't seen combat. The war had produced its own fraternity. When a motivated, high-and-tight wearing infantryman who hadn't been to Iraq tried to trash-talk "those damn pogues," other veterans would speak up in their defense. *He might be a pogue,* they thought, *but at least he was getting mortared and shot at with me while you were in the rear with the gear.*

The most difficult for the Marines to stomach were their encounters with senior enlisted men or officers who had used their rank to avoid duty in combat, but still wanted to lord their authority and power over the junior men. Having lived for months in Disorder surviving on their wits, instincts, and judgment, the Marines found it insulting to take an Order from those who had never confronted anything more difficult than a challenging paperwork deadline or annoying boss.

Sometimes the veterans felt like these armchair warriors just wanted to put them back into a sealed glass case marked "BREAK IN CASE OF WAR" and treat them as ordinary cogs in the system. Only the glass had already been broken. And the returning warriors weren't about to continue blindly following what they saw as chickenshit regulations for their own sake.

After World War II, the Department of Defense formalized a pension and retirement plan that allowed military personnel to leave the service after twenty years, drawing half of their base pay for the rest of their life. As a result, the idea of retiring—as early as age thirty-eight—became a major incentive for those choosing to remain in military service. As Marines increased in rank, some decided to remain in the military because, like Lieutenant General Mattis, they loved working with and being Marines. Others, however, calculated that the fiscal benefits of military service were more to their advantage. After all, where else in today's society can parents find free health care and housing, discounts on food and clothing, and aspire to retirement at such a young age? Just do your twenty and then punch out. Many who were waiting to cash in on their pension no longer had any enthusiasm for the Disorder of combat leadership.

In this fashion, almost any given day of the week at Marine bases like Camp Lejeune, Camp Pendleton, or Twentynine Palms, a clean, well-manicured Gunnery Sergeant Order with a soft face and some gray in his high-and-tight might decide to stop and devil dog a Corporal Disorder in the chow hall for his appearance.* "Hey devil dog, look at you! What to you mean, coming in here with that filthy uniform? And when was the last time you got a haircut? Hell, your hair's so long, you look like a damn Navy corpsman!"

Corporal Disorder and his infantry battalion might have just returned from Iraq (or Afghanistan, the Philippines, Djibouti, or wherever else Disorder has been since 9/11). He had been out in the field training the new boots in the battalion on convoy operations, returning to the barracks late last night. Truthfully, he had a clean uniform, and he knew he should have worn it into the chow hall instead of his field gear. He just didn't want to screw with it. He was being lazy. And he knew it.

But the condescending comment about the Navy corpsman was too much. Corporal Disorder's corpsman had saved his life when they were back in the shit. Insulting him like that, even over a haircut (which Corporal Disorder actually did need) was way out of line.

---

* In Marine-speak, "devil dog" is both a noun (indicating a Marine) and a verb. In this context, the phrase means to arrogantly counsel a subordinate. When a senior begins a conversation with "Hey, devil dog," typically some form of reprimand—from minor correction to fierce ass-chewing—ensues. Grunts especially hate being devil dogged.

So Corporal Disorder, who had been submitted for two decorations for valor in combat, would scream at Gunny Order, dressing him down with the fury that Howell had shown to the bouncer. Then, with Gunny Order stunned in surprise, he would stroll away, throwing a "go fuck yourself" over his shoulder.

Invariably, it turned out that Gunny Order worked in the admin section for the regiment. Soon after being punished for his outburst of temper, Lance Corporal Disorder had a pay problem. So he went up to regiment, to the admin section, where Gunny Order was staring back at him.

Disorder spun away in contempt, cursing the Marine Corps for screwing up his pay, and counting the days until his beloved End of Active Service date when could finally escape this Orderly monstrosity.

And who the hell could understand this craziness?

Only those who had been there.

On April 12, 2004, a day after Cpl Dan Amaya was killed, Brian Zmudzinski called home. His mother answered the phone. The corporal didn't even say hello.

"I need to talk to Dad."

Dad was Marine veteran John Zmudzinski, a calm, friendly, optimistic man who proudly flew an American and Marine Corps flag outside of his house. That sad day in April, John Zmudzinski, who had served with a motor transport company in Vietnam that was often attacked while running supply convoys, had consoled his son with understanding rather than words. He knew how he had felt. He had seen it all before.

Of course it was a lot more difficult for John as a parent than it had been as a participant. Like Bev Atkins, the Zmudzinski family had banned use of the doorbell. Eventually, they stopped watching television. They didn't want to let themselves imagine the worst.

And so when Cpl Brian Zmudzinski of Kilo 3/4 returned to Twentynine Palms and his father's welcoming embrace, John instinctively knew when to prod and when to stay silent. He knew what his son was going through—the bitter sweetness of returning, the disillusionment of rosy, ill-founded government predictions ("the insurgency is in its last throes"), the confusion of trying to explain war's realities to those who just couldn't understand. He had been there thirty years ago. The wars themselves may have been different, but the effects of their politics had certain similarities.

A few weeks after returning, Brian Zmudzinski, like Dusty Soudan after OIF I, earned a competitive meritorious promotion to sergeant. Kilo 3/4 had a couple of weeks off before they would begin their training cycle for their February 2005 return to Iraq. New boots came in. Veterans left for schooling or new duty stations.

Others, Sergeant Zmudzinski included, were planning to leave for their old home. They had finished their enlistment and they wanted to pursue the freedoms they had earned. Like the days before coming home, they counted down until their End of Active Service date. Their next duty station?

1st Civilian Division.

CHAPTER 15

Our Way of Life

*Freedom isn't free, but the U.S. military
will pay your part of it.*

—*Anonymous former Marine*

On a Wisconsin evening in February 2005, Brian Zmudzinski was tending the bar at Matty's in New Berlin, south of Milwaukee. The job at Matty's Bar and Grille had been a relaxing change of pace after his trials of the previous year. He had sent in applications and started the interview process with the US Secret Service while also flirting with the idea of local law enforcement.

Zmudzinski wasn't completely finished with the Marine Corps. He still had a four-year commitment as a sergeant in the inactive ready reserves. He sometimes wished for a phone call from someone in Kilo 3/4, or Blue Diamond, or even Headquarters, Marine Corps. He wondered if one day he would hear: "Sergeant Zmudzinski, you are ordered back to active duty. The Marine Corps and the war effort demand a man of your caliber. You've been goofing off as a civilian for long enough—it's time for you to get back to work."

But of course that phone call never came. Other than volunteers, the Marines hadn't dipped into the inactive ready reserves since World War II. Back then, it was a much different Marine Corps, different country, and different war. Zmudzinski didn't waste too much time indulging in that fantasy. He had earned his freedom in his own eyes. He had to figure out what to do with it.

Brian Zmudzinski had gotten to a point of normalcy with his civilian friends. He told them as many stories as he would ever feel comfortable talking about. What he hadn't fully come to grips with was the guilt. The emotion struck insidiously, at random times. It wasn't guilt at Dan Amaya's death anymore; that had become sadness, a different form of grief. It was guilt at leaving, as though he might have let his Marines or the Corps down by choosing freedom over duty.

"And now we take you live to March Air Force Base, California, where the Third Battalion of the Fourth Regiment is preparing to return to Iraq for their third time . . ." the FOX News anchorman said.

Why can't those people on TV ever get it right? Zmudzinski thought as he looked up from the bar. *It's just Three Four. Two Numbers. Why is that so hard for them to figure out?*

Even after growing the scraggly goatee that almost every Marine tries out when he leaves the Corps (most eventually shave it off), Brian was still imbued with the Spartan Way. No matter where he went, he would always see the world through a warrior's eyes. Even if he no longer wore Kevlar and carried an M-16, combat had eternally altered his worldview. They hadn't been joking in the Marine recruiting brochures—the change really is forever.

Zmudzinski took a break, walking out from behind the bar to watch the TV report. The patrons weren't paying attention. As soon as the news turned to Iraq, they turned their heads away, returning to their conversations and their beers.

It isn't important to them that 3/4 is in Iraq for their third time, he thought, staring into the TV with a tunnel vision that reflected his guilt. As he listened to the anchorman's thirty-second report and thought about Ward, Hoyt, McNeil, and the rest of 3rd Platoon, he felt the ache of emptiness return. Some even made a joke of it: "Did you hear? Another car bomb in Iraq today!" Zmudzinski used to joke like that, too, but only when he was there, facing the car bombs. It wasn't funny when civilians joked.

Of course, most of the folks at the bar had their yellow ribbon magnets and support the troops stickers, which had been sold wrapped in clear plastic ironically stamped Made in Taiwan. He knew that many of them did and said things because they were culturally acceptable things to do and say, not necessarily because they felt that way. They were unwaveringly supportive of "the troops," even though they had no idea who the troops really were. For most of Zmudzinski's friends, he was the only person they knew who had been to Iraq. The war only touched them, vicariously, through him.

Most of them thanked him for his service and for abstractions like "fighting for our freedom." When it really got down to it, some were actually thanking him for volunteering to serve so *they didn't have to.* After all, if there weren't enough people like Brian Zmudzinski who had decided—either because of family lineage, personal conscience, or the perquisites of military service—that they just *had* to serve, then all those people thanking him might have been forced by the government to do more than just say words.

When civilians would criticize the war, Zmudzinski—with the dispassionate, thoughtful, and intellectual bearing of a Spartan— would debate with them, articulating a strong belief that was borne from the same moral purpose that sculpted Mad Dog Mattis's "Why We Are Here" message. Above all else, loyalty meant never breaking faith with the Marines that were in harm's way. He was proud that he had served; that he had gone where others refused to. He would not—could never—accept that his country would let men like Cpl Dan Amaya die in vain.

Privately, among other Marines who had served in Iraq, Zmudzinski questioned whether they would succeed in changing a tribal and religious culture that predated democracy by centuries. "We all knew it wouldn't be the last time 3/4 was in Iraq," he said. "There was no sense of closure or accomplishment. We fought for each other, and that was it."

Three months later, in May 2005, a friend of Zmudzinski's from his days at Bangor visited him in Muskego. The former Marine had also spent time in Iraq. They visited a local VFW bar called The Bunker, catching up on old times as they waited for Zmudzinski's father, John, to finish work and join them at the pub.

"It's hard for me to believe that Iraq will be any different ten, twenty, or even thirty years from now," Brian Zmudzinski said.

"You know," said the other former Marine, "there's only so much we can do. In a lot of ways, us being there is making it more difficult for the Iraqis to fix their own problems."

Zmudzinski nodded.

His friend paused as they each reflected on their journey, sipping his beer before continuing. "But whatever happens ten, twenty, or thirty years from now, at least we can say that we did our duty. We went where they asked us to go and gave it all we had. That's more than a lot of other people can say."

Zmudzinski nodded again in agreement. They glanced around the room laden with camouflage and military memorabilia. Looking around at the plaques and the faces of the veterans of other misunderstood conflicts that surrounded the bar, they actually felt comfortable.

When they talked to the old-timers, they didn't discuss politics or war stories. They chatted about the weather, the Brewers, and the economy. They talked about work, family, and life. They didn't go out of their way to avoid talking about war, but other things just seemed more interesting.

When the subject did come up, the communication was mostly nonverbal. It happened through firm handshakes and nods of mutual admiration. *You guys did your duty,* both parties said with their eyes, *and so did we. Sleep well in your beds, young men,* the wrinkled, wizened warriors seemed to say. *You've earned it.*

While Brian Zmudzinski was bartending, Jason Howell was trimming tree limbs away from power lines. He had wanted to spend six months at a low-stress menial labor job—"I want to be the little guy and not give orders to anybody"—before backpacking all summer in Europe and then applying for the L.A. County Sheriff's police academy. Only two months into his new routine, Howell had become impatient. He wanted to find something new to excel at. Tree trimming was not as satisfying as he had pictured.

Howell, who had also been promoted to sergeant soon after returning home, spent his last few months in the Marine Corps teaching classes to Marines preparing to go to Iraq. The classes took only a few hours each morning, so he spent the afternoons surfing. *That* was his idea of decompression time.

The teacher at the Transition Assistance Program—a reentry-into-civilian-life class the Department of Defense requires all who are leaving the military to attend—had said: "Be sure that when you get out, you have a plan." When he left the Marines, Howell was looking forward to, effectively, being a lance corporal again. "I just wanted to dig ditches or something for a while," he said. "I wanted a low stress job where I could do hard labor and not have to give orders to anybody."

Howell got what he wanted, but it didn't make him feel the way he had thought it would. "Hey Jason," the tree-trimming crew foreman said, "go pick up all that brush and drag it over to the wood chipper."

"Okay, boss." Obediently, Jason grabbed the limbs. *I used to be Sergeant Howell,* he thought to himself as he mindlessly fed the branches into the machine. *I was the guy who had all the answers. I led Marines. I took care of my guys. And now look at me. I'm just another piece of shit trying to squeeze out a buck.*

A few weeks later, the manager of the tree-trimming company decided to lay off some of his workforce. There was no perform-ance review. The newest on the job would be fired first. Jason Howell was one of them.

Howell gave up on the idea of backpacking through Europe. After spending a month unemployed and living off the money he made in Iraq, he took a job making pizzas at Costco while he was waiting to finish background checks and testing for the police departments, including the Los Angeles County Sheriffs, that he hoped to join. As he had suspected, the two years of pro-bation left over from his drinking and driving incident at Taco Bell in Washington State would make it difficult for him to get his foot in the door.

One of Howell's coworkers at Costco was a woman who seemed intent on flaunting her seniority as a pizza employee. The woman's primary purpose in life, it appeared, was to scruti-nize the way Jason Howell made pizzas. She would tell him *exactly how much* mozzarella was supposed to go on each pie and *precisely* the amount of sauce and toppings that should be meted out for each of the pre-cut circular crusts. She threatened to report him to the manager if he dared to make brazen, independent decisions like adding too much pepperoni.

"I have this arrogant feeling I can't escape," Howell said. "I look around at a lot of my old friends and I wonder what the hell they are doing with their lives. They're lazy. They've been living at home and going to college for four years, and I was a Marine. I was twice as busy as they were and had ten times as much responsibility, but somehow I also wound up with more college credits.

"I hate arrogant people," Howell continued. "But I look at myself and I feel so disconnected. I feel better than the people around me. I led Marines in combat. I'm getting shit done. What's *wrong* with them? Can't they get their lives together?"

Howell started thinking a lot about going back in.

Before he had gotten himself into trouble and reduced in rank, LCpl "Shady" Stevens had decided to volunteer for another seven-month tour in Iraq. A few more months of tax-free income had sounded good to him. He could deal with the risk of mortars as long as he could keep running his black market enterprise.

After his punishment, it was too late to back out of the extension. While Capt Bill Anderson and the other familiar faces headed back to Camp Pendleton, Shady would be stuck at Camp Fallujah until February 2005 as a lance corporal in the MEF Headquarters Group. The fifth circle of hell sounded more appealing.

Even after the alcohol incident, Shady didn't completely give up his black market operation. Although he did quit selling alcohol, Shady continued a brisk trade in Iraqi dinar. The currency was a popular souvenir item for Marines, who wanted to demonstrate their "investment" in Iraq by purchasing a few hundred dollars worth of Iraqi money. If the country prospered, and the dinar stabilized, their cash would theoretically be worth millions. Although not officially banned, the move was discouraged, as it weakened the already fragile monetary unit.

The only up side to his extension was that Shady received two weeks of leave. While the other Marines were returning home and decompressing, Jarod Stevens was cramming in all the good times he could. The first week he was home, he went out to the bars in Dallas every night. He did not go to get plastered. He just wanted to relax and feel normal for a while.

One of those nights, while Shady was playing darts and trying to feel normal, a girl with long black hair and attractive, professional savvy walked into the bar. Shady immediately noticed her. So did another man, who was considerably larger and considerably drunker.

The wasted man approached the girl, whose name was Andrea, and started talking to her. As he belched and spouted his way through a stream of gibberish, he grabbed Andrea's arms and pinned both of them to the bar rail.

Andrea caught Shady's eye. She was scared.

Shady walked up and said hi to Andrea, like they were old friends. They had never seen each other.

"Hey, duuuude. I was talkin' to her," the drunk said.

"Well, sorry man. Now I'm talking to her."

"Why th' fuuuuck are yew mooovin in on me?" the man slurred, pushing Shady.

"Listen, pal, I'm a Marine on leave from Iraq," Shady said evenly, "and I was just talking with this girl before you came over. I'd really like to finish my conversation. If you'd like to hang out with us later, that's fine. But either you let me talk to her or we'll go outside and fight about it.

"By the way," Shady finished as he flashed his military identification card, "I've probably killed better men than you."

Stunned, the emotionally castrated paramour waited a couple of seconds before responding. "Yeah man, that's cool. I don't want to mess with you or anything."

"Thanks." Shady smiled, and extended his hand. "I'm Jarod Stevens. Now, if you don't mind, perhaps we can catch up later on tonight." As the drunk stumbled off, Shady turned back to Andrea and gave her his full attention. "You okay?"

Andrea was impressed.

Before he went to combat, Cpl Craig Atkins had told Deb that he planned to leave the Marines at the end of his enlistment, return to St. Anthony, Indiana, and open up a woodworking shop. Instead, Atkins changed his mind.

He reenlisted.

He briefed Deb about it later.

Deb responded to her boyfriend's independent decision by promptly breaking up with him. This lasted for a couple of months, but eventually they got back together. Having waited like Penelope for Odysseus throughout his tour in Iraq, Deb realized she wasn't willing to let Atkins go that quickly.

Corporal Atkins got orders to Quantico, where he would be an instructor on the rifle range. He would be teaching second lieutenants how to shoot. Since Atkins had held his first gun before learning to walk, his new job and duty station seemed tailor-made.

When career Marines transfer from one duty station to another, they usually take several weeks of leave—vacation—that they had accumulated at their last command. Atkins used four weeks of leave to drive across from southern California to northern Virginia. Deb accompanied him.

Along the way, they stopped for a visit in St. Anthony, Indiana. During the visit, they were driving around Dubois County with some of his friends and sipping beer in the back seat of his buddy's truck. Craig Atkins wanted to take Deb to see the local sights, including the fire tower, a popular place for high school lovers to go and spend, as those from southern Indiana might say, a bit of alone time.

Deb enjoyed St. Anthony and all of Dubois County. The first time she had visited, one of Atkins's friends had picked them up in a Cessna at the Dayton, Ohio, airport and flown them to a private airstrip. Deb was shocked when they landed, literally, in the middle of a cornfield. Deb often told her boyfriend that she would be happy to move to the village-like St. Anthony. She admired the rugged self-sufficiency of the town's inhabitants; the sense of community was so different from her own suburban upbringing. But as long as Atkins stayed in the Marines, Deb reminded him, they could never move back to St. Anthony.

One of his friends asked him how long he was planning to stay in the Corps. Was he going to make it a career? "I just take it one enlistment at a time," Atkins said.

That wasn't enough for Deb. "Baby, I thought you said after this one, we'd get out and settle down . . ." Her tone was pleading, defiant, and frustrated. She had desires, too, and they didn't include being a camp follower, traipsing across America from one Twentynine Palms–like hovel to another.

"We'll see. I don't know if I'll get to deploy again on this enlistment."

"But you've already gone over there once! Why do you have to go again?"

"Deb," Atkins said, "I gotta be out there doin' what I'm supposed to do."

"And what's that?" She already knew his answer.

"Hookin' and jabbin' with my Marines," Atkins replied as though it was obvious what he was supposed to be doing. Deb's glare suggested that other things should be on his mind, including, perhaps, the needs of their relationship and potential family.

Although at times he could be eminently practical, Atkins could not deny that the emotions of Iraq—and particularly the night at the River with Dustin Schrage—had permanently altered his plans. For reasons God only knew, Craig Atkins had been next to Gunny Lens and the pack. Why did he live instead of Dustin? It was a mystery.

But he had lived. And, in a way, Schrage lived on through him, just as the spirit of every Spartan lived on through the warriors they left behind. Atkins liked the idea of being a part of that. Perhaps nobly, perhaps selfishly, being a part of that legacy for an indefinite period of time mattered more to him than Deb's musings.

In November 2004, LtGen James N. Mattis took command of Marine Corps Combat Development in Quantico, Virginia. Formally, his job was to "develop warfighting concepts and determine associated required capabilities to enable the Marine Corps to field combat-ready forces." In this mission, Mattis reported directly to the Commandant of the Marine Corps.

Informally, Mattis continued to look for ways to infuse the reservoirs of spiritual power into the men and women on the front lines. He coordinated the printing of World War II–style motivational posters: pictures of bloodied, exhausted Marines with captions like "What Have You Done For Him Today?" "He Is The Reason For Our Daily Routine," and "Killing Time Kills Marines." In his off time on weekends, the general frequently traveled up to Maryland to visit Marines and sailors wounded in Afghanistan and Iraq at Bethesda Naval Medical Center. His highest priority continued to be the spirits of the men. His grunts. His Marines.

One day in the fall of 2005, Mattis was discussing his thoughts on the war with another Iraq veteran. "In this kind of a fight, spiritual power not only wins wars, sometimes it also wins or loses the battles as well as the wars," Mattis said. "Today, symbolism is often more important than physical destruction. Spiritual power is that sense of abandon, where you give part of yourself up for something bigger and come out stronger.

"I still look back on the Palouse Hills of Washington State in a symbolic, spiritual way," Mattis reflected. "For me, they represent what we're fighting for: the American people, the natural beauty of the land, and our free way of life."

In 2005 the American military—in particular the Army, Marine Corps, and their Reserve components—were at war. The people of the United States—whom Brian Zmudzinski and Jason Howell interacted with each day—were not. Why have the American people themselves not been asked to play a stronger part in this global war or terror? Are their spirits that weak? Are they that unwilling to sacrifice? "I don't think so. But telling people to

go to the mall as their part of winning a war is probabl
cient," the general said.

Mattis's voice shifted; his even cadence took on an edge of battlefield-like intensity. "What would happen if we made, say, energy independence a major national priority so we were no longer dependent on foreign oil? What if we had a weekly day of reflection at town centers that revolved around discussing the war effort? What if we plastered the message throughout America—UNCLE SAM NEEDS YOU—and we told them exactly what we needed them to do? Why aren't we explaining the moral purpose to our citizens for this war?"

What should a citizen's duty be during wartime? To serve? To conserve? "All of those," Mattis said. "But even more important, those in government should ask themselves if they have done their duty in explaining *why* they are bleeding on foreign soil. We *must not* surrender the moral high ground to our enemies."

On the war itself, Mattis, who believed that brutal honesty was also an essential element of spiritual power, was candid. "I recognize that morally, ethically, and even legally going after Saddam Hussein was absolutely the right thing to do. This man was a hideous, evil thug. But was it strategically correct? Or will we bleed our armies and leave them high and dry?

"I'm only asking questions; I don't have the answers. But our spirits must be strong enough to be able to handle any reality, even the realities that are not optimistic."

In ancient Sparta, the ethos of discipline and self-sacrifice was society-wide. Fathers, mothers, wives, and children all reinforced the code of the body politic. The beautiful, Amazonian women

(Helen of Troy was a Spartan) famously admonished their husbands and sons to return from battle "either carrying their shield or being borne on it." Dishonor in battle was grounds for divorce. Weak-kneed sons were disowned, or even killed, by their own mothers.

As Zmudzinski and Howell learned when they left the Marine Corps, the Spartan Way had no civilian crossover. Their experience had made them aliens within their own country. Although their faithful devotion to the religion of the Way made them feel as though they had earned their citizenship, they found little that inspired them in the country whose way of life they had fought to defend. They were Marines inside their hearts, but staring back in the mirror was, once again, a nasty civilian.

Although they gravitated toward jobs like firefighting, law enforcement, or manual labor, they still found themselves reflecting on the good old days. They didn't miss the institutional foolishness or the violence and death. They missed the purity of being surrounded by a group of men who, whether they loved or hated them, were fully devoted to giving their blood, sweat, and lives for the sake of their mission or their Corps.

In the Marines, comrades who reinforced their Spartan values surrounded them. In the Athens of America, the only values being celebrated were instant gratification, glib self-interest, and love of material things. The Spartans abhorred these crass pursuits. Once a Marine, always a Marine.

They were constantly fielding questions about the war. "So what's it really like over there? Is it as bad as they say? The media's all wrong, aren't they?" As the civilians fought the war over the war, they looked for Marines who would tell them what they wanted to hear—who would say, "All the good news isn't getting reported" or who would testify, "It's all a lie and we need to leave."

The true Spartans held neither opinion. They were honest about the mistakes they had made and candid about the strains. They knew the United States was in a war—a long war—that pundits, talk-show hosts, and even ordinary citizens could not fully understand unless they had years of study and on-the-ground experience.

Most of all, their experience taught them that the Marines could not fully win the war against enemies of humanity like Osama bin Laden or Abu Musab al-Zarqawi. Of course, they would be handed the hardest part—separation from families, psychological stress, risk of injury and death—but the ultimate victory, if it came, would happen within the culture of Islam itself. Marines would have to function like soil for a seed. There would be no Iwo Jima for this war, only years of toil in the sand.

So they steeled themselves for the labor, not worrying about where the work needed to be done. Those were other people's decisions—the schemes of politicians or academics or policy experts or the myriads of "thousand-pound heads" whose lofty plans they would be left to execute. They girded themselves for a complex fight, asking only that the natives of their country, regardless of their politics, would never break faith with their warriors.

Like the Spartans who stood on Mount Olympus for the old man who was scorned, America's Athenians—particularly in this world-flattened age of global information—look at the Marines and expect them to always have the discipline to do what is right. Some might view such a standard as capricious and unfair, but—as Marines themselves often say when pondering their fate—it is what it is.

The lack of a "war effort"—for example, a man-on-the-moon style push for energy independence, or a call for some form of mandatory national service—indicates that America has become a nation that holds its warriors to a standard far above that of ordinary citizens. If no sacrifice is asked of the nation at war, by what moral authority do those Athenians expect to exercise control of their Spartans? Like those who mocked the old man while contenting themselves with their own revelry, the Athenians admire the Spartans from afar—their tunics lily-white—as warriors grapple with the detritus, seeking valor, triumph, and perhaps someday even peace.

Although the final outcome of the American venture into Iraq remains to be seen, if victory is achieved, it will come from young, rugged men who wear the blood stripes of sacrifice teaching their boots the proper balance of Order and Disorder. It will come from maintaining their favorite general's code of honor: first, do no harm; no better friend; no worse enemy. It will come as they pursue their Highest Good—their unflinching commitment to each other and their dedication to being authentic warriors rather than amoral killers. And it will come once the moral virtue of the nation they represent can be seen, in the eyes of themselves and their current adversaries, as matching that of the most devoted followers of their faith, the Spartan Way.

Citizens

cit·i·zen—
(1): an inhabitant of a city or town; especially: one
entitled to the rights and privileges of a free man
(2) a: a member of a state; b: a native or naturalized
person who owes allegiance to a government and
is entitled to protection from it

L t Kealoha Stokes, formerly 3rd Platoon commander, Kilo 3/4, left the Marine Corps soon after returning from Iraq. "Everyone still calls me Stokes," he said. "Even my mother. Hell, I call myself Stokes." Stokes and his wife, another former Marine who served in Iraq, spent a few months in Twentynine Palms before moving to Boston.

Stokes also made a pilgrimage to the doorstep of David and Kacey Carpenter, Dan Amaya's stepfather and mother, in Odessa, Texas. The visit was cathartic. Stokes knew that he would carry Amaya's memory with him for the rest of his life. Since Dan Amaya would always be his younger brother, those who loved him had become part of his permanent family as well.

In August 2005, Stokes traveled back to California to welcome home 3/4 from their third deployment to the Root of All. They were stationed inside Fallujah, which had been retaken from the

315

Muj in November 2004. Kilo Company was quartered in a section of houses on the southwest corner, not far from where Capt Jason Smith led the rescue of Bravo 1/5 and the destroyed amtrack. They called their base Camp Amaya.

Morgan Savage was promoted to major. After returning from Haditha in 2004, Savage left the Thundering Third and reported to Officer's Candidate School in Quantico. He is the officer in charge of the academics division, where he leads corporals and sergeants who are screening and evaluating potential Marine officers.

In the summer of 2005, after finishing his stint at Matty's, Brian Zmudzinski was accepted to the Burlington City Police Department. He attended the Academy that autumn, and now serves as a member of Burlington's finest.

At the War Memorial at Veteran's Park in Milwaukee, a new red brick sits amongst the granite columns where John Zmudzinski's service in Vietnam was remembered. Perhaps someday, John Zmudzinski's grandchildren will see their father's brick—SGT BRIAN ZMUDZINSKI, USMC 2001-2005—placed adjacent to their grandfather's.

And there they will sit, and quietly ponder life. The way fathers and sons do.

Jason Smith, who also picked up major, left Bravo 1/5 in the summer of 2004. His new assignment was with 3/23, a reserve battalion stationed in Baton Rouge, Louisiana, which was about two hours south of his Washington Parish home. On July 14, 2005, Smith was awarded the Silver Star for his actions in Fallujah the year before. His father Walter, who had earned a Distinguished Flying Cross in Vietnam, drove down from the family cattle farm to be present at the ceremony.

Six weeks later, when Hurricane Katrina devastated the Gulf Coast region, Smith took a few days of leave and returned home to Washington Parish in southeastern Louisiana. He rigged generators, mended fences, and helped his family keep the farm running until services were restored. Jason Smith never said it, but there was a glint in his eye that suggested he got a small thrill from Hurricane Katrina. Not only had he triumphed over the Muj in combat; he had faced down nature's fury as well.

LCpl Mathew Puckett, who drove the burning amtrack through Fallujah that Smith eventually rescued, was killed when his convoy was attacked on September 13, 2004. He had been in Iraq for six months. Puckett was posthumously promoted to corporal.

Bob Dawson reenlisted and was promoted to sergeant. He took orders to Officer's Candidate School in Quantico, where he evaluates officer candidates on leadership potential as they negotiate obstacles and perform team-building exercises. His commanding officer is Maj Morgan Savage.

Dirty Steve Nunnery was promoted to corporal. He became a squad leader in 1st Platoon, Bravo 1/5, and deployed with them to Ramadi from February–September 2005. Like 3/4, 1/5 was on their third tour in Iraq, broadcasting their motto to the Muj: Make Peace or Die.

While in Ramadi, Dirty Steve reportedly purchased candy, soda, and, of course, cigarettes, from a little Iraqi girl. Returning unscathed from his tour, Dirty Steve left the Corps. He is now attending MassBay Community College in Massachusetts.

Lt Stephen Lewis became the executive officer for Bravo 1/5. According to several Marines, he was "kind of a jackass" when

Bravo was in Ramadi. But they also trusted his judgment. Maj Jason Smith once had a similar reputation.

In the summer of 2005, Jason Howell received a phone call from the Kitsap County Courthouse in Washington State. A probation hearing had been scheduled for his DUI from the Taco Bell. He was told he did not need to attend, that it was a normal administrative procedure.

Howell went anyway. He hired an attorney, drove eighteen hours up to Washington, crashed with some of his old Bangor friends, and then donned his best suit and tie for the hearing. "I was better dressed than my attorney," he said.

The clerk read his case number off the docket.

"Jason Howell?" the female judge asked.

"Yes, ma'am."

"I have spoken with the prosecutor. We have already reached a decision on your case."

Howell waited. His future depended on her verdict. If he remained on probation, he would never become a police officer.

The judge removed a piece of paper from a file. It was the award citation for the Navy/Marine Corps Commendation Medal with V that Jason Howell had earned in Fallujah and Karmah.

She began reading. "For heroic achievement in the superior performance of his duties while serving as squad leader in support of Operation Iraqi Freedom from 5 April to 17 June 2004. Throughout this time period, Corporal Howell distinguished himself under the most arduous conditions. In Fallujah, Corporal Howell fearlessly led his Marines through continuous enemy fire in the pursuit of insurgents . . ."

The award went on, but the judge stopped. Howell later learned that the judge found the rest of the citation too emotionally moving for her to read aloud. She thought she would lose her courtroom composure.

The judge put the paper down and smiled at Howell. "Case dismissed."

On October 28, 2005, Jason Howell became a member of the L.A. County Sheriffs. He graduated from the Sheriff's Academy at the top of his class. In the audience to congratulate Howell on his achievement was his old platoon commander, Lt Stephen Lewis.

Sgt Peter "Link" Milinkovic negotiated his reenlistment on a handshake with the Lima Company 3/7 first sergeant. He was only going to sign up for another four years if he could be guaranteed the job of 3rd Platoon sergeant. In combat. When 3/7 took over for 1/5 in September 2005 in Ramadi, Link got what he asked for.

Unfortunately, this lifestyle choice did not suit Link's wife, Caitlyn, whom he had met in high school. She divorced him before he left for his third tour in Iraq, returning to her home outside of Chicago.

Prior to serving with 3/7, the late Maj Richard J. Gannon II had been an instructor at the U.S. Naval Academy. On October 31, 2004, the Naval Academy Parent's Club of Kentucky and the Oceanside Band of Sisters—a Marine wife/fiancé/girlfriend club—ran the Marine Corps Marathon in Washington, D.C., in Major Gannon's honor. For his actions on April 17, 2004, Gannon was posthumously awarded the Silver Star. His wife, Sally, and children, Richard III, Patrick, Conner, and Maria, accepted the award in his memory.

Capt Dominique Neal finished his tour with 3/7. He was transferred to the school of infantry in Camp Pendleton and commands a company.

Lieutenant Benatz became the executive officer for Lima Company. By all accounts, including Dusty Soudan's, he has matured into a widely respected officer. It did not hurt that Sergeant Link, one of Lima's veterans, believed in his growth potential, which helped bolster his reputation with younger Marines. "Going into our deployment to Ramadi, Benatz was strong and decisive," Link said.

In a rare moment of hesitation and indecision, Dusty Soudan thought twice about civilian life. The private security contractors who worked in Iraq—Blackwater USA, DynCorps, Wackenhut—called him a couple of times. He looked through their brochures and web sites. Six figures. Tax-free. Plus he could get back into the action. He wanted to do something he was good at, and combat had suited him well.

He had considered reenlisting, but Krista and his parents talked him out of it. They didn't have to talk very hard. After everything that he had gone through in Husaybah, his energy was spent. He had been either training for or in Iraq for over half of his entire enlistment. Soudan decided that was enough.

Dusty Soudan eventually found work with the Pennsylvania Carpenter's Union. A recommendation letter from Capt Dominique Neal helped him land the job. On September 27, 2005, Krista Soudan gave birth to their first child, a girl they named Madison. The Soudan family lives south of Erie, in their hometown of Girard.

Nina Schrage—a tan, slender Floridian transplanted from New York—was angry. Angry that her son, Cpl Dustin Schrage, had drowned. Angry with the Marine Corps for asking them to swim across a flooded river. Angry that she couldn't find a healthy outlet for her anger. Believing in the rightness of the war or protesting the wrongness of it didn't matter to her. Neither one of those actions would bring Dustin back.

In November 2004, Nina and her husband Preston had been honored guests at the Marine Corps Birthday Ball for 2/4. Retired LtCol Oliver North, the Iran-Contra scandal figure who also commanded a platoon of Magnificent Bastards during Vietnam, was the guest speaker. Meeting North and hearing him express personal condolences was significant for the Schrage family, especially Preston, who viewed Lieutenant Colonel North as a charismatic and exemplary figure.

That night, Nina and Preston also met Capt Mark Carlton, who had been Dustin's company commander the night he died. "He had tears in his eyes," Nina said. They talked briefly. Nina and her husband were welcome to call him anytime.

A mother of four—Dustin and his three siblings—Nina wanted answers, but she wasn't ready to ask for them. A year after Dustin died, she called Mark Carlton, who had been sent to Quantico as a student at the Expeditionary Warfare School, a graduate-level course of study for captains.

Although the formal results of the investigation remained classified, Captain Carlton was able to tell Nina what she needed to know. She heard him apologize to her for everything that went wrong. The fins. The current. The vortex. The inadequate training. The decisions. Everything. In speaking with each other, they both, according to Nina, found a measure of peace.

Additionally, Nina asked Captain Carlton to help her contact the Scout Swimmer's Course in Coronado, California. She wanted them to add instruction on avoiding an attempted deep river crossing unless properly trained. The captain supported the idea.

Nina is working with Mark Carlton and Scout Swimmer officials to accomplish her goal. She has also become involved with the Statues of Servicemen Fund, a nonprofit organization working to sculpt bronze busts of every person in the military killed in Afghanistan or Iraq.

Justin Oliver left active duty and returned to Oswego, Illinois. He started classes at Waubonsee Community College in the summer of 2005. He had an interesting perspective on being interviewed. "I think it's pretty weird that my name will be in a book," Oliver said. "Maybe it will help me get laid."

After serving with 2/4 for seven months in Ramadi, Doc Jared White, who Oliver said was more of a Marine at heart, volunteered to serve with 3/5 in the Second Battle of Fallujah in November 2004. After he finished his tour and returned, he requested a third tour. "I am happy serving my country," White said, according to a Joplin, Missouri, NBC affiliate's website. The corpsman/Marine is currently with 3/1.

After his freshman year of college, Garrett Atkins dropped out of the University of Southern Indiana and enlisted in the Marine Corps in the spring of 2005 as an infantryman, graduating from boot camp that summer. Pfc Garrett Atkins is now stationed at Camp Lejeune as a grunt with 3/2.

Mitch Atkins, who was finishing his junior year in high school in 2006, had similar plans. The rest of the Atkins family, according to Bev, is working to persuade Mitch to get a wrestling scholarship, go to college, and become an officer. Regardless of the path, Mitch intends to become a Marine. Gordon and Bev Atkins are both nervous and proud.

After reporting to Quantico, Cpl Craig Atkins found out that the nearby Aquia Harbor had good fishing. Most of the time, that kept him busy on weekends. He made friends quickly with other outdoor enthusiasts, especially other Iraq vets, which kept him from getting too lonely. Deb had stayed in California, but the long distance challenged their relationship.

One weekend, Atkins took a trip out of town with a buddy from West Virginia. He had a few beers. He met a girl. They wound up having some alone time.

He felt guilty and told Deb about it. She broke up with him. A month later, they started talking again. In October 2005, Deb flew out to the east coast for a visit. That seemed to patch things up.

At press time, the couple is back together.

Father Bill Devine was promoted to captain (the Navy equivalent of colonel). He remained Chaplain, 1st Marine Division, until October 2005. He is currently stationed in Japan as the chaplain for the Seventh Fleet.

H-Money continued working for the Titan Corporation and remained with Marines. He was with 3/1 during the Second Battle of Fallujah in November 2004. Throughout the battle, H-Money carried a sniper rifle. According to a sergeant who was with 3/1, Maj Jason Smith's blood brother fought "like a lion."

In June 2004, Naval Submarine Base, Bangor, was renamed Naval Base Kitsap. The Marines stationed there can still neither confirm nor deny the presence of national strategic assets.

The Shahwanis were officially dissolved in late December 2004, immediately after the Second Battle of Fallujah. One of the Marine Shahwani advisors, Capt Jason Vose, led a small group of former Shahwanis that became a mobile Iraqi special operations team called Freedom's Guard. Most of the other Shahwanis were incorporated into the Iraqi Intelligence Agency, which is headed by the group's namesake.

As of September 2005, Toby Keith had journeyed back and forth from Iraq with three different USO tours. In the meantime, he recorded a new album, *Honkytonk University*. Keith plans to continue performing in support of American military forces at locations throughout the world.

Ted Nugent kept asking to go back to Iraq as well, but the USO staff told him the tour was already full. Nugent stays busy bowhunting, rock-and-rolling, and hosting The Outdoor Channel's *Spirit of the Wild* as well as his new reality-TV show *Wanted: Ted or Alive*. He has publicly considered running for governor of Michigan.

Before the Second Battle of Fallujah, Fatima was transferred to a U.S. Army base south of Baghdad, befriending a number of people in the Army Special Forces. Through one of the contacts she made while working with the Americans, she was introduced to a generous individual living in Washington, D.C., familiar with the labyrinth of the immigration system. In March 2005, Fatima arrived in the United States. Three months later, she obtained a work visa. She is now working as a civilian for a Marine cultural studies center and trying to obtain American citizenship.

Jamie "Boner" Cox was promoted to lieutenant colonel and transferred from his aviation duties in Iraq to a headquarters job in Washington, D.C. Capt Bill Anderson was one of the officers Lieutenant Colonel Cox asked to pin on his new rank insignia. Cox now works at the Office of Legislative Affairs, where he represents the Marine Corps to senators and congressmen. Anderson left active duty and works as a consultant.

Before he ended his leave in August 2004, Jarod "Shady" Stevens and Andrea had already started a romance. In February 2005, Shady returned unharmed from Iraq. He carried the boar's tooth back with him, which had retained its streak of good luck. Shady had not gotten into any more trouble and had been recognized as a productive member of Marine Corps society for the rest of his time in the combat zone.

On June 1, 2005, eleven months after he had been stripped of his rank, Colonel Bruder called Lance Corporal Stevens into his office.

"Stevens, do you still have your old corporal chevrons?"

"Yes, sir." Shady had carried the faded insignia around with him, hoping for an occasion to wear the rank again. Becoming a corporal always means more the second time. Or the third.

"I think it's time for you to put them back on." Ten minutes later, Colonel Bruder pinned the collar devices onto Shady's uniform. The MHG sergeant major tapped the chevrons with his fists. "Wear 'em with pride, Marine."

Cpl Jarod Stevens and Andrea were married in July. That summer, he submitted a reenlistment package. Because of his NJP, it was denied. However, an arcane Defense Department regulation required that Stevens receive $15,000 in separation pay for his hardships. It seemed every cloud had a silver lining.

Shady and Andrea left the Corps in December 2005. They returned to Dallas. Jarod Stevens is now a partner with a professional landscaping company and plans to become a successful civilian businessman.

The boar's tooth is with a Marine in Iraq.

Muhammad remains alive and continues to fight the Americans. Most expect this kind of war to go on for many, many years.

Glossary of
Marine/Iraqi Terms

abu: Arab honorific meaning "father of," as in Abu Musab al-Zarqawi

baksheesh: Arabic word for payoffs or bribes involving government bureaucracy, law enforcement, or other aspects of social infrastructure

bin: Arab honorific meaning "son of," as in Osama bin Laden; also written as *ibn*

Blue Diamond: a nickname for the 1st Marine Division.

CAAT: Combined Anti-Armor Team: infantry Marines who train to fight on vehicles using heavy weapons systems (Mark-19 grenade launchers and .50-caliber machine guns)

CamelBak: a water bladder, holding two to three quarts of water, carried like a backpack with a small hose and valve attached; Marines bite and suck from the hose

chai: a thick, sweet Arabic tea popular in Iraq

Corpsman: US Navy enlisted medical personnel; Corpsmen are assigned to Marine Corps units to provide immediate first aid and emergency response for the wounded

cover: Marine word for hat

devil dog: jargon for Marine; mostly used when correcting the deficiency of a junior Marine, as in "Hey, devil dog, fix your cover"; also used as a verb: to be corrected is to be "devil dogged"

dishdasha: one-piece garment worn by men; made with wool and darker colors for the winter, and white cotton or polyester for the summer

EOD: Explosive Ordnance Disposal: the roadside bomb squad in Iraq

flex-cuffs: a type of handcuff made from hard plastic that military personnel often use when detaining a suspected enemy combatant

General Order 1-A: the US Central Command's order prohibiting "the introduction, possession, sale, transfer, manufacture or consumption of any alcoholic beverage by military personnel"

GPS: Global Positioning System: a satellite receiver commonly used as a navigation aid

grunt: an infantryman; also used to generally describe a person who lives without the luxuries available in the "rear" and/or someone who regularly goes into combat

hajji: American slang term for an Iraqi or Arab; also, an honorific for someone who has completed the *hajj,* or pilgrimage, to Mecca

head: Navy/Marine Corps term for restroom

hijab: a scarf-like piece of material that covers a woman's hair

hubbous: a thick flatbread eaten in Iraq

hukka: a water pipe used in the Middle East for smoking tobacco; also called the *sheesha* pipe, or *narghile;* men often sit in a circle and smoke it communally

IED: Improvised Explosive Device: a homemade bomb often built using artillery shells, mortar, or rockets; the term is also often used as a verb, as in "We were IEDed today out in Karmah"

I MEF: First Marine Expeditionary Force: higher headquarters of 1st Marine Division.

ibn: see *bin*

jundi: a junior enlisted man in the Iraqi Army

kheffiyah: head covering for a man; also called a *yashmagh*

madrassa: school; specifically, a religious center of education

MEDEVAC: Medical Evacuation of wounded or killed persons

MOS: Military Occupational Specialty: the specific type of job the military teaches an individual to perform

MRE: Meal, Ready to Eat: vacuum-packed meals served in tan-colored plastic pouches; twenty-four different types of MREs are available, including vegetarian, halal, and kosher varieties

mosque: Islamic house of worship

Muj: American slang for *Mujahideen*; a male who views himself as an Islamic holy warrior who has dedicated his life to fighting infidel; the ideal death for any *mujahideen* is in combat against infidels

NCO: Non-Commissioned Officer: corporals and sergeants; they are directly responsible for the leadership and welfare of the junior Marines in their unit

Nine-line: standard military briefing format used by leaders for calling in MEDEVACs, IEDs, air strikes, or other necessary information to higher headquarters

OIF: Operation Iraqi Freedom: originally planned as a single military effort, the constant period of deployment and redeployment caused the various OIFs to be numbered to delineate between the units involved. Further complicating the nomenclature was the division of each seven-month rotation into A and B in 2004. Beginning in 2005, OIF phases were designated by calendar year rather than Roman numeral. As this book went to print, Marines were engaged in OIF '06

OIF I: December 2002 (Kuwait) to September 2003 (Iraq)

OIF II-A: February to September 2004, Al Anbar Province, Iraq; OIF II-B ran from September 2004 to February 2005

POAG: Persons Other than Actual Grunts; more commonly known as "pogue"; slang term used to differentiate between those who are or are not engaged in combat

pos: shorthand for "position"; a unit's current location, often corresponding to a terrain feature or map coordinate

rig: gear carried by an individual Marine, often including a flak jacket with Kevlar plates inserted and ammunition pouches, first aid kits, GPS receivers, radios, night vision devices, and other gear

RPG: Rocket Propelled Grenade: a conical-shaped explosive often used by the Muj in combat

SITREP: Situation Report: an update on what's going on

Skipper: USMC captain or company commander; a company commander is also called the "Six"

SOP: Standard Operating Procedure; also known as a "battle drill"

tamur: date (fruit)

VBIED: Vehicle Borne Improvised Explosive Device: a car or truck bomb

wasta: "connections" or "network"; having the ability to survive and prosper based on an expansive web of interpersonal relationships and family/tribal connections

WIA: Wounded In Action

United States Marine Corps Rank Chart

From junior to senior[*]

ENLISTED RANKS

Non-rates
> Private
> Private First Class
> Lance Corporal

Non-commissioned officers (NCOs)
> Corporal
> Sergeant

Staff NCOs
> Staff Sergeant
> Gunnery Sergeant
> Master Sergeant
> First Sergeant
> Master Gunnery Sergeant
> Sergeant Major

OFFICER RANKS

Company grade officers
> Second Lieutenant
> First Lieutenant
> Captain

Field grade officers
> Major
> Lieutenant Colonel
> Colonel

General officers
> Brigadier General
> Major General
> Lieutenant General
> General

---

[*] Both Master Sergeant and First Sergeant are the same pay grade (E-8); however, a First Sergeant is considered senior. The same applies for Master Gunnery Sergeant and Sergeant Major. Warrant officers rank between enlisted and officers, but since no warrant officers are featured in this book, they have been removed from this chart. No offense, gunners. And infantry weapons specialists.

Acknowledgments

I n preparing this book, I chose to research the lives of a few to provide a broad general sketch of a deployment to Iraq in 2004. Because of this, events at the battalion level and up are not detailed. I tell little, for example, about *why* senior commanders did many of the things they did. Nor do I explain the martial mechanisms that made something happen, such as logistics, communications, and operational planning. These things are important, but not essential, to the way a grunt sees his life on the battlefield.

The scenes in *Blood Stripes* were reconstructed from the descriptions of the Marines I interviewed. In each case, I asked as many of the participants involved whom I could contact to review my account of the event. Several did not return my requests for interviews; others could not be reached for comment because they were out of the country. Although some were reluctant to discuss their experiences, more often the problem was a matter of timing. When I was doing research, most of these units were either training for or engaged in their next phase of combat operations, either in Iraq or in some other place of Disorder.

Interviews, photographs, and e-mailed comments from the following people helped to create *Blood Stripes*. On the Blue Diamond staff: LtGen James N. Mattis, Cdr Bill Devine, and Col Clarke Lethin. Kilo 3/4: Maj Andrew Petrucci, Maj Morgan Savage, Lt "Stokes" Stokes, Lt Ed Slavis, and Sgt Brian Zmudzinski. Bravo 1/5: Maj Jason Smith, Sgt Bob Dawson, "Doc" Mark Perkins, Sgt Jason Howell, and Cpl "Dirty Steve" Nunnery. Lima 3/7: Capt Dominique Neal, Sgt Peter "Link" Milinkovic, and Sgt Dusty Soudan. Fox 2/4: Lt Matt Brooks, Cpl Craig Atkins, and LCpl Justin Oliver. MHG: LtCol David Pere, LtCol Jamie "Boner" Cox, and Cpl Jarod "Shady" Stevens. Thanks also to David and Kacey Carpenter, Gordon and Bev Atkins, Mitch Atkins, Deb Edwards, John and Fran Zmudzinski, and Nina Schrage for their contributions.

I also interviewed LtGen James Conway and Col John Toolan, who, respectively, commanded the 1st Marine Expeditionary Force (Blue Diamond's higher command) and the 1st Regimental Combat Team (which handled the April 2004 Fallujah fight). With the exception of one quote from General Conway in Chapter 4, material from those interviews was not used in the book. Nonetheless, they were generous with their time, and I thank them both.

The original outline of this book included material on the MHG's motor transport platoon—which ran convoys throughout Iraq—as well as a reserve infantry company, India 3/24, that secured Camp Fallujah. For several reasons, I chose to cut this part of the narrative. However, I thank all those in these units who sat for interviews and reviewed drafts, particularly Capt Jacob Berry, Capt John Lewis, Sgt Michael Renfro, and Cpl John Cruse.

Collectively, I thank the members of the U.S. Naval Academy class of 1998; Basic School class 5-98 (Echo Company); Infantry Officer Course 3-99; 1st Battalion, 7th Marines (1/7); and Marine Security Force Company, Bangor, for professional development, insight, and camaraderie during my decade of military service and beyond. And I thank those I worked with and met while deployed to Iraq with I MEF for friendship and for enduring the highs and lows of the fight with the spirit of Spartans. You all know who you are. Listing your names would take another book.

I thank Steven Pressfield for his mentorship and alliance as a writer, his gifts to the warrior ethos, and his extremely kind foreword. I also thank two other mentors: Robert Timberg, for providing brilliant, patient instruction in good nonfiction technique, and James Webb, for his explanation of what it means to be a writer instead of a propagandist. Thanks to Jack Glasgow for his timely review of the manuscript. For guidance as a peer, both in navigating the confusion of publishing and the challenges of leaving the Corps to write, I thank Nathaniel Fick.

It's a movie cliché, but agents who are "ambassadors of qwan" really do exist. I was fortunate to meet up with E. J. McCarthy, who is both a professional and a friend, and I thank Col T. X. Hammes for his recommendation. At Stackpole Books, I thank my editor, Chris Evans, for championing this project. I also thank David Reisch, Judith Schnell, Pat Moran, Peter Rossi, Susan Drexler, Tracy Patterson, and Wendy Reynolds for their efforts.

I thank my family and friends for their encouragement. Most of all, I thank my wife, Mary, who supported my decision to leave the battlefield and become a writer and has chosen to share the challenges that this vocation brings. If the best parts of ourselves are reflected in those whose love we share, then I am, without question, the luckiest guy on the planet.

Finally, I thank those soldiers, sailors, airmen, Marines, and civilians who have volunteered to serve their nation. I appreciate, and share, your willingness to sacrifice for something greater than yourselves. That virtue is sacred and should be esteemed in our free land. Those who govern should ask as much of the rest of us.

Index